WORKING [illegible] HEROES

The Histo[illegible]ecordings

Neville Stannard & John Tobler

Virgin

Virgin Books

ARE YOU BRIGHT, HARDWORKING, INTELLIGENT AND AMBITIOUS, WITH A KEEN INTEREST IN CONTEMPORARY MUSIC, A FRIENDLY PERSONALITY AND A SMART APPEARANCE?

Then what are you doing reading this?

If you are bright then you'll probably have realised that this is an advertisement for Paul McCartney's new single 'Temporary Secretary.'

Only available as a limited edition 12" record, the B-Side is the 10½ minute, previously unavailable "Secret Friend."

No previous experience necessary.

Apply in person at your local record store.

First published in Great Britain in 1983 by Virgin Books
Ltd., 61-63, Portobello Road, London W11 3DD.

ISBN 0 907080 92 8

Printed and bound in Great Britain by Richard Clay
(The Chaucer Press) Ltd, Suffolk.
Photoset by A.J. Latham Limited, Dunstable, Beds.
Designed by Phil Smee and Cally
at Waldo's Design
Production services by Book Production Consultants
Cambridge.
Distributed by Arrow Books.

CONTENTS

Mull of Kintyre is number one.

Graham Hughes

Thanks a lot, folks!
Paul McC... Thanx a half-Million
up your Kilt, Denny Laine
Linda

Wings

R6018 mpl EMI

ACKNOWLEDGEMENTS

Every attempt has been made to contact holders of copyright material reproduced in this book, and any infringement of copyright is accidental. In the case of any question arising out of the use of copyright material, the authors will be pleased to make the necessary corrections in any further editions of the book. The authors are indebted to the following for permission to use copyright material:

A&M Records Ltd.,
Apple Records,
© 1964-82 by Billboard Publications Inc. All chart data compiled by the Billboard research department and printed with permission,
Capitol Records Inc.,
CBS Records (for CBS, Epic & Ode),
Decca Records,
DJM Records Ltd.,
EMI Records UK Ltd., (for EMI, Harvest, Music For Pleasure & Parlophone),
Ganga Publishing,
K-tel International (UK) Ltd.,
MPL Ltd.,
New Musical Express,
PolyGram Records,
RCA Records,
WEA Records (for Atlantic, Dark Horse, Geffen & Warner Brothers)

Chart information © Music Week/BBC/Gallup

The authors wish to express their gratitude to the following: Brian Southall, James Devereux, Adrian Vogel, Colin Miles, Eugene Manzi, Claire Fielding Griffiths, Denise Jerome, Paul Davis, Peter Wilkinson, Diana Robertson, Neil Aspinall, Beebe Jennings,Georgina Challis and Frances Rogers.

The following music papers were researched for recording information and record sales:
New Musical Express
Melody Maker
Disc
Record Mirror
Sounds

The following record sales charts were used for chart positions and statistics:
New Musical Express (British Beatles records)
Billboard (American Beatles records)
Music Week/British Market Research Bureau/BBC (other artists' hits and British Beatles records)

Every major country has a screw in its side, in England it's Oz. Oz is on trial for its life. John and Yoko have written and helped produce this record – the proceeds of which are going to Oz to help to pay their legal fees. The entire British underground is in trouble, it needs our help. Please listen – 'God Save Oz'.

Apple 36

PREFACE

Having been described (by others, I hasten to add) as a rock historian, it is particularly pleasing to be associated with this discography of the solo careers of the Beatles. I cannot claim to have compiled very much of the information – this chore was undertaken with his usual application and thoroughness by Neville Stannard, whose knowledge of the Beatles and their music seems to me to be second to none in Great Britain, and possibly in the world.

After the success of Neville's first book, *The Long And Winding Road*, which dealt with the records released by the Beatles as a group, it was an obvious step to prepare a companion volume featuring the records released by the erstwhile Beatles as individuals (and their participation on records which did not bear their names).

This volume is the result of that decision, and is as up to date as publishing schedules will allow (and anyway complete to the end of 1982). As the three surviving Beatles continue to release new records, *Working Class Heroes* will inevitably become outdated, but it is our intention to update both *The Long And Winding Road* and *Working Class Heroes* on a regular basis until it becomes evident that the Beatles – both individually and collectively – are no longer of interest. It has not escaped our notice that this may turn out to be a life work. . .

Our thanks for their help to Robert Devereux, John Brown, Catherine Ledger, Felix Dennis, Dick Pountain, Malcolm Eade, Liz Cruickshanks, Adrian Vogel, Harold Bronson, Phil Smee and Cally.

John Tobler
May 1983

INTRODUCTION

The first part of this book is divided into four sections; each covers the Beatles' individual British and American releases, using a record and song numbering system identical to that in *The Long And Winding Road* (the companion volume to *Working Class Heroes*). In each section, all solo releases are given a "record number" – to the left of the "record title" – although compilation albums and certain solo Beatle related records are not numbered. Each song is given a "song number" – appearing to the left of each "song title" – and this receives a suffix letter for subsequent appearances of the song, i.e., "a" indicates the first appearance, "b" the second appearance, etc., while a song number without a suffix indicates the first appearance of the song. Where albums receive a straight re-release (Paul McCartney's Columbia releases in America, for instance) the track listings are not repeated in order to economise on space; therefore the song numbering and letters do not apply.

The artist credits for John and Paul's releases have changed throughout their careers, and these varying credits are given after each record title, but since George and Ringo have so far only released records under their own names, these are not repeated. Some might argue that neither John's *Elastic Oz Band* nor Paul's *Country Hams* and *Percy Thrillington* are truly solo releases. However, for simplicity they have been included in the appropriate sections, although they do not receive record or song numbers. Likewise, Linda McCartney's solo releases under "Suzy And The Red Stripes" have been included in Paul's section, as they do not warrant separate listing. The early John and Yoko albums are included in John's section, but Yoko's solo recordings are featured in Appendix 4.

JOHN LENNON

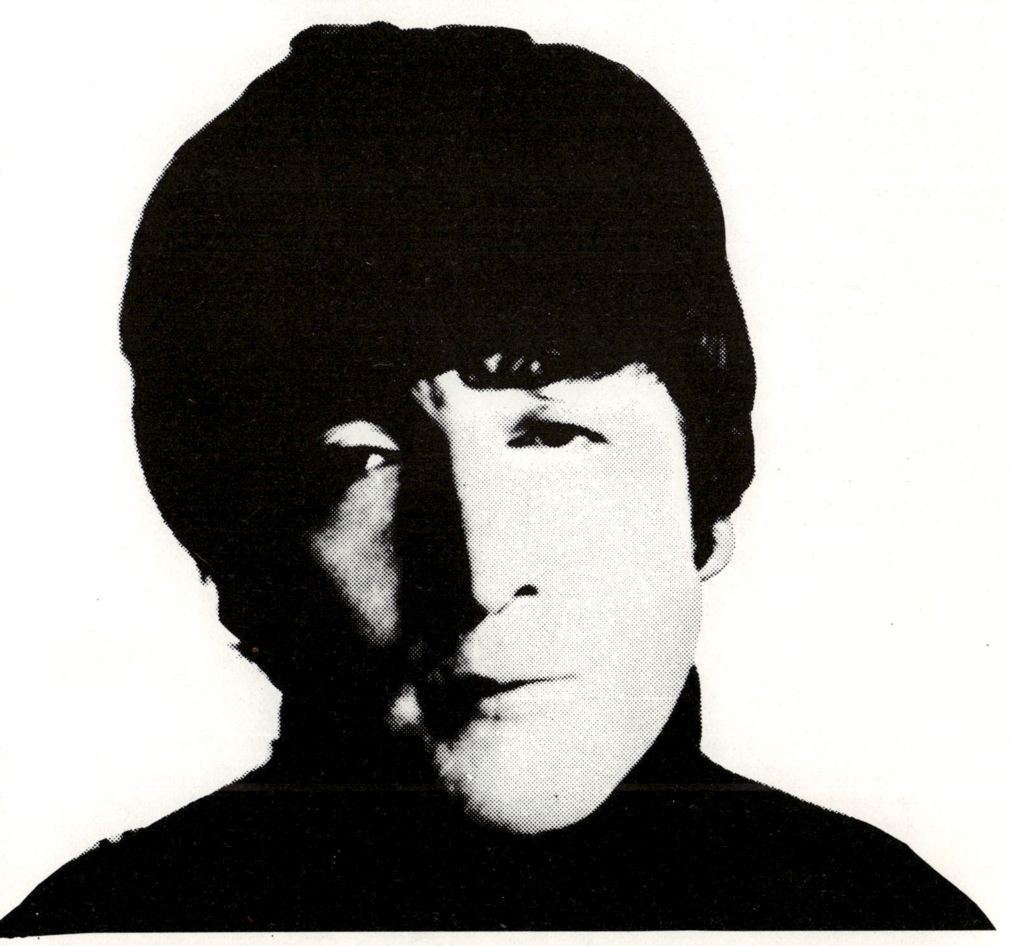

1 UNFINISHED MUSIC No. 1 – TWO VIRGINS

By John Lennon and Yoko Ono

Apple SAPCOR 2 (Released as Track 613012 – see below) – November 29, 1968

John's first recording venture without his three fellow Beatles was into the realms of the avant-garde, with this mysterious album of sound effects, bodily noises and snatches of "music". It was recorded one May morning, between midnight and dawn, in 1968, when John had invited Yoko to his Kenwood mansion in Weybridge, after his wife, Cynthia, had departed for a holiday in Greece with Jennie Boyd and Apple "inventor" Magic Alex. John had previously been experimenting with various recordings of his own, using his home recording studio, and Yoko was interested in his rather "way-out" recordings, and they decided to record an album together.

The naked cover photographs for the album were taken in the basement of Ringo's flat, in Montagu Square, London, in early October, 1968, with John using a delayed action shutter release, as he was too embarrassed to allow a professional to take the nude pictures. It took John five months to get approval from the other Beatles to allow him to use the pictures and even so, EMI refused to handle the album unless John changed the sleeve photographs. However, John was adamant in wanting to use the photographs, and personally appealed to Sir Joseph Lockwood, chairman of EMI, who assured John that he would do all he could. Eventually the album was distributed by Track Records in Britain, under the condition that it was wrapped in brown paper bags before going on sale. Even then, problems arose with printing the sleeves and, even when it was ready for release, many shops refused to stock the record. No advertisements for the album appeared in the music press, as no editors would accept advertising copy for the album. Even though Paul McCartney was strongly opposed to the album being issued because of the sleeve, he still supplied a sleeve note which read: "When two great Saints meet, it is a humbling experience. The long battle to prove he was a Saint".

Understandably, the album never entered the British charts, as it only sold about 5,000 copies, and was the first Beatles' solo album to be deleted by EMI. It was later reinstated into the catalogue via European Imports, distributed by Charmdale, in January 1975, before being again deleted in 1978.

A SIDE

1 **TWO VIRGINS 1**
2 **TOGETHER (De Silva, Brown & Henderson)**
3 **TWO VIRGINS 2**
4 **TWO VIRGINS 3**
5 **TWO VIRGINS 4**
6 **TWO VIRGINS 5** *(Total time 14.13)*

B SIDE

7 **TWO VIRGINS 6**
8 **HUSHABYE, HUSHABYE**
9 **TWO VIRGINS 7**
10 **TWO VIRGINS 8**
11 **TWO VIRGINS 9**
12 **TWO VIRGINS 10** *(Total time 15.11)*

Although the label lists twelve titles, it is almost impossible to distinguish between each track.

2 UNFINISHED MUSIC No. 2 – LIFE WITH THE LIONS

By John Lennon and Yoko Ono

Zapple ZAPPLE 01 – May 9, 1969

John and Yoko's second instalment in the series of recordings meant to chronicle their lives together again featured very avant-garde performances, this time recorded at a live concert in Cambridge and in a London hospital.

No 1173 Week ending July 5, 1969

BATH, ALBERT HALL SHOWS: WORDS AND PICS

PRESLEY SPEAKS

AT HOME WITH THUNDERCLAP

* FAMILY DOGG

TOP POP NEWS

* CHICKEN SHACK

STONES NEW SINGLE

WORLD'S **LARGEST** CIRCULATION OF **ANY** MUSIC PAPER

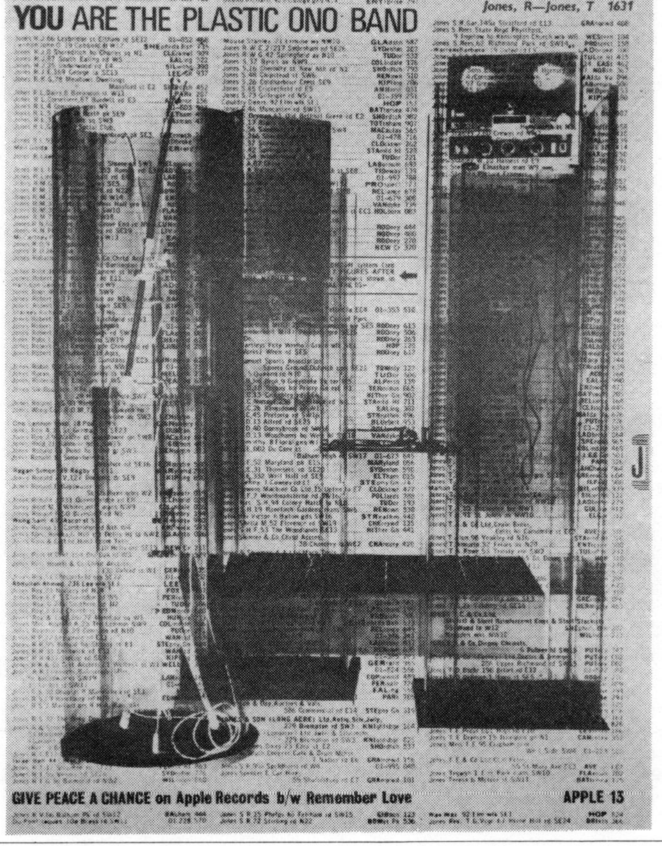

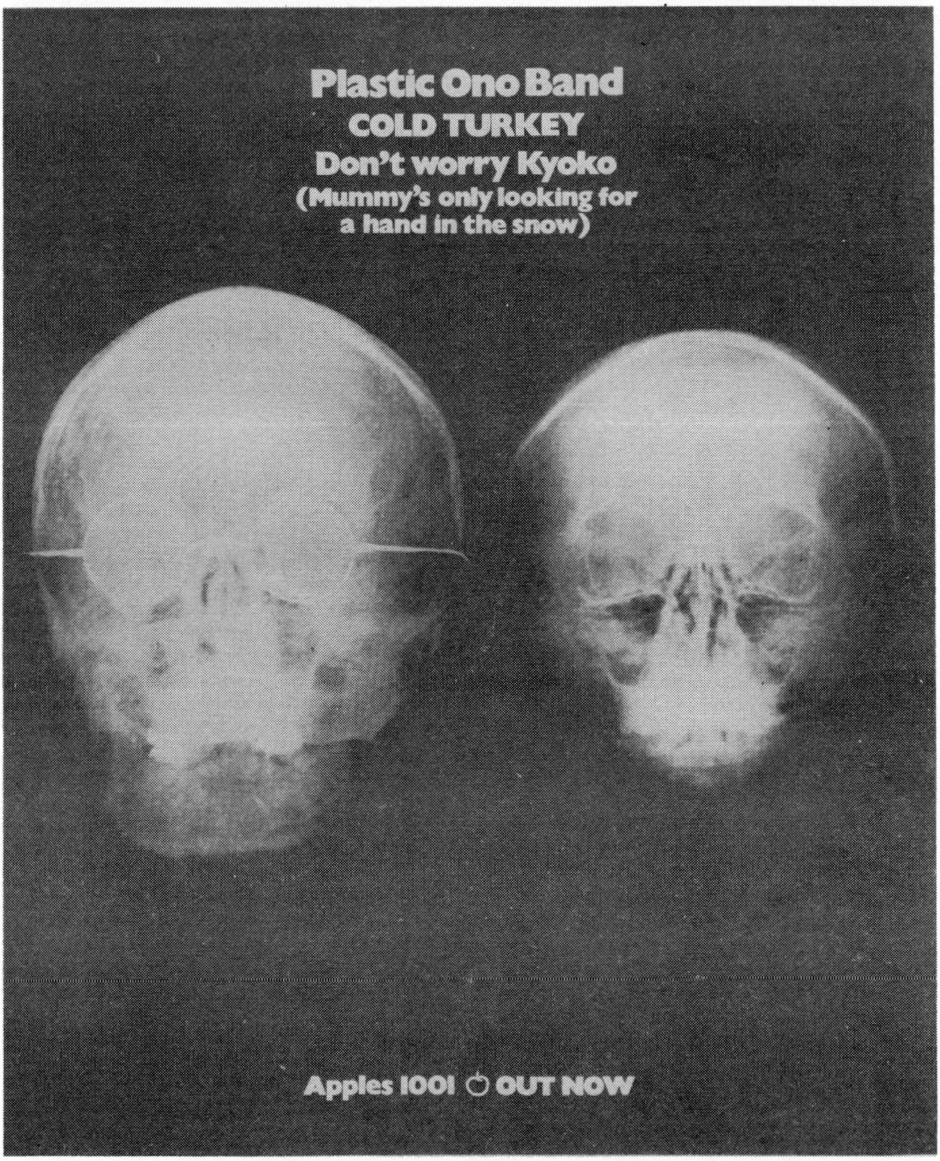

Apples 1001 OUT NOW

The front cover photograph was taken by Susan Wood in Room No 1, Second West Ward, Queen Charlotte Hospital, Hammersmith, London, during November 1968. The back cover photograph was taken by a *Daily Mirror* photographer outside the Marylebone Magistrates Court, 181 Marylebone Road, London, on October 19, 1968, after John and Yoko had appeared in court upon charges of possession of hashish. On October 18, John and Yoko had been arrested in Ringo's Montagu Square flat, where police had found amounts of the drug, which John always insisted were planted. In court the following day John pleaded guilty, allowing charges against Yoko to be dropped, as she was pregnant at the time. It was this drugs charge which caused John his "Green Card" problems in America during the seventies.

The album was produced by John and Yoko, and the album sleeve includes a quote from Beatles' producer, George Martin: "No comment".

As with *Two Virgins*, John and Yoko did not enjoy any chart success with this album, as once again it only sold about 5,000 copies.

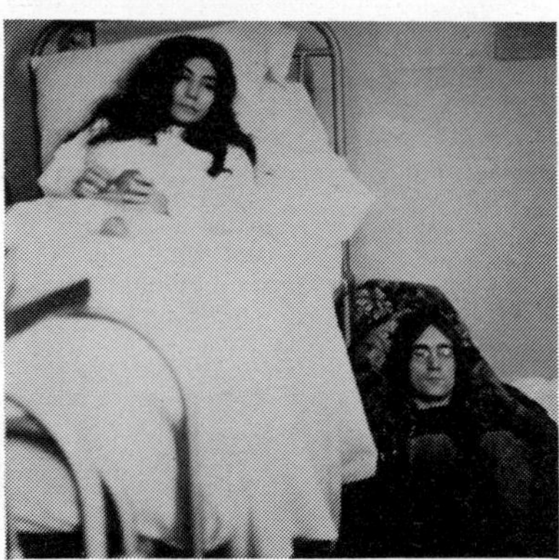

A SIDE

13 **CAMBRIDGE 1969** *(26.30)*

B SIDE

14 **NO BED FOR BEATLE JOHN** *(4.50)*

15 **BABY'S HEARTBEAT** *(5.10)*

16 **TWO MINUTES SILENCE** *(2.01)*

17 **RADIO PLAY** *(12.33)*

Cambridge 1969 was recorded live on March 2, 1969, at Lady Mitchell Hall, Cambridge, England, with Yoko Ono/vocals, John/guitar, John Tchikai/saxophone, and John Stevens/percussion, who emerge towards the end of the piece. The recordings consist mainly of Yoko singing in a free form style, with John producing feedback sounds from his guitar. John's appearance at the concert constituted the first solo Beatles' performance anywhere.

The whole of the second side of the album was recorded on a cassette machine in Room No 1, Second West Ward, Queen Charlotte Hospital, Hammersmith, London, between November 4 and 25, 1968, during Yoko's pregnancy, which resulted in a miscarriage on November 21. All of the "songs" are credited to Lennon/Ono, *No Bed For Beatle John* being Yoko and John "singing" various newspaper reports of John's problems in keeping a bed in the hospital, and the *Two Virgins* cover fiasco. John was originally staying in a bed in the hospital to be with Yoko, but the bed was later needed for a patient and John had to use a sleeping bag in Yoko's room (see cover photo). *Baby's Heartbeat* is simply that, a recording of Yoko's unborn child's heart. *Two Minutes Silence* speaks for itself, and *Radio Play* is recordings of Lennon fiddling with the dials of a radio, with various pieces of conversation in the background.

3 (18) GIVE PEACE A CHANCE *(4.50)* (19) REMEMBER LOVE *(4.00)*

By The Plastic Ono Band

Apple APPLE 13 – July 4, 1969

Between May 26 and June 3, 1969, John and Yoko (with Kyoko, Yoko's daughter by a previous marriage) held their second "bed-in" in the Hotel La Reine Elizabeth (The Queen Elizabeth Hotel), Montreal, Canada, in Room 1742. During their stay, John and Yoko wrote *Give Peace A Chance*, their first composition together, and John decided to record it immediately, so he ordered an eight-track recorder to be moved into their bedroom. Within hours, the André Perry Studios had installed the required equipment and, with John and Yoko singing, John and Tommy Smothers playing guitars, and Yoko banging a wardrobe, the song was recorded on June 1, 1969. Helping out with the infectious chorus were Allen Ginsberg, Rosemary and Timothy Leary, Murray The K, Dick Gregory, Petula Clark, Derek Taylor, Rabbi Geinsberg, a priest, various members of the hotel staff, reporters, camera men, a film crew and the Canadian Chapter of the Radha Krishna Temple. John called this hastily assembled group of chanters The Plastic Ono Band and continued to use the name for many of his various back-up bands, although the musicians varied from album to album and concert to concert. *Remember Love,* written solely by Yoko, was also recorded in the hotel room.

The single entered the *NME* Top 30 on July 9, 1969, at No. 22, rising to No. 2 on July 30 for one week. The record was in the Top 30 for ten weeks, selling over 250,000 in the UK, and over two million world-wide.

A press reception was held for the single at the Chelsea Town Hall on July 3, but John and Yoko were unable to attend, due to their involvement in a car accident in Golspie, Scotland, two days previously. The Plastic Ono Band were represented by an abstract design of pieces of clear plastic and recording equipment, while Ringo and Maureen Starr deputised for John and Yoko.

Give Peace A Chance has subsequently become a frequently used campaign song by those protesting for peace or against the establishment. The most well known performance of this kind was at the Peace March in 1969, at the Washington Monument, where 250,000 people joined Pete Seeger in a moving rendition of the song.

4 (20) COLD TURKEY *(5.00)* (21) DON'T WORRY KYOKO (Mummy's Only Looking For A Hand In The Snow) *(4.00)*

By The Plastic Ono Band

Apple APPLES 1001 – October 24, 1969

In the August 1969 issue of *Beatles Monthly,* a news item reported that the next Plastic Ono Band record would be "a long and heavy instrumental single" called "Rock Peace", to be released at the end of August 1969. The single never materialized, but instead *Cold Turkey* appeared in October 1969 and, although not an instrumental, it did turn out to have a very heavy sound, produced by John's latest incarnation of The Plastic Ono Band: John/guitar and vocals; Eric Clapton/lead guitar; Klaus Voorman/bass guitar; Ringo Starr/drums; and Yoko/backing vocals. John collected this band of top musicians together to record his latest song because Paul refused to record the song as The Beatles, and therefore John decided it was time to drop the "Lennon and McCartney" composing credits from his songs, *Cold Turkey* being solely credited to John Lennon. The song was recorded on September 30, 1969, with John and Yoko producing, and the "B" side, featuring a song written by Yoko to her daughter Kyoko, was recorded using the same line up of musicians, and later appeared on her solo album, *Fly.*

The single entered the *NME* Top 30 on November 5, 1969, at No. 23, rising to No. 13 on November 19 for one week. The single stayed in the Top 30 for six weeks. During the week ending November 26, *Cold Turkey* dropped to No. 17 and, on November 25, John returned his MBE to Buckingham Palace to protest, so he said, against Britain's involvement in the Nigerian-Biafran War, against Britain's support of America in Vietnam and because *Cold Turkey* had slipped down the charts. John returning his MBE caused as much trouble as when he was initially awarded the decoration in 1965.

5 THE WEDDING ALBUM

By John Lennon and Yoko Ono

Apple SAPCOR 11 – November 7, 1969

JOHN & YOKO
KLAUS VOORMANN
ALAN WHITE
ERIC CLAPTON
courtesy of Polydor
Records
With fab pics and poetry
in 1970 calendar!
PLASTIC ONO BAND–LIVE PEACE IN TORONTO APPLE RECORDS CORE 2001 OUT NOW

John and Yoko's third episode in their "Unfinished Music" series – although not titled as such – was a souvenir of their marriage, which took place on March 20, 1969, in Gibraltar. Due to the elaborate packaging, comprising a boxed set containing the album, a poster of wedding pictures, a photograph of a piece of wedding cake inside a plastic bag titled "Bagism", a cartoon strip by John depicting the wedding, a booklet of press cuttings, a postcard, a strip of "passport" pictures, and a copy of the marriage certificate, the album took eight months to produce. The whole package was designed by John Kosh, with photographs taken by Mlle Daniau, Richard DiLello (the Apple "House Hippie", author of the book *The Longest Cocktail Party,* a very informative and enjoyable insider's look at the Apple fiasco), John Kelly, Nico Koster, David Nutter and John and Yoko.

When preview copies of the album were sent out prior to release, the two recordings were pressed as two single-sided LPs with apparently empty grooves on the two blank sides. *Melody Maker* reviewer Richard Williams reported that the album was a double LP, with sides two and four consisting "entirely of single tones maintained throughout, presumably produced electronically". He also apparently believed that, if listened to intently, the pitch of the tones altered frequently by a microtone or a semitone, thus producing an uneven "beat". In fact, what Williams "reviewed" was an engineer's test signal, as EMI test pressings, unlike those used by many other labels, were single-sided. A week later he received a telegram from John and Yoko in Bombay which read: "DEAR RICHARD THANK YOU FOR YOUR FANTASTIC REVIEW ON OUR WEDDING ALBUM INCLUDING C-AND-D SIDE STOP WE ARE CONSIDERING IT FOR OUR NEXT RELEASE STOP MAYBE YOU ARE RIGHT IN SAYING THAT THEY ARE THE BEST SIDES STOP WE BOTH FEEL THAT THIS IS THE FIRST TIME A CRITIC TOPPED THE ARTIST STOP WE ARE NOT JOKING STOP LOVE AND PEACE STOP JOHN AND YOKO LENNON."

The album did not enter the British charts.

A SIDE

22 **JOHN AND YOKO***(22.38)*

B SIDE

23 **AMSTERDAM***(24.54)*

John and Yoko consists of the couple calling out each other's names in varying ways; shouting, crying, whispering, pleading, laughing, wailing etc., to the sound of their own heartbeats. The second side, *Amsterdam,* was recorded on a cassette during John and Yoko's honeymoon "bed-in" in the Hilton Hotel, Amsterdam, on March 26, 1969. The recording consists mainly of John and Yoko talking to reporters about peace, "bagism" and their bed-ins, but also includes four musical items. The opening song by Yoko is called *John, Let's Hope For Peace* (which would later be performed at the Toronto Rock 'n' Roll Revival Concert), while the second offering is from John, who strums a guitar and sings *Goodbye Amsterdam Goodbye.* John and Yoko then sing a song probably called *Stay In Bed* or *Bed Peace,* with John supplying the guitar accompaniment, and finally John sings a very off-key rendition of *Goodnight,* sung by Ringo on the Beatles' *White Album,* released during 1968.

6 THE PLASTIC ONO BAND – LIVE PEACE IN TORONTO 1969

By The Plastic Ono Band

Apple CORE 2001 – December 12, 1969

While John and Yoko were in Toronto, during their bed-ins, they met some friends who were planning to stage a "Rock 'n' Roll Revival Concert", and were invited to appear. At very short notice, on September 12, 1969, John and Yoko contacted Eric Clapton (guitar), Alan White (drums), Klaus Voorman (bass guitar), Anthony Fawcett (John and Yoko's personal assistant), Terry Doran (George Harrison's assistant) and Jill and Dan Richter (who were filming John and Yoko), and this group of people boarded a Boeing 707 bound for Toronto, Canada. During the flight, John and Yoko's band rehearsed several songs in the rear of the plane, and the following day walked out in front of 25,000 Canadians to perform eight numbers in the Varsity Stadium as part of the Toronto Rock 'n' Roll Revival Concert. The concert also featured rock and roll legends such as Little Richard, Gene Vincent, Chuck Berry and Bo Diddley (Jerry Lee Lewis withdrew at the last minute).

The album of this September 13 concert was produced by John and Yoko and featured a very stark sleeve design by John Kosh. Original copies included a John and Yoko Calendar for 1970, featuring pictures of John and Yoko, plus various poems and songs by both. Several of the poems were taken from John and Yoko's books *In His Own Write, A Spaniard In The Works* and *Grapefruit* (Yoko), but particularly interesting are the poems by John on the top leaf, which originally appeared in recorded form on the Beatles 1968 Christmas record; they appear in print here for the first (and only) time.

The album did not enter the *NME* Top 30 album charts.

A SIDE

24 **BLUE SUEDE SHOES***(2.11)*

25 **MONEY***(2.59)*

26 **DIZZY MISS LIZZY***(3.02)*

27 **YER BLUES***(3.35)*

28 **COLD TURKEY***(3.00)*

29 **GIVE PEACE A CHANCE***(3.05)*

B SIDE

30 **DON'T WORRY KYOKO (Mummy's Only Looking For A Hand In The Snow)***(4.20)*

31 **JOHN JOHN (LET'S HOPE FOR PEACE)** *(12.00)*

John kicked off the performance with three vintage rock 'n' roll classics, two of which, *Money* and *Dizzy Miss Lizzy*, had been previously recorded by the Beatles on *With The Beatles* and *Help* respectively. *Blue Suede Shoes* was written by Carl Perkins, who took it to No. 4 in the United States during the 1950's, selling two million copies world-wide. The song was also covered with great success by Elvis Presley. The *White Album* song, *Yer Blues*, followed, with Yoko introducing *Cold Turkey* as a new number, as it was being performed live for the first time. It was later re-recorded by John in London as a Plastic Ono Band single, the follow up to *Give Peace A Chance*, which itself closes the first side, with John admitting that while he could remember the chorus, he had forgotten the lyrics of the verses. The second side features two songs written by Yoko, *Don't Worry Kyoko* (also being performed live for the first time and later released as the "B" side to *Cold Turkey*). *John John (Let's Hope For Peace)*, which originally appeared on *The Wedding Album*, features Yoko "singing" over the feedback guitars of John, Eric and Klaus, who at the end of the number placed their guitars against their amplifiers (thus continuing the feedback sounds), walked to the centre of the stage, lit cigarettes, and then walked off. Mal Evans then walked onstage and turned each amplifier off in turn.

7 (32) INSTANT KARMA*(3.19)* (33) WHO HAS SEEN THE WIND*(2.01)*

By Lennon/Ono With The Plastic Ono Band

Apple APPLES 1003 – February 6, 1970

The follow up single to *Cold Turkey* was originally reported as being, at different times, either "Make Love Not War" ("Mind Games") or "You Know My Name (Look Up The Number)", but neither appeared. On January 27, 1970, John wrote, recorded and mixed *Instant Karma,* with Phil Spector producing, and with The Plastic Ono Band consisting of John/vocals, guitar and electric piano; Yoko/vocals; George Harrison/guitar and grand piano; Klaus Voorman/bass guitar and electric piano; Alan White/drums and grand piano; Billy Preston/organ; Mal Evans/clapping and chimes; and, helping with the chorus, Allen Klein and a couple of dozen late-night revellers from London's Hatchetts Club, rounded up by Billy Preston at the last minute and conducted by George Harrison. The heavy piano sound was achieved by Lennon, Harrison, Voorman and White all playing grand pianos or electric pianos. The "B" side, *Who Has Seen The Wind,* written and sung by Yoko, was produced by John. The single was released ten days after being recorded, on February 6, 1970, thus being probably one of the fastest singles of modern times to be completed.

The single entered the *NME* Top 30 on February 18 at No. 17, rising to No. 5 the following week, where it remained for three weeks, and staying in the Top 30 for seven weeks. The record was the first Beatle solo single to sell a million in America, and has probably sold over two million globally.

8 JOHN LENNON/PLASTIC ONO BAND

By John Lennon and The Plastic Ono Band

Apple PCS 7124 – December 11, 1970

John's first true solo album was the result of several months of treatment at Arthur Janov's Primal Institute in Los Angeles. After John and Yoko had read Dr Janov's book, *The Primal Scream,* Janov gave them three weeks of intensive private treatment in London during March, 1970, followed by five months of treatment,

between April and August, in Los Angeles, where John wrote most of the songs for the album.

The album was mainly recorded in early October 1970, in England, at EMI Studios in Abbey Road, where John and Yoko and Phil Spector produced the sessions. The Plastic Ono Band consisted of John/vocal, guitar and piano; Ringo Starr/drums; Klaus Voorman/bass guitar; Billy Preston/piano on *God;* Phil Spector/piano on *Love;* while Yoko is credited with "wind". The sleeve was designed by John and Yoko, featuring a front cover photograph by Dan Richter, and a back cover photo showing a young John. (The front cover photograph is almost identical to Yoko Ono's solo album released at the same time – except that John and Yoko reverse places.) The inner sleeve contains the song lyrics, but one word in *I Found Out* and two words in *Working Class Hero* are replaced with asterisks, as EMI had refused to handle the album if lyrical profanities were to appear in print. EMI eventually won their battle, but Apple added the legend "omitted at the insistence of EMI".

The album entered the *NME* album chart on January 13, 1971, at No. 17, rising to No. 13 on February 3 for four weeks, and staying in the chart for ten weeks.

A SIDE

34 **MOTHER***(5.31)*

35 **HOLD ON***(1.49)*

36 **I FOUND OUT***(3.34)*

37 **WORKING CLASS HERO***(3.47)*

38 **ISOLATION***(2.48)*

B SIDE

39 **REMEMBER***(4.32)*

40 **LOVE***(3.18)*

41 **WELL WELL WELL***(5.55)*

42 **LOOK AT ME***(2.51)*

43 **GOD***(4.07)*

44 **MY MUMMY'S DEAD***(0.48)*

Mother and *Isolation* were written in England, while *Look At Me* was left over from the *White Album* period. *Remember* was edited down from an extended jam session in the studio, while *My Mummy's Dead* was recorded by John alone on a cassette recorder. John supposedly wrote *God* in answer to George's religious beliefs.

9 (45) POWER TO THE PEOPLE*(3.21)* (46) OPEN YOUR BOX*(3.31)*

"A" side by John Lennon and The Plastic Ono Band

"B" side by Yoko Ono and The Plastic Ono Band

Apple R 5892 – March 12, 1971

Both sides of John and Yoko's fourth single were recorded in February 1971, with Phil Spector and John and Yoko producing the "A" side, and John and Yoko producing the "B" side. Yoko had to re-record parts of the vocal for her song *Open Your Box* on March 4, 1971, due to EMI insisting that the lyrics be "cleaned-up", as Mr Philip Brodie, then Managing Director of EMI Records, considered them "distasteful". *Open Your Box* was recorded with a Plastic Ono Band line-up of Yoko/vocals; John/guitar; Klaus Voorman/bass guitar and Jim Gordon/drums. *Power To The People* featured John/vocals, with the addition of Rosetta Hightower and forty-four others helping with backing vocals.

The record should have been released on March 6, 1971, but the problems with Yoko's song held up release until a week later. It entered the *NME* Top 30 on March 17, at No. 20, reaching No. 6 on April 14 and staying seven weeks in the chart. The record has sold a global million.

GOD SAVE US*(3.09)* DO THE OZ*(3.07)*

"A" side by Bill Elliot and The Elastic Oz Band

"B" side by The Elastic Oz Band

Apple APPLE 36 – July 16, 1971

During 1971, the three main figures behind the publication of *Oz*, the "underground" magazine of the late sixties and early seventies, Jim Anderson, Felix Dennis and Richard Neville, were prosecuted under the Obscene Publications Act, the offending publication being issue No. 28, known as "The School Kids" issue. To help pay their court costs, John and Yoko wrote the two songs on this single, and donated their royalties to help the defence fund. Anderson, Dennis and Neville were found guilty on several counts and sentenced to prison terms of between nine and fifteen months on August 4, 1971. The magazine continued publication until the winter of 1973, when the last issue, No. 48, was published.

The vocalist on *God Save Us* is Bill Elliot, who later teamed up with Bob Purvis to form Splinter (who recorded for George Harrison's Dark Horse Records). The song was produced by John, Yoko, Mal Evans and Phil Spector, while *Do The Oz* features lead vocals by John, with Yoko supporting on backing vocals, and was produced by John and Yoko and Phil Spector.

The passing of time and failing memories have made it difficult to discover with any accuracy precisely who played on these tracks, but it has been suggested that among those who participated on the recording were: Lennon and Charles Shaar Murray (acoustic guitars), Ringo (drums), Klaus Voorman (bass), Bobby Keyes (saxophone), a black girl known as Michelle (acoustic guitar), and an unnamed white girl (keyboards). Charles Shaar Murray reveals that the lead vocal was originally sung by one Michael, and that Bill Elliot's voice was only added at a later date.

On the rear of the picture sleeve,

GOD SAVE US
ELASTIC OZ BAND

OUTCRY AS OZ EDITORS ARE JAILED
Labour MPs attack 'act of revenge'
Daily Telegraph

FURY OVER OZ JAILINGS
Angry MPs join the wave of protest
The Sun

OZ: OBSCENE! BUT WHY THE FEROCIOUS SENTENCES?

NEVILLE Sentenced to fifteen months

ANDERSON Sentenced to [illegible]

THE JUDGE Accused of an 'act of revenge'

Fury as three editors are jailed
Daily Mirror

Oz sentences – Labour MPs sign protest
Daily Express

COMMENT

Personal reactions —

Kenneth Tynan, of "Oh! Calcutta" [illegible]: "Battle has been joined between Judge Argyle's England and a Free England."

Mrs. Mary Whitehouse, TV campaigner: "It is a very good thing the [illegible] has been drawn."

John Lennon called it all "disgusting fascism."

Lord Soper thought the verdict was right but the sentence "savage."

Kingsley Amis, author, member of Lord Longford's committee on pornography: "My instinct is to cheer anything nasty that might happen to this unsavoury [illegible]. At the same time nobody should be sent to prison for obscenity—whatever that is."

John Trevelyan, former film censor: "I have seen Oz and I don't like it. But I think the sentences are much too severe in relation to the offences."

John Braine, author, said he had no sympathy with Oz but "I don't see why these people should be singled out for this severe treatment."

Mick Jagger: "If there has been a moral crime committed [illegible] police and the judge."

Organisations joined in:—

● National Council for Civil Liberties: "The sentences are savage and vindictive."

● The Young Liberals described it as "a sordid and snivelling little political trial."

● The Haldane Society of progressive lawyers said the case "will bring the law into [illegible]."

MPs condemn OZ gaolings as 'Establishment revenge'
The Guardian

Demonstrations and protests against 'Oz' jail sentences
The Times

'Shocked MPs protest: It looks like revenge

STORM OVER OZ SENTENCES
Daily Mail

THE prison sentences on three editors of Oz magazine unleashed a storm of controversy last night

Apple are donating royalties on this record to the Oz Obscenity Fund

several individuals connected with *Oz* are featured; while the two males standing in the middle at the back have not been positively identified, the remaining people are (back row, left to right): Sue Miles (who worked at *Oz*, and is now a high-class caterer in London); Jim Anderson (now apparently Mayor of the town of Bolinas, California, where hippies out-number others); the two mystery men; Stan Demidjuk (or Demajug), an Australian antique dealer of Yugoslav extraction (who was mail order manager and connected with fund-raising activities for Oz, and was last heard of in France); and Felix Dennis himself (now Chairman of the successful Bunch Books organisation, and resident in New York). And finally (front row, left to right): Debbie Knight (secretary at Oz, and still living in London); and Bill Elliot.

The single was recorded at John's studio in Ascot. Lyrics were written by Yoko, and the tracks were recorded in a "semi-live" manner to resemble the successful *Give Peace A Chance*. Charles Shaar Murray was an actual contributor to "The School Kids" issue of *Oz*. He subsequently went on to become a well-known rock writer (particularly for the *New Musical Express*), and during the 1970s he led his own band – originally known as Blast Furnace and The Heat-waves but then, following an injunction by another group known as Heatwave, as Blast Furnace and The Copyright Violations.

The record had no chart success.

10 IMAGINE

By John Lennon and The Plastic Ono Band, with The Flux Fiddlers.

Apple PAS 10004 – October 8, 1971

John's second non-experimental solo album was recorded in July 1971, in the eight-track recording studio built in his home at Tittenhurst Park which he called Ascot Sound Studios. The album was produced by John and Yoko and Phil Spector, and the strings, credited as The Flux Fiddlers, were overdubbed at the

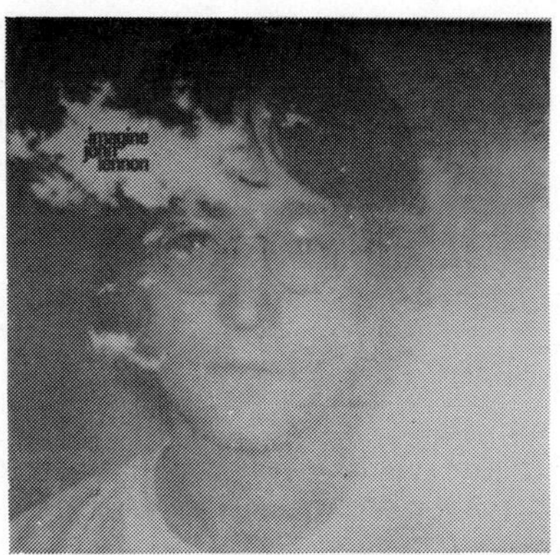

Record Plant, New York. The cover was designed by Yoko, who also took the photograph of John. Original copies of the album, as well as including a printed inner sleeve containing lyrics and credits, also contained a large poster of John at his white grand piano, and a small postcard size picture of John holding a pig by the ears (a parody of Paul's *Ram* album cover).

The album entered the *NME* Top 30 album charts on October 20, at No. 11, and rose to No. 1 on November 3 where it remained for three weeks. It featured in the charts for thirty-two weeks, and was listed in the Top Ten for fourteen weeks. After Lennon's tragic murder in December 1980, sales of his and all Beatles records escalated dramatically. *Imagine* re-entered the chart on January 17, 1981, at No. 4, its highest position, and remained in the chart for a further nine weeks, making a combined total of forty-two weeks.

A SIDE

47 **IMAGINE** *(3.01)*

48 **CRIPPLED INSIDE** *(3.46)*

49 **JEALOUS GUY** *(4.13)*

50 **IT'S SO HARD** *(2.24)*

51 **I DON'T WANT TO BE A SOLDIER MAMA, I DON'T WANT TO DIE** *(6.03)*

B SIDE

52 **GIVE ME SOME TRUTH** *(3.11)*

53 **OH MY LOVE** *(2.42)*

54 **HOW DO YOU SLEEP?** *(5.32)*

55 **HOW?** *(3.39)*

56 **OH YOKO** *(4.15)*

Imagine was originally inspired by poems in Yoko's book, *Grapefruit* (several poems in the book start with an instruction to "Imagine . . ."), although

John did not give Yoko any composing credit. The song became the theme for the "One To One" Charity Foundation in America, and features John/piano; Klaus Voorman/piano; and Alan White/drums.

Crippled Inside supposedly attacks Paul, as John insisted that Paul's song *3 Legs*, from *Ram*, was directed at him. The song features John/guitar; Nicky Hopkins/piano; Klaus Voorman and Steve Brendell/upright basses; George Harrison/dobro; and a trio of acoustic guitars played by Ted Turner, Rod Linton and John Tout.

Jealous Guy was apparently inspired by, and co-written with, Yoko, although her contributions are not credited. The song features John/electric guitar; Klaus/bass guitar; Jim Gordon/drums; John Barham/harmonium; and Alan White/vibes. After Lennon's death in 1980, Roxy Music recorded the song as a tribute to its composer. It entered the *NME* Top 30 on February 28, 1981, at No. 14, rising to No. 1 for two weeks from March 14, and featuring in the chart for seven weeks.

It's So Hard features a simple line-up of John/guitar; Klaus/bass; Jim Gordon/drums; and King Curtis/saxophone.

I Don't Want To Be A Soldier features the largest Plastic Ono Band aggregation on the album with John/guitar; Nicky Hopkins/piano; Klaus/bass; Jim Gordon/drums; George Harrison/slide guitar; King Curtis/saxophone; Badfinger members Joey Molland and Tom Evans/acoustic guitars, Steve Brendell/maracas; and Moody Blue Mike Pinder/tambourine.

Give Me Some Truth was written in India in 1968, and was originally rehearsed (but not officially released) by The Beatles during the "Let It Be" sessions. Here, John plays guitar, with George Harrison/lead guitar; Nicky Hopkins/piano; Klaus/basses; Alan White/drums; and Rod Linton and Andy Cresswell-Davis (who is credited as simply "Andy" on the sleeve)/acoustic guitars. Andy Cresswell-Davis was a founder member of the West Country band, Stackridge, and later co-leader of The Korgis.

Oh My Love, co-written by John and Yoko (who on this occasion is credited on the sleeve) features George Harrison/guitar; John/piano; Klaus/bass; Alan White/drums and Tibetan cymbals; and Nicky Hopkins/electric piano.

How Do You Sleep?, John's bitter attack on Paul, features John/guitar; Nicky/piano; Klaus/bass; Alan White/drums; and George Harrison/slide guitar.

How features both John and Nicky playing piano, with Klaus/bass, Alan/drums; and John Barham/vibes.

Oh Yoko, written in 1968 by John and Yoko, features John/guitar and mouth organ; with Nicky/piano; Klaus/bass; Alan/drums; and acoustic guitars by Rod Linton and Andy Davis.

11 SOME TIME IN NEW YORK CITY

Record One by John and Yoko/Plastic Ono Band with Elephant's Memory plus Invisible Strings

Record Two by The Plastic Ono Supergroup and The Plastic Ono Mothers

Apple PCSP 716 – September 15, 1972

This double album was released in America three months before its British appearance, the delay being caused by copyright problems concerning Yoko's co-composing credits with John, as Northern Songs would not acknowledge Yoko's composing claims for some of the songs. As a result by the time the album was released in Britain, many copies had been imported from America. The British release, although with the same cover

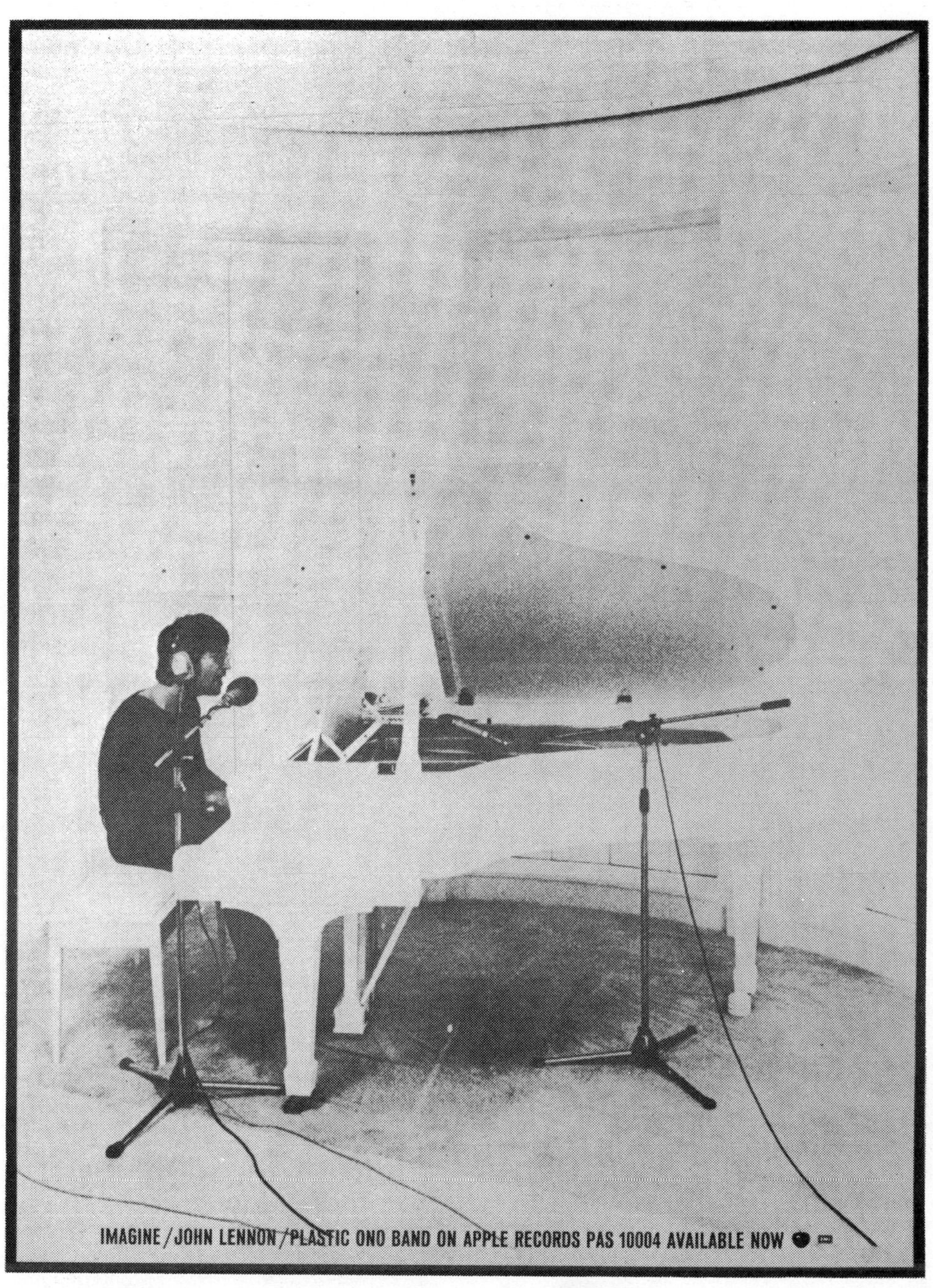
IMAGINE / JOHN LENNON / PLASTIC ONO BAND ON APPLE RECORDS PAS 10004 AVAILABLE NOW

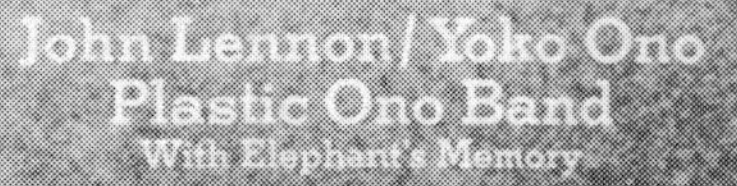
John Lennon/Yoko Ono
Plastic Ono Band
With Elephant's Memory
"Some Time in New York City"
"The People's Album"
—Melody Maker
Ring 01-247 6693

design (by Michael Gross) as the American version, did not include the insertion of a postcard of the Statue of Liberty, and a petition about John's expulsion from the US. The album was supposedly to be sold as a single LP, with a free bonus album of the "Live Jam" set, but in both Britain and America it had a slightly higher retail price than a normal album. The album entered the *NME* Top 30 album chart on October 10 at No. 22, staying in the chart for five weeks and dropping out from No. 19 its highest position.

The first and second sides of the album were recorded between March 1 and 20, 1972, in New York, with John and Yoko and Phil Spector producing. The Plastic Ono Band, consisting of John/vocals and guitar; Yoko/vocals and drum; and Jim Keltner/drums and percussion, were augmented by Elephant's Memory, a New York rock band, who contributed to the soundtrack of the film, *Midnight Cowboy.* The line-up of the band was Stan Bronstein/saxophone and flute; Richard Frank Jnr/drums and percussion; Gary Van Scyoc/bass; Adam Ippolito/piano and organ; and Wayne (Tex) Gabriel/guitar.

RECORD ONE A SIDE

57 **WOMAN IS THE NIGGER OF THE WORLD** *(5.14)*

58 **SISTERS, O SISTERS** *(3.45)*

59 **ATTICA STATE** *(2.52)*

60 **BORN IN A PRISON** *(4.02)*

61 **NEW YORK CITY** *(4.30)*

RECORD ONE B SIDE

62 **SUNDAY BLOODY SUNDAY** *(4.58)*

63 **THE LUCK OF THE IRISH** *(2.55)*

64 **JOHN SINCLAIR** *(3.26)*

65 **ANGELA** *(4.04)*

66 **WE'RE ALL WATER** *(7.11)*

Woman Is The Nigger Of The World, written by John and Yoko, and sung by John, was originally scheduled as a single in Britain (Parlophone number R 5953) to be released on December 5, 1972, but was withdrawn although promotional copies were distributed to radio stations.

Sisters, O Sisters, written solely by Yoko, features Yoko multi-tracked on solo vocals. *Attica State* was written by John and Yoko about the killing of prisoners and guards at the Attica State Prison in New York, during the "Attica Uprising", where troops were sent in by Governor Rockerfeller. John and Yoko sing together.

The second Yoko song, *Born In A Prison,* on which she again takes solo vocal, features John La Bosca on piano. Lennon's *New York City* features John singing solo.

Sunday Bloody Sunday was written by John and Yoko to protest about the "Bloody Sunday" massacre in Ireland on January 3, 1972, and features John singing lead, with Yoko assisting with the chorus.

The Luck Of The Irish, another Lennon/Ono composition, complaining about British interference in Northern Ireland, features John singing the first, second and fourth verses, with Yoko singing the third and fifth, and both singing the last. This song was nearly released as the main track on an EP featuring four numbers recorded live at a concert in Ann Arbor, Michigan, on December 18, 1971, when John and Yoko performed, with Jerry Rubin on bongos, *Attica State, The Luck Of The Irish, Sisters, O Sisters* and *John Sinclair.* The EP was withdrawn due to the reception Paul's political statement, "Give Ireland Back To The Irish", received.

John Sinclair features John on slide guitar and singing solo, and was written as a protest against Sinclair's imprisonment for ten years for the possession of a very small amount of marijuana.

Angela, written jointly by John and Yoko, is yet another protest song, supporting Angela Davis, who was on trial for conspiring in the prison escape of her husband, George Jackson. John and Yoko sing together.

We're All Water features Yoko singing her own composition.

RECORD TWO A SIDE

67 **COLD TURKEY** *(6.40)*

68 **DON'T WORRY KYOKO** *(14.48)*

RECORD TWO B SIDE

69 **WELL (BABY PLEASE DON'T GO)** *(3.38)*

70 **JAMRAG**

71 **SCUMBAG**

72 **AÜ** *(total time 16.59)*

The "free bonus" record with the album, titled *Live Jam,* featured two live sessions from John and Yoko recorded with various superstars during 1969 and 1971. The first side was recorded on Monday, December 15, 1969, at a concert in aid of UNICEF (United Nations Children's Fund), staged in the Lyceum Ballroom in London. Due to record company contractual problems, the record sleeve gives a list of pseudonyms for the many superstars who appeared with John and Yoko performing *Cold Turkey* and *Don't Worry Kyoko.* The full line-up for the Plastic Ono Supergroup was: John/vocals and guitar; George Harrison, Eric Clapton, and Delaney Bramlett/guitars; Klaus Voorman/bass; Jim Gordon, Keith Moon and Alan White/drums; Billy Preston/organ (which was "lost" during the recording, and was replaced by Nicky Hopkins' electric piano, overdubbed in New York); Bonnie Bramlett and "Friends"/percussion and brass – "Friends" included Bobby Keyes/saxophone, Jim Price/trumpet, with Bobby Whitlock and Carl Radle; and also assisting was "Legs" Larry Smith (from the Bonzo Dog Doo Dah Band); and Dino Danelli, the drummer from The (Young) Rascals.

The second side was recorded at the famous Fillmore East auditorium in New York on June 6, 1971. John and Yoko appeared unannounced for this performance with Frank Zappa's Mothers Of Invention, which consisted at the time of Frank Zappa/vocals and guitar; Ian Underwood/woodwinds, piano and vocals; Don Preston/mini moog; Bob Harris/vocals and piano; Aynsley Dunbar/drums; Mark Volman and Howard Kaylan/vocals; with John on vocals and guitar, and Yoko/vocals. Although not present at the concert, Klaus Voorman later overdubbed bass onto *Well (Baby Please Don't Go)* in the studio.

John announces, before performing *Well (Baby Please Don't Go),* that he used to sing the number in the Cavern days. The song was written by Walter Ward, and was originally recorded by The Olympics as the coupling to their 1958 hit, *Western Movies,* which reached No. 8 in the US, and No. 12 in the UK. The last three numbers on the album are basically a free-form jam between John and Yoko and The Mothers, it being very difficult to distinguish the point where one number finishes and the next starts. *Jamrag* and *Aü,* credited to Lennon/Ono, largely comprise Yoko "wailing" over feedback and synthesizers, while *Scumbag,* credited to Lennon/Ono/Zappa, does boast an actual tune, plus a lyric of a sort, consisting of the title being repeated over and over again.

These live recordings were mixed at the Record Plant in New York, with John and Yoko producing the Lyceum side, and John and Yoko and Phil Spector the Fillmore side (the inner sleeve notes contradict the record label, as the label credits production on both sides to John and Yoko and Phil). The inner sleeve for the *Live Jam* album is a replica of The Mothers of Invention's 1971 live album *Fillmore East – June 1971,* appropriately altered by Al Steckler and John and Yoko.

12a **(73) HAPPY XMAS (WAR IS OVER)** *(3.32)*
(74) LISTEN THE SNOW IS FALLING *(3.09)*

12b **(73) HAPPY XMAS (WAR IS OVER)** *(3.32)*
(74) LISTEN THE SNOW IS FALLING *(3.09)* **(green vinyl)**

"A" side by John and Yoko/Plastic Ono Band with The Harlem Community Choir

"B" side by Yoko Ono and The Plastic Ono Band

Apple R 5970 – November 24, 1972

Due to publishing difficulties over Yoko's composing credits (which had also held up the *Some Time In New York City* album) this single was delayed in Britain by a year, being released in America in 1971, when it was recorded on October 28 to 29 in New York. The session, which also provided the "B" side, was produced by John and Yoko and Phil Spector. The record entered the *NME* Top 30 on December 5, 1972, at No. 22, rising to No. 2 for one week on December 26 (the top position being held by (ironically) *Long Haired Lover From Liverpool* by Little Jimmy Osmond), and remained in the chart for seven weeks. After Lennon's death in 1980, the record re-entered the charts on January 3, 1981, at No. 12, rising to No. 3 on January 17, and staying in the chart for five weeks. The single has become a regular "re-release" during each Christmas season, and invariably enters the lower regions of the BMRB chart and, by mid-February, 1973, was reported to have sold two million globally. Less than two weeks after Lennon's murder, EMI received advance orders for *Happy Xmas* of 300,000, and the record must have sold well over half a

Listen To This Ad.

"Whatever Gets You Thru' The Night"

John Lennon

R 5998

On apple records
Marketed by EMI Records

million copies in Britain alone.

This was the first Lennon single not to feature the "Apple" logo on the record label. As with *Sometime In New York City*, it was replaced with the "John and Yoko merging heads" design, which shows five pictures of John and Yoko, with John predominantly on the left merging into Yoko from the right. The record was also released in special green vinyl, and both versions have a special Christmas message from the cutting engineer, engraved on the inner run-out groove area: the "A" side reads "Happy Xmas – Porky", while the "B" side reads "and New Year – Pecko". "Porky" and "Pecko" are nicknames for George Peckham, EMI's cutting engineer, who has engraved many pieces of graffiti on records.

Happy Xmas features a dozen guitars played by John and Hugh McCracken, Nicky Hopkins playing chimes, piano and glockenspiel, while Jim Keltner performed on sleigh bells and drums. John sings the verses solo, while Yoko and thirty youngsters from the Harlem Community Choir support John for the choruses. *Happy Xmas* was co-written by John and Yoko, while *Listen The Snow Is Falling* was written solely by Yoko, who also takes solo vocal, being supported instrumentally by John, Klaus Voorman and Hugh McCracken on guitars, and Nicky Hopkins on piano and chimes. *Happy Xmas* starts with a whispered message from John and Yoko; Yoko says "Happy Christmas Kyoko" while John follows with "Happy Christmas Julian".

The photograph on the sleeve of the single features John and Yoko surrounded by the children from the Harlem Community Choir along with Phil and Ronnie Spector, Klaus Voorman, Jim Keltner and Hugh McCracken.

13 (75) MIND GAMES *(4.09)* (76) MEAT CITY *(2.59)*

By John Lennon

Apple R 5994 – November 16, 1973

John's only singles release of 1973 was a trailer for his forthcoming album of the same name, *Mind Games*. With this release, John finally dropped The Plastic Ono Band tag, crediting the record only to himself, although the later album did credit the session men backing him, as "The Plastic U.F. Ono Band". The single also saw the end of John's association with Phil Spector (until the later *Rock 'n' Roll* album): John is the only credited producer.

The song was recorded in September 1973 at the Record Plant in New York, although an earlier version must exist, as the song was originally called "Make Love Not War", and was suggested for release as a follow up to *Cold Turkey* in 1969.

The single entered the *NME* Top 30 on November 27 at No. 25 and rose to No. 19 the following week, but stayed in the chart for only four weeks.

Both sides of the single were written by John Lennon, and appear on the *Mind Games* album.

14 MIND GAMES

By John Lennon (with The Plastic U.F. Ono Band)

Apple PCS 7165 – November 16, 1973

John's first self-produced solo album, which entered the *NME* Top 30 album charts on December 4, 1973 at No. 21, and rose to No. 9 on January 1, 1974, for one week, staying in the chart for seven weeks.

The album was recorded at the New York Record Plant in September 1973, using the following musicians: Ken Ascher/piano, organ and mellotron; David Spinozza/guitar; Gordon Edwards/bass; Jim Keltner/drums; Michael Brecker/saxophone; Sneaky Pete Kleinow/pedal steel guitar; with John supplying percussion, guitar and clavinet, being credited as Dr Winston O'Boogie, one of his many pseudonyms; while the backing vocals are supplied by "Something Different".

The sleeve was designed by John, and the inner sleeve, as well as containing the song lyrics, also includes John and Yoko's "Declaration of Nutopia", an imaginary country consisting of only people, all of whom are ambassadors of that country.

A SIDE

75a **MIND GAMES** *(4.11)*

77 **TIGHT A$** *(3.36)*

78 **AISUMASEN (I'M SORRY)** *(4.42)*

79 **ONE DAY (AT A TIME)** *(3.07)*

80 **BRING ON THE LUCIE (FREDA PEEPLE)** *(4.10)*

81 **NUTOPIAN INTERNATIONAL ANTHEM (silent track)** *(0.03)*

B SIDE

82 **INTUITION** *(3.07)*

83 **OUT THE BLUE** *(3.20)*

84 **ONLY PEOPLE** *(3.25)*

85 **I KNOW (I KNOW)** *(3.47)*

86 **YOU ARE HERE** *(4.09)*

76a **MEAT CITY** *(2.47)*

"Aisumasen" is Japanese for "I'm Sorry", and the song was John's apology to Yoko during their separation. *Bring On The Lucie* features an extra drummer in Rick Marotta, and is followed by a silent track, which many people have probably never noticed. Both *Out The Blue* and *You Are Here* were inspired by Yoko, while the latter was the title for Lennon's "White Art" exhibition in the Robert Frazer Gallery in 1968. *Meat City* also features Rick Marotta on drums.

15 (87) WHATEVER GETS YOU THRU THE NIGHT *(3.18)* (88) BEEF JERKY *(3.26)*

"A" side by John Lennon with The Plastic Ono Nuclear Band

"B" side by John Lennon with The Plastic Ono Nuclear Band/Little Big Horns and Booker Table and The Maitre D's.

Apple R5998 – October 4, 1974

John's seventh single became his least successful thus far in commercial terms, managing only two weeks in the chart. Entering on October 15 at No. 24, it dropped to No. 27 the following week.

Up to this point, all John's British singles releases had appeared in picture bags, but this release was the first in an ordinary paper sleeve. The songs on the single were taken from the "Walls And Bridges" sessions, recorded between June and August 1974 at the New York Record Plant.

Whatever Gets You Thru The Night features Elton John on organ and piano and joining John for backing vocals. Other musicians comprising The Plastic Ono Nuclear Band were: Jim Keltner/drums; Eddie Mottau/acoustic guitar; Jesse Ed Davis/guitar; Ken Ascher/clavinet; Klaus Voorman/bass; Arthur Jenkins/percussion; and Bobby Keyes/tenor saxophone; while John is credited as Hon. John St. John Johnson playing guitar. *Beefy Jerky*, the "B" side instrumental, features Jim Keltner/drums; Klaus Voorman/bass; Arthur Jenkins/percussion; with Jesse Ed Davis, Dr Winston (John) and Booker Table and The Maitre D's (a spoof on the name of Booker T and The MGs) on guitars; while the Little Big Horns (consisting of Bobby Keyes, Steve Madaio, Howard Johnson, Ron Aprea and Frank Vicari) supply brass backing.

16 WALLS AND BRIDGES

By John Lennon (with The Plastic Ono Nuclear Band)

Apple PCTC 253 – October 4, 1974

Walls And Bridges entered the album charts on October 8 at No. 23, rising to No. 5 three weeks later on October 29, and eventually staying in the chart for eight weeks.

John produced and recorded the album between June and August 1974 in New York's Record Plant, with one track, *Nobody Loves You (When You're Down And Out)* being recorded in Los Angeles.

The sleeve, designed by Roy Kohara, features several photographs of John plus

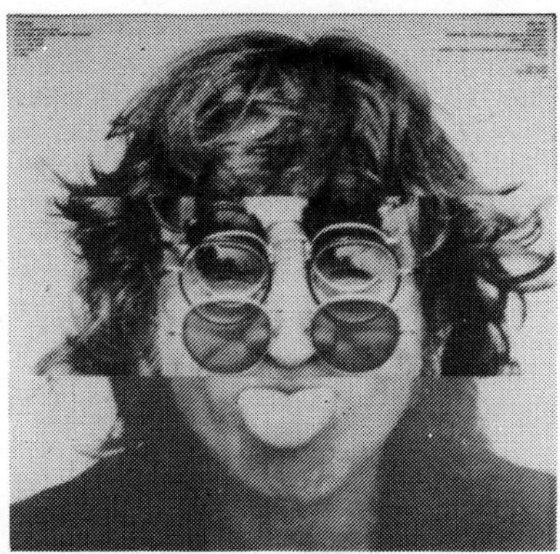

three school paintings by John, in an "identikit" overlay design. Included in the album is a booklet of lyrics, illustrated with five of John's school paintings from 1952.

The album features a basic instrumental line-up of Jim Keltner/drums; Jesse Ed Davis/guitar; Eddie Mottau/acoustic guitar (all tracks except *Beef Jerky*); and Klaus Voorman/bass, who appear on all tracks except *Ya Ya*, with the addition of John (under various pseudonyms) playing guitar, acoustic guitar and piano on various tracks. Other keyboards are supplied by Ken Ascher, Nicky Hopkins, and Elton John while, on nine of the tracks, Arthur Jenkins supplies extra percussion (not on *Old Dirt Road, Beef Jerky* and *Ya Ya*). Seven tracks feature the Little Big Horns. Orchestration, although credited to the Philharmonic Orchestrange, was provided by the New York Philharmonic Orchestra, conducted by Ken Ascher, who also supplied the orchestral arrangements.

A SIDE

89 **GOING DOWN ON LOVE** *(3.54)*

87a **WHATEVER GETS YOU THRU THE NIGHT** *(3.23)*

90 **OLD DIRT ROAD** *(4.09)*

91 **WHAT YOU GOT** *(3.04)*

92 **BLESS YOU** *(3.37)*

93 **SCARED** *(4.36)*

B SIDE

94 **No. 9 DREAM** *(4.47)*

95 **SURPRISE SURPRISE (SWEET BIRD OF PARADOX)** *(2.52)*

96 **STEEL AND GLASS** *(4.37)*

88a **BEEF JERKY** *(3.26)*

97 **NOBODY LOVES YOU (WHEN YOU'RE DOWN AND OUT)** *(5.10)*

98 **YA YA** *(1.03)*

Going Down On Love features Ken on electric piano, and Nicky on piano, while John plays guitar as Dr Winston O'Ghurkin. *Old Dirt Road* features Nicky and John (as Rev. Thumbs Ghurkin) on pianos and Ken on electric piano, while Harry Nilsson supplies backing vocals, and also assisted John with the lyrics to the song. *What You Got* features "Kaptain Kundalini" (John) on guitar, while Ken plays clavinet and Nicky piano. John, as Rev. Fred Ghurkin, plays guitar on *Bless You,* while Ken Ascher plays both electric piano and Mellotron. *Scared,* which begins with the howls of a wolf, features electric piano by Ken, and acoustic pianos by Nicky and Mel Torment (John) while the Little Big Horns showcase Howard Johnson on baritone saxophone.

John and Yoko always considered nine to be their lucky number, John being born on October 9, and the number seemed to continually feature in their lives: During their separation, John wrote *No. 9 Dream* on a ninth day to Yoko. The number features John on acoustic guitars with Eddie Mottau (John as Dr Dream), while Nicky and Ken play electric piano and clavinet respectively. Backing vocals are supplied by The 44th Street Fairies, consisting of May Pang, Lori Burton, Joey Dambra and John.

Surprise Surprise is another song about Yoko, who used to work in a restaurant called "Paradox" in Greenwich Village in the sixties. The song features Nicky on piano, Ken on clavinet and Elton John supplying backing vocals. John does not play an instrument on this song. *Steel And Glass,* John's vicious attack on Allen Klein, features John on acoustic guitars (as Dr Winston O'Reggae) with Nicky on piano and Ken on clavinet. *Nobody Loves You (When You're Down And Out)* has Nicky on piano, Ken on organ and John on acoustic guitar (as

Dwarf McDougal). The short version of *Ya Ya* written by Robinson, Lewis and Dorsey, features John's son, Julian, on drums, with John singing and playing piano.

17 (94a) No. 9 DREAM *(4.44)* (91a) WHAT YOU GOT *(3.07)*

By John Lennon

Apple R 6003 – January 31, 1975

The second single from the *Walls And Bridges* album, which did little, if at all, better than the first, entering the *NME* charts on March 4, 1975, at No. 23, then dropping to No. 29 the following week (its final chart week).

18 ROCK 'N' ROLL

By John Lennon

Apple PCS 7169 – February 21, 1975

John's oldies album entered the *NME* chart on March 4, at No. 23, rising to No. 10 on March 18, and dropping out after seven weeks. On May 6, it re-entered at No. 27 for a five-week run, rising to No. 14. On June 17 it re-entered for a second time, at No. 29, for one week, thus featuring in the Top 30 for a total of thirteen weeks.

John started to record his collection of oldies (originally called "Oldies But Moldies") in 1973 between October and December, with Phil Spector producing in Los Angeles, but disagreements between the two caused a temporary stoppage. Phil Spector disappeared with the tapes, and was allegedly involved in a car accident, and Lennon was unable to retrieve the tapes from him. When Lennon did eventually manage to acquire the tapes, he found that many of the recordings were unsuitable; only four numbers, *You Can't Catch Me, Sweet Little Sixteen, Bony Moronie* and *Just Because* were, John felt, up to standard. John then entered the New York Record Plant for an intensive recording session between October 21 and 25, 1974, to lay down another ten tracks to complete the album. At this time, *Walls And Bridges* had just been released, so it was decided to delay the oldies album until April 1975.

Then, at the beginning of February 1975, an album titled *Roots – John Lennon Sings The Great Rock & Roll Hits* appeared in America, with TV advertising promoting the LP, released by the mail order firm, Adam VIII Ltd. The album stated that the release was authorized by John Lennon and Apple and featured numbers from the Spector recording sessions, including two tracks, *Angel Baby* and *Be My Baby*, which did not appear on the later official release.

The story goes that Morris Levy, publisher of Chuck Berry's song catalogue, had sued Lennon for alleged copyright infringement of Berry's song *You Can't Catch Me*, from which Levy claimed Lennon had plagiarised *Come Together*. In an out of court settlement, Lennon agreed to record several Chuck Berry songs for his next album, including *You Can't Catch Me*. In late 1974, Lennon gave Levy tapes from the Spector sessions which Levy then used to produce the *Roots* album, claiming that Lennon and Apple had given him a verbal agreement to release the record.

This was later denied by both Lennon and Apple. To combat sales of the "pirate" album, Apple immediately brought forward the release date of *Rock 'n' Roll* to February, and Lennon and Apple promptly sued Levy. The *Roots* album was subsequently taken off the market, and Lennon was awarded $45,000 compensation in April 1976.

The cover photograph of John by Jurgen Vollmer, a student from Hamburg,

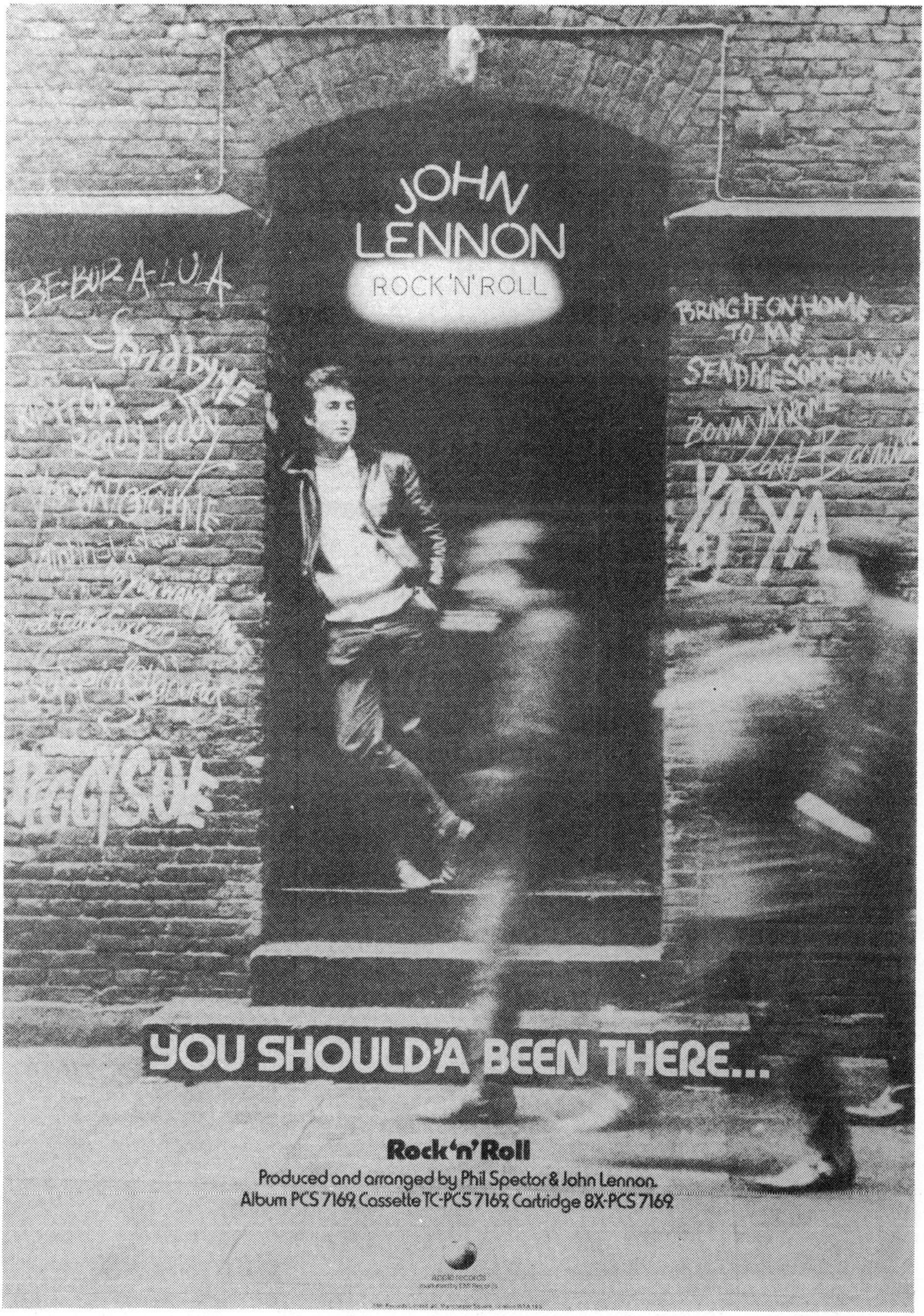

JOHN
LENNON
ROCK 'N' ROLL

YOU SHOULD'A BEEN THERE...

Rock 'n' Roll

Produced and arranged by Phil Spector & John Lennon.
Album PCS 7169, Cassette TC-PCS 7169, Cartridge 8X-PCS 7169.

JOHN
LENNON
Rock 'N' Roll
PCS 7169
including 'Stand by Me'
latest single
"Stand By Me"
R6005
Both albums available on tape
Walls And Bridges
PCTC 253
including "# 9 Dream"
Marketed by EMI Records EMI Records Limited, 20, Manchester Square, London W1A 1ES

who was introduced to the Beatles by Klaus Voorman, was taken in 1961 when the Beatles were performing in the German clubs. The blurred figures walking past John are George and Paul and either Pete Best or Stuart Sutcliffe. The cover was designed by Roy Kohara.

The Spector sessions, recorded at the Record Plant, Los Angeles, and A&M Studios, featured the following musicians: Jim Keltner/drums; John and Jesse Ed Davis/guitars; Jose Feliciano/acoustic guitar; Leon Russell/keyboards; Nino Tempo/saxophone; with Steve Cropper/guitar, Hal Blaine/drums, Jeff Barry and Barry Mann guesting. The sessions produced by John in the Record Plant in New York featured the same musicians as used on the *Walls And Bridges* album: Jim Keltner/drums; John and Jesse Ed Davis/guitars; Klaus Voorman/bass; Ken Ascher/keyboards; Arthur Jenkins/percussion; Bobby Keyes/brass; with four guest musicians – Peter Jameson, Joseph Temperley, Dennis Morouse and Frank Vicari.

A SIDE

99 **BE-BOP-A-LULA** *(2.36)*

100 **STAND BY ME** *(3.26)*

101-2 **RIP IT UP/READY TEDDY** *(1.32)*

103 **YOU CAN'T CATCH ME** *(4.52)*

104 **AIN'T THAT A SHAME** *(2.30)*

105 **DO YOU WANNA DANCE** *(2.52)*

106 **SWEET LITTLE SIXTEEN** *(3.00)*

B SIDE

107 **SLIPPIN' AND SLIDIN'** *(2.16)*

108 **PEGGY SUE** *(2.03)*

109-10 **BRING IT ON HOME TO ME/SEND ME SOME LOVIN'** *(3.40)*

111 **BONY MORONIE** *(3.48)*

112 **YA YA** *(2.17)*

113 **JUST BECAUSE** *(4.25)*

Be-Bop-A-Lula was written by Sheriff Tex Davis and Gene Vincent – Vincent's single version was released in 1958 and became a million seller. *Stand By Me* was written by Ben E. King, Jerry Leiber, Mike Stoller and Ollie Jones, and produced hits for Ben E. King in 1961 and Kenny Lynch in 1964.

Rip It Up and *Ready Teddy* were composed by Robert Blackwell and John Marascalo and recorded by Little Richard in 1956. The tracks were released as the two sides of one single, giving Richard a million-selling US No. 27 hit and a UK No. 30 hit, although *Rip It Up* fared better in the UK charts when covered by Bill Haley and His Comets (No. 4) and Elvis Presley (No. 27).

You Can't Catch Me was written and recorded by Chuck Berry in 1956, with no British chart success, while *Ain't That A Shame*, written by Antoine "Fats" Domino and Dave Bartholomew, charted four times in Britain; once for Fats Domino (No. 23) in 1957, twice for Pat Boone in 1955 (No. 7) and 1957 (No. 22), and lastly for The Four Seasons (No. 38) in 1963.

Do You Wanna Dance was written and recorded by Bobby Freeman, who took it to No. 5 in the US in 1958, and attracted three cover versions – by Cliff Richard (No. 2 in 1962 in the UK), The Beach Boys (No. 12 in 1965 in the US) and Bette Midler (No. 17 in 1972 in the US). The second Chuck Berry number, *Sweet Little Sixteen*, gave Berry his fifth million-selling single, reaching No. 2 in the US and No. 16 in the UK charts.

Slippin' And Slidin' written by Richard Penniman, Edwin J. Bocage, Albert Collins and James Smith, was recorded by Little Richard as the "B" side to his 1956 million seller, *Long Tall Sally*.

Peggy Sue was written by Jerry Allison, Norman Petty and Buddy Holly, and recorded by the latter in 1957, giving him a No. 3 US and a No. 6 UK hit, which sold over a million.

Bring It On Home To Me was written and recorded by Sam Cooke in 1962, giving him a No. 13 US hit, and was later covered by The Animals, giving them a No. 7 UK and a No. 32 US hit.

Send Me Some Lovin', written by Leo Price (Lloyd's brother) and John Marascalo is the fourth song previously recorded by Little Richard on the album, being the coupling for his 1957 million seller *Lucille*, which went to No. 10 in the UK and No. 27 in the US.

Bony Moronie was recorded by its composer, Larry Williams, in 1957, reaching No. 11 in the UK and No. 18 in the US, and selling a million.

Ya Ya, which John originally recorded with his son Julian for the *Walls And Bridges* album, was written by Morgan Robinson, Clarence Lewis and Lee Dorsey. Dorsey recorded it in 1961, reaching No. 7 in the US and selling a million, and it was later recorded by Petula Clark, giving her a No. 14 UK hit.

Just Because was written by Lloyd Price and released as a single in 1957, reaching No. 29 in the US.

PHILADELPHIA FREEDOM
I SAW HER STANDING THERE *(3.49)*

"A" side by The Elton John Band

"B" side by The Elton John Band featuring John Lennon with The Muscle Shoals Horns

DJM DJS354 – February 28, 1975

During the recording of John's *Walls And Bridges* album, Elton John assisted by playing organ and piano and supplying backing vocals on *Whatever Gets You Thru The Night.* Elton told John that he thought John had a certain No. 1 with the song, and made John promise that if the single did reach the top of the charts, he would appear at one of Elton's concerts. The single did get to No. 1 in America, and John did keep his promise, appearing with The Elton John Band at Madison Square Garden, New York, on November 28, 1974. As well as *I Saw Her Standing There* (which appears on the "B" side of this Elton John Band single, *Philadelphia Freedom*) John performed *Whatever Gets You Thru The Night* and *Lucy In The Sky With Diamonds.* Elton John's band featured Dee Murray/bass, Nigel Olsson/drums, Davy Johnstone/guitar, and Ray Cooper/percussion.

Philadelphia Freedom entered the *NME* charts on March 18, 1975, at No. 19, rising to No. 12 for one week on April 1, and being listed in the charts for seven weeks.

The record label erroneously states, however, that the concert took place on November 26, 1974.

19 (100a) STAND BY ME *(3.27)*
(114) MOVE OVER MS. L *(2.54)*

By John Lennon

Apple R 6005 – April 18, 1975

John's second single of 1975 entered the *NME* Top 30 on May 6 at No. 27 for one week, dropping out the following week, and re-entering at No. 30 for another week, thus staying in the chart for two weeks only.

The single was released in an attempt to boost the sales of the *Rock 'n' Roll* album, from which it was taken, and which had dropped down the charts. The release seems to have had the desired effect, as the album re-entered the charts, rising to No. 14.

The "B" side, *Move Over Ms. L,* written by Lennon for Keith Moon's 1974 album, *Two Sides Of The Moon,* was recorded during the October 1974 sessions for the *Rock 'n' Roll* album, using the same musicians.

The single was re-released (although it had never actually been deleted) on April 17, 1981, but didn't enter the charts.

20 (47a) IMAGINE *(3.00)*
(37a) WORKING CLASS HERO *(3.46)*

By John Lennon

Apple R 6009 – October 24, 1975

Imagine entered the *NME* Top 30 on November 4, 1975 at No. 23, rising two weeks later to No. 5, and staying in the charts for seven weeks. Following Lennon's death on December 8, 1980, sales of all Beatle recordings increased, and by December 20, 1980, there were orders of over 300,000 for *Imagine,* even though it had not been re-released or promoted in any way. It re-entered the Top 30 on January 3, 1981, at No. 17, rising to No. 1 the following week, where it stayed for four weeks. It featured in the chart for ten weeks, making a combined total of seventeen weeks in the Top 30. The single passed the million sales mark in Britain during its 1981 chart run, thus taking six years to achieve platinum status.

The 1975 release was Lennon's first British picture sleeve single released since *Mind Games* in 1973 (but the 1980 "re-release" – it had never been deleted – did not sport this cover) and proved to be his last single release for five years.

21 SHAVED FISH (COLLECTABLE LENNON)

By John Lennon

Apple PCS 7173 – October 24, 1975

John's "greatest hits" or "best of" album, depending on whether it is looked at from an American or British point of view, entered the *NME* album chart on November 11, 1975, at No. 19. It rose to No. 6 on December 9 for one week, being in the Top 30 for twelve weeks. After the increased sales of Beatle material due to Lennon's death, *Shaved Fish* re-entered the Top 30 album charts on January 17, 1981, at No. 25, rising to No. 7 on February 21, and staying for a further eight weeks in the chart, making a combined total of twenty weeks.

The sleeve was designed by Roy Kohara, with illustrations by Michael Bryan, who illustrated each song with an appropriate picture. The illustration for *Power To The People*, for example, celebrated John receiving his "Green Card" on October 7, 1975, after three years of fighting to be allowed to stay in the United States. The printed inner sleeve features the lyrics to each song, although as with the original song sheet to *Give Peace A Chance*, EMI substituted "mastication" for "masturbation" (a subtle difference!). Moreover, the whispered introduction to *Happy Xmas* is incorrect, as Yoko does not say "Happy Xmas Yoko" and neither does John say "Happy Xmas John"; the first two lines should read "Happy Xmas Kyoko, Happy Xmas Julian".

The sleeve notes erroneously credit Phil Spector as co-producer of *Cold Turkey* with John and Yoko, but Spector did not officiate until *Instant Karma*, the following single.

In his review of the album in *NME* of November 1, 1975, Charles Shaar Murray mentioned Spector in conjunction with *Cold Turkey* and also stated that neither *Mother* nor *Woman Is The Nigger Of The World* were singles, and asked why certain other songs (e.g. *Working Class Hero, Don't Worry Kyoko, How Do You Sleep?* and *Oh Yoko*) were omitted in favour of these two "album" tracks. Murray eventually received an answer to his queries from none other than Mr Lennon himself, who wrote a letter to Murray, which was printed in the *NME* of December 13, 1975. In it, Lennon stated that *Cold Turkey* was not produced by Spector ("There's no echo on it") and that he thought that all the tracks were singles (except *Imagine*) in Britain, and that they were saving *Don't Worry Kyoko* for *The Best Of Yoko* album. Lennon also apologised for the mistakes on the sleeve, saying that he was unable to keep an eye on Capitol and EMI because he was having his baby, as it were.

A SIDE

18a **GIVE PEACE A CHANCE** *(0.58)*

20a **COLD TURKEY** *(5.02)*

32a **INSTANT KARMA** *(3.12)*

45a **POWER TO THE PEOPLE** *(3.03)*

34a **MOTHER** *(5.06)*

57a **WOMAN IS THE NIGGER OF THE WORLD** *(4.36)*

B SIDE

47b **IMAGINE** *(3.00)*

87b **WHATEVER GETS YOU THRU THE NIGHT** *(3.03)*

75b **MIND GAMES** *(4.10)*

94b **No. 9 DREAM** *(4.45)*

73a **HAPPY XMAS (WAR IS OVER)** *(3.22)*

115 **GIVE PEACE A CHANCE** *(0.58)*

The album starts and finishes with two different versions of *Give Peace A Chance*, the first being part of the single version and the second a live recording taken from the "One To One" Concert at Madison Square Garden, New York, on August 30, 1972. The concert was a benefit in aid of the Willowbrook School for Children, and John and Yoko performed with the Elephant's Memory Band. Only part of *Give Peace A Chance* is included on this album, but the whole song, along with the other numbers performed by John and Yoko, was recorded and therefore remains "in the can". John and Yoko also sang: *Sisters, O Sisters, Instant Karma, Come Together, Imagine, Cold Turkey, Hound Dog, New*

York City, *We're All Water*, *Woman Is The Nigger Of The World*, *Mother* and *Born In A Prison*. Helping on *Give Peace A Chance*, as well as Elephant's Memory, were Stevie Wonder, Sha Na Na and Roberta Flack, all of whom performed individually at the concert.

A MONUMENT TO BRITISH ROCK VOLUME 1 – 20 Rock/Pop Classic From EMI

By various artists

Harvest EMTV 17 – May 4, 1979

The first compilation album to feature a John Lennon track, *A Monument To British Rock* was released in EMI's TV advertised series. (The album also featured *Get Back* by The Beatles; see The Beatles British section in *The Long and Winding Road*, page 110, for complete track listing and sleeve illustration.) Although subtitled "Volume 1", EMI have yet to release a follow up album, despite having by now released over thirty-five albums in their EMTV series.

B SIDE TRACK 5

47c **IMAGINE** *(3.00)*

22 (116) JUST LIKE STARTING OVER *(3.57)* (117) KISS KISS KISS *(3.38)*

"A" side by John Lennon

"B" side by Yoko Ono

Geffen Records K79186 – October 24, 1980

John and Yoko's first record since 1975 released exactly five years after *Imagine*. It entered the *NME* charts on November 15, 1980, at No. 13, rising to No. 9 on November 29, and dropping to No.

11 on December 6. On December 8, at approximately 11 pm (New York time) John Lennon was mercilessly gunned down and died on the way to hospital. As always seems to happen when a top recording artist dies, Lennon's records swamped the charts, and *Starting Over* jumped back to No. 4 on December 20, and by January 3, 1981, it was No. 1. In the same week, *Happy Xmas* and *Imagine* re-entered the charts at No.'s 12 and 17 respectively. *Imagine* jumped to No. 1 the following week, knocking *Starting Over* back to No. 2. *Starting Over* stayed in the chart for eleven weeks and, by February 1981, had sold over 500,000 in Britain, and has therefore sold well over a million globally.

The record was produced by John and Yoko and Jack Douglas at the Hit Factory, New York, sometime during August 1980. (See *Double Fantasy*.)

23 DOUBLE FANTASY

By John Lennon and Yoko Ono

Geffen Records K99131 – November 17, 1980

John's first album for five years (during which time he was bringing up his son, Sean) entered the album charts on November 29 at No. 9 rising one position the following week, but dropping to No. 17 on December 13. With Lennon's death on December 8, *Double Fantasy* moved back up the charts to No. 5 on December

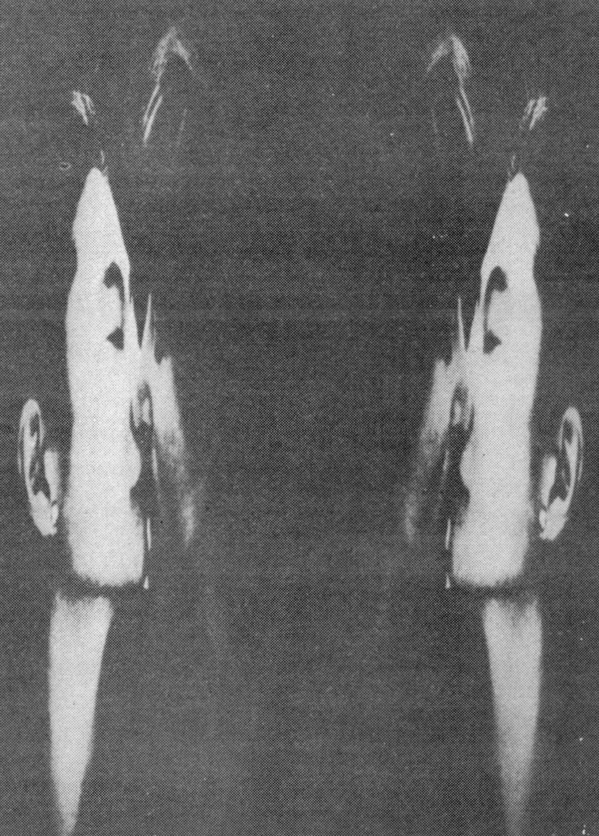
JOHN LENNON
YOKO ONO
NEW ALBUM
DOUBLE FANTASY
INCLUDES THE SINGLE
(JUST LIKE) STARTING OVER

Distributed by WEA Records Limited © A Warner Communications Company
K99131 Also available on cassette

28th November 1974...

...was Thanksgiving Day as well as the date that an Elton John concert at New York's Madison Square Garden turned into a very special event. Towards the end of the evening Elton was joined onstage by close friend and fellow musician John Lennon. Together they performed three numbers – 'Whatever Gets You Through The Night', 'Lucy In The Sky With Diamonds' and 'I Saw Her Standing There'. Lennon's performance of the last number surprised many as he has never been known to sing a McCartney song before. This was the last concert appearance by John Lennon.

Special 15-minute single
picture bag – out now!

(DJS 10965)

20, and by January 10, 1981, was at No. 1 for one week. It returned to the No. 1 position on three separate occasions during January and February 1981, thus being at No. 1 for a total of four weeks, and eventually staying in the charts for twenty-four weeks. For the three week period between January 17 and March 7, 1981, three of Lennon's albums were in the charts: *Double Fantasy* (between No. 1 and No. 6), *Imagine* (4-20) and *Shaved Fish* (7-27).

The reason for John's self-imposed exile in 1975 for five years was, he stated, in order to bring up his son, Sean, born to Yoko on October 9, 1975. John had missed his first son, Julian, growing up, due to his commitments to the Beatles, and he therefore intended to retire until Sean was five years old. On August 4, 1980, John and Yoko started recording at the Hit Factory, New York, and eventually produced, with Jack Douglas, twenty-two songs. Musicians helping on the sessions included guitarists Earl Slick and Hugh McCracken, bass player Tony Levin, keyboard player George Small, drummer Andy Newmark, percussionist Arthur Jenkins Jnr, and Ed Walsh playing an Oberheim and Randy Stein an English Concertina, with John playing guitar. Backing vocals were supplied by Michelle Simpson, Cassandra Worten, Cheryl Mason Jacks, Eric Troyer, The Benny Cummings Singers and The Kings Temple Choir. The horn section featured Howard Johnson, Grant Hungerford, John Parran, Seldon Powell, George "Young" Opalisky, Roger Rosenberg, David Tofani and Ronald Tooley. Also present during the sessions were Ralph McDonald, Robin Zander and keyboard player Jean Roussell.

The remaining tracks from the session were originally scheduled to be released during 1981, but with Lennon's death, the album (provisionally titled "Milk and Honey") has never appeared.

The cover photographs were taken by Kishin Shinoyama, the back cover shot being taken outside John and Yoko's apartments in New York's Dakota building during the summer of 1980, and the album sleeve was designed by Christopher Whorf of Art Hotel.

A SIDE

116a **(JUST LIKE) STARTING OVER** *(3.54) (John)*

117a **KISS KISS KISS** *(3.39) (Yoko)*

118 **CLEAN UP TIME** *(2.53) (John)*

119 **GIVE ME SOMETHING** *(1.52) (Yoko)*

120 **I'M LOSING YOU** *(3.59) (John)*

121 **I'M MOVING ON** *(3.17) (Yoko)*

122 **BEAUTIFUL BOY (DARLING BOY)** *(3.57) (John)*

B SIDE

123 **WATCHING THE WHEELS** *(3.31) (John)*

124 **I'M YOUR ANGEL** *(3.34) (Yoko)*

125 **WOMAN** *(3.31) (John)*

126 **BEAUTIFUL BOYS** *(2.53) (Yoko)*

127 **DEAR YOKO** *(2.30) (John)*

128 **EVERY MAN HAS A WOMAN WHO LOVES HIM** *(4.00) (Yoko)*

129 **HARD TIMES ARE OVER** *(3.12) (Yoko)*

As with many of John's solo songs, most of his seven numbers on *Double Fantasy* are either about, or dedicated to, Yoko, the one exception being *Beautiful Boy (Darling Boy)* which is John's song to his son, Sean, and features steel drum by Robert Greenidge. *Watching The Wheels*, with Matthew Cunningham on hammer dulcimer, was John's answer to all of the questions from the public about his exile for five years. Yoko's song, *I'm Your Angel*, was the subject of a law suit filed in New York on June 15, 1981, by the publishers of *Makin' Whoopee*. The publishers claimed that Yoko's song "was very similar to and a copy of *Makin' Whoopee*" (which was written in 1928) and were seeking one million dollars damages and demanding that the song be removed from further pressings of the album.

24 MIND GAMES

By John Lennon

Music For Pleasure MFP 50509 – November 27, 1980

Along with Ringo's *Ringo*, George's *Dark Horse* and the Beatles *Rock 'n' Roll Music* albums, this was part of the first batch of Beatle product to appear on a budget label from EMI. The album features a revised front cover, showing a multiple image of the original sleeve, with track listings on the back cover, but without lyrics printed on the inner sleeve, as contained on the original release.

A SIDE

75c **MIND GAMES** *(4.11)*

77a **TIGHT A$** *(3.36)*

78a **AISUMASEN (I'M SORRY)** *(4.42)*

79a ONE DAY (AT A TIME) *(3.07)*

80a BRING ON THE LUCIE (FREDA PEEPLE) *(4.10)*

81a NUTOPIAN INTERNATIONAL ANTHEM *(0.03)*

B SIDE

82a INTUITION *(3.07)*

83a OUT THE BLUE *(3.20)*

84a ONLY PEOPLE *(3.25)*

85a I KNOW (I KNOW) *(3.47)*

86a YOU ARE HERE *(4.09)*

76b MEAT CITY *(2.47)*

25 (125a) WOMAN *(3.27)* (126a) BEAUTIFUL BOYS *(2.51)*

"A" side by John Lennon

"B" side by Yoko Ono

Geffen Records K 79195 – January 16, 1981

Just after *Starting Over* had been released as a single, John and Yoko had insisted that *Woman* be issued as the follow up. It entered the *NME* Top 30 on January 31, 1981, at No. 3, the highest entry position attained by any of John's singles. The following week it rose to No. 2 where it remained for three weeks (the No. 1 position being held for the first two weeks by the first solo single from Genesis vocalist/drummer Phil Collins, *In The Air Tonight* and for the third week by *Vienna* by Ultravox). In the BMRB charts, *Woman* went to No. 1, giving Lennon a hat trick of three number ones in a row as *Starting Over* and *Imagine* had both topped the charts.

By February 1, 1981, just fifteen days after release, *Woman* had sold 250,000 in Britain.

I SAW HER STANDING THERE *(3.34)* WHATEVER GETS YOU THRU THE NIGHT *(4.24)*/ LUCY IN THE SKY WITH DIAMONDS *(6.10)*

By The Elton John Band featuring John Lennon and the Muscle Shoals Horns.

DJM DJS10965 – March 13, 1981

After Lennon's death, DJM acquired permission from EMI to release all three numbers recorded at the Elton John Band concert on November 28, 1974, when John Lennon made a guest appearance to honour a promise made to Elton. With Lennon's death, this guest appearance became even more important, as it constituted the last concert performance by John, thus making the recordings of historical interest. The three recordings were released on a 33⅓ r.p.m. single in a picture sleeve. The two photographs on the sleeve were taken at the concert by Chuck Pulin, of Elton and John.

The "A" side features the song performed last during the concert, *I Saw Her Standing There,* which John introduces as a number by an estranged fiancé, Paul. The second side, lasting over ten minutes, features *Whatever Gets You Thru The Night* on which Elton guested when the song was originally recorded by John, and *Lucy In The Sky With Diamonds*, which had previously been recorded by the Elton John Band, with John guesting on guitar and backing vocals.

The single entered the *NME* charts for one week on April 4, at No. 24.

26 (123b) WATCHING THE WHEELS *(3.29)* (124a) YES I'M YOUR ANGEL *(2.48)*

"A" side by John Lennon

"B" side by Yoko Ono

Geffen Records K 79207 – March 27, 1981

The third single release from the *Double Fantasy* album entered the *NME* Top 30 for one week only at No. 27 on April 18, 1981.

27 JOHN LENNON (box set)

By John Lennon

Apple JLB8 – June 15, 1981

In January 1981, EMI stated that they did not intend releasing any posthumous or memorial record of John Lennon material, but in June 1981 a boxed set containing eight albums was released as a limited edition. The set contained the following albums: *Live Peace In Toronto 1969, John Lennon/Plastic Ono Band, Imagine, Some Time In New York City, Mind Games, Walls And Bridges, Rock 'n' Roll* and *Shaved Fish*. Each album was as the original release, except that *Live Peace In Toronto* did not include the calendar, and *John Lennon/Plastic Ono Band* and *Imagine* did not include their original printed inner sleeves. *Imagine*, however, did contain the original postcard, although the poster was slightly different, having a double image of Lennon at his piano. The set also included a magazine titled *Lennon – The Liverpool Echo's Tribute To John Lennon*, which featured pictures and articles from various stages in the Beatles' careers as covered by that newspaper.

28 ROCK 'N' ROLL

By John Lennon

Music For Pleasure MFP 50522 – November 25, 1981

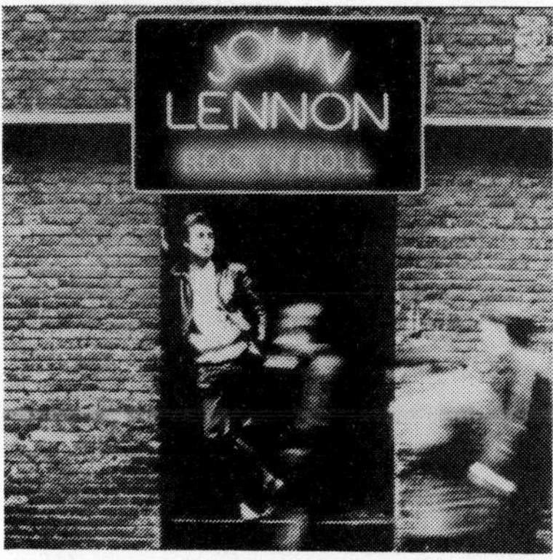

The second selection of Beatle solo albums to be released on EMI's budget label, Music For Pleasure, included John's *Rock 'n' Roll, The Best of George Harrison* and Ringo's *Blast From Your Past.*

The cover for the album retained the original photograph by Jorgen Vollmer, but featured a slightly enlarged title on the front, with a new back cover (crediting *Stand By Me* more correctly to "King-Leiber-Stoller" – the original cover credited the song to "King-Glick", "Elmo Glick" being a joint pseudonym for Jerry Leiber and Mike Stoller).

A SIDE

99a	**BE-BOP-A-LULA** *(2.36)*
100b	**STAND BY ME** *(3.26)*
101-2a	**RIP IT UP/READY TEDDY** *(1.32)*
103a	**YOU CAN'T CATCH ME** *(4.52)*
104a	**AIN'T THAT A SHAME** *(2.30)*
105a	**DO YOU WANNA DANCE** *(2.52)*
106a	**SWEET LITTLE SIXTEEN** *(3.00)*

B SIDE

107a	**SLIPPIN' AND SLIDIN'** *(2.16)*
108a	**PEGGY SUE** *(2.03)*
109-10a	**BRING IT ON HOME TO ME/ SEND ME SOME LOVIN'** *(3.40)*
111a	**BONY MORONIE** *(3.48)*

112a YA YA *(2.17)*

113a JUST BECAUSE *(4.25)*

29 THE JOHN LENNON COLLECTION

By John Lennon

Parlophone EMTV 37 – November 8, 1982

This TV advertised collection of the best of John Lennon entered the *NME* charts on November 27 at No. 9, rising to No. 2 on December 11, and hitting the No. 1 spot on December 25, staying there for five weeks. The album sold 300,000 copies in its first week in Britain. It received a platinum disc, and by the third week in January, 1983, had passed the million mark in the UK alone – thus selling approximately 17,000 copies per working day.

The album was originally planned by EMI in 1981, but due to difficulties in getting permission from Yoko and David Geffen for the inclusion of *Double Fantasy* recordings, it was delayed for over a year. Final negotiations between EMI and Geffen resulted in the American album being released on Geffen Records with a slightly differing track listing.

The album, featuring all but one of John's British singles (*Cold Turkey* being the missing release) plus six of his *Double Fantasy* tracks, was compiled by John David Kalodner, with assistance from Yoko and David Geffen. The album sleeve features pictures taken by Annie Leibovitz at John's last photographic session, in December 1980, for *Rolling Stone* magazine.

As with *Shaved Fish*, the inner sleeve features the lyrics to each song, and *Give Peace A Chance* finally appears with the correct lyric, i.e. "masturbation" and not "mastication", but the first two lines of *Happy Xmas* are still incorrect, as they should read "Happy Xmas Kyoko, Happy Xmas Julian".

A SIDE

18b GIVE PEACE A CHANCE *(4.48)*

32b INSTANT KARMA *(3.17)*

45b POWER TO THE PEOPLE *(3.00)*

87c WHATEVER GETS YOU THRU THE NIGHT *(3.23)*

94c No. 9 DREAM *(4.37)*

75d MIND GAMES *(4.10)*

40a LOVE *(3.20)*

73b HAPPY XMAS (WAR IS OVER) *(3.32)*

B SIDE

47d IMAGINE *(3.01)*

49a JEALOUS GUY *(4.13)*

100c STAND BY ME *(3.27)*

116b (JUST LIKE) STARTING OVER *(3.55)*

125b WOMAN *(3.29)*

120a I'M LOSING YOU *(4.00)*

122a BEAUTIFUL BOY (DARLING BOY) *(4.00)*

123b WATCHING THE WHEELS *(3.33)*

127a DEAR YOKO *(2.32)*

30 (40b) LOVE *(3.12)* (52a) GIVE ME SOME TRUTH *(3.11)*

By John Lennon

Parlophone R 6059 – November 15, 1982

Released as a trailer for the *John Lennon Collection* album, *Love* entered the *NME* Top 30 for one week only on November 20 at No. 27.

The single version of *Love* differs from the original album track and that on the *Collection*, as it was re-mixed to boost the very quiet introductory and ending piano passages. EMI decided that if the song were released with its original mix, with the piano fading in and out very quietly, DJs might be prone to ignore the record as unsuitable for broadcasting.

JOHN – US SECTION

1 UNFINISHED MUSIC No. 1 – TWO VIRGINS

By John Lennon and Yoko Ono

Apple T 5001 – November 11, 1968

John and Yoko's first solo album bubbled under the Billboard Hot Hundred album charts for eight weeks during February and March 1969, rising no higher than No. 124. As with EMI in Britain, Capitol refused to handle the album, and it was eventually distributed by Tetragrammaton, with 25,000 being sold, although 30,000 copies were confiscated by police from a warehouse in Newark, New Jersey.

(Tracks and cover as British release.)

2 UNFINISHED MUSIC No. 2 – LIFE WITH THE LIONS

By John Lennon and Yoko Ono

Zapple ST 3357 – May 26, 1969

As with *Two Virgins, Life With The Lions* did not enter the Billboard Top 100 album charts, managing only eight weeks in the lower regions of the Top 200, rising no higher than No. 179. The album did, however, outsell *Two Virgins,* as 60,000 copies were sold in the US. (Track listing and sleeve same as British release.)

3 (18) GIVE PEACE A CHANCE (19) REMEMBER LOVE

By The Plastic Ono Band

Apple 1809 – July 7, 1969

The first Plastic Ono Band single entered the Billboard Hot Hundred on July 26 at No. 62, rising to No. 14 on September 6, and staying in the Top 100 for nine weeks. The single sold 800,000 in America, and was released with the same picture sleeve as in Britain.

4 (20) COLD TURKEY (21) DON'T WORRY KYOKO (MUMMY'S ONLY LOOKING FOR A HAND IN THE SNOW)

By The Plastic Ono Band

Apple 1813 – October 20, 1969

Cold Turkey entered the Billboard Hot Hundred on November 15 at No. 86, rising to No. 30 for one week on January 17, 1970, being in the Top 100 for twelve weeks. The single appeared in the same picture sleeve as the British release.

5 THE WEDDING ALBUM

By John Lennon and Yoko Ono

Apple SMAX 3361 – October 20, 1969

As with their first two albums, *The Wedding Album* only managed to creep into the lower regions of the Top 200, rising no higher than No. 178 during three weeks in the chart. (Track listing and sleeve same as British release.)

6 PLASTIC ONO BAND – LIVE PEACE IN TORONTO – 1969

By The Plastic Ono Band

Apple SW 3362 – December 12, 1969

The Plastic Ono Band's first album entered the Top 200 album charts on January 10, 1970, at No. 136, rising to No. 10 for two weeks from February 7, being in the Top 200 for thirty-two weeks, and spending twenty-three weeks in the Top 100. The record received a Gold Award from RIAA for sales of more than $1,000,000 on March 17, 1970. (Tracks and sleeve same as British release.)

7 (32) INSTANT KARMA (33) WHO HAS SEEN THE WIND

By Lennon/Ono with The Plastic Ono Band

Apple 1818 – February 20, 1970

Instant Karma was the first solo Beatles single to sell a million copies in America. It entered the US Top 100 on February 28 at No. 85, rising to No. 3 on March 28 for three weeks, and staying in the charts for thirteen weeks. The American single features a mix of *Instant Karma* by Phil Spector which was not approved by Lennon.

8 JOHN LENNON/PLASTIC ONO BAND

By John Lennon and The Plastic Ono Band

Apple SW 3372 – December 11, 1970

John's first true solo album had an advance order of 250,000 in America, and entered the Top 200 album charts on December 26 at No. 14, rising at No. 6 on January 30. It was in the Top 100 for eighteen weeks, and the Top 200 for twenty-two weeks, selling a million copies by the end of January, 1971. (Tracks and sleeve the same as British release.)

9 (34a) MOTHER WHY

"A" side by John Lennon/Plastic Ono Band

"B" side by Yoko Ono/Plastic Ono Band

Apple 1827 – December 28, 1970

Not released as a single in Britain, *Mother* was taken from the *John Lennon/Plastic Ono Band* album, using a slightly different mix, and coupled with Yoko's *Why* from her *Yoko Ono/Plastic Ono Band* album, as a single in the States. The single entered the Top 100 on January 9, 1971, at No. 87, but only managed to rise to No. 43 for two weeks, on January 30, being in the chart for six weeks.

10 (45) POWER TO THE PEOPLE TOUCH ME

"A" side by John Lennon/Plastic Ono Band

"B" side by Yoko Ono/Plastic Ono Band

Apple 1830 – March 22, 1971

In Britain, *Power To The People* was coupled with *Open Your Box* by Yoko but, in America, Capitol would not allow Yoko to use the song due to its suggestive lyrics. Therefore another number from *Yoko Ono/Plastic Ono Band* album was used. The single entered the US Top 100 on April 3 at No. 73, rising to No. 11 for two weeks from May 1; it remained in the chart for nine weeks.

GOD SAVE US DO THE OZ

"A" side by Bill Elliot and The Elastic Oz Band

"B" side by The Elastic Oz Band

Apple 1835 – July 7, 1971

As in Britain, John's record for the Oz Defence Fund did not enter the charts.

11 IMAGINE

By John Lennon

Apple SW 3379 – September 9, 1971

Imagine entered the US album charts on September 18 at No. 163, rising to No. 1 for one week on October 30. The album stayed in the Top 100 for twenty-five weeks, and in the Top 200 for thirty weeks, achieving sales of over one million dollars by October 1, 1971, and subsequently selling a million in America. (Tracks and sleeve the same as British release.)

12 (47a) IMAGINE (50a) IT'S SO HARD

By John Lennon

Apple 1840 – October 11, 1971

The *Imagine* single entered the Billboard

Top 100 on October 23, at No. 20 (the highest entry position since *Let It Be* entered at No. 6 on March 21, 1970) making it tenth equal with the Beatles *Something* in the list of highest entry positions. The Top Ten in this chart is as follows:
1 *Let It Be* (No. 6) The Beatles (1970);
2 = *The Purple People Eater* (No. 7) Sheb Woolley (1958) & *Wear My Ring Around Your Neck* (No. 7) Elvis Presley (1958);
4 = *Hey Jude* (No. 10) The Beatles (1968) & *Get Back* (No. 10) The Beatles (1969);
6 = *Mrs Brown You've Got A Lovely Daughter* (No. 12) Herman's Hermits (1965);
7 = *Jailhouse Rock* (No. 15) Elvis Presley (1957) & *Hard Headed Woman* (No. 15) Elvis Presley (1958);
9 = *Poor Little Fool* (No. 18) Ricky Nelson (1958);
10 = *Something* (No. 20) The Beatles (1969) & *Imagine* (No. 20) John Lennon (1971).

Imagine rose to No. 3 on November 13 for two weeks, staying in the charts for nine weeks. The single did not appear in a picture sleeve, and did not receive a British release as a single until 1975.

13 (73) HAPPY XMAS (WAR IS OVER) (74) LISTEN THE SNOW IS FALLING

"A" side by John & Yoko/Plastic Ono Band with The Harlem Community Choir

"B" side by Yoko Ono and The Plastic Ono Band

Apple 1842 – December 1, 1971

In America, *Happy Xmas* appeared a year before its British release, but did not enter the Billboard Hot Hundred. The single appeared in a picture sleeve, on clear green vinyl. (Picture sleeve same as British release.)

14 (57) WOMAN IS THE NIGGER OF THE WORLD (58) SISTERS O SISTERS

"A" side by John Lennon/Plastic Ono Band with Elephant's Memory and Invisible Strings

"B" side by Yoko Ono/Plastic Ono Band with Elephant's Memory and Invisible Strings

Apple 1848 – April 24, 1972

The trailer for the *Sometime In New York City* album entered the Billboard Hot Hundred on May 20 at No. 76, rising to No. 57 for one week on June 10, and featuring in the chart for only five weeks.

15 SOMETIME IN NEW YORK CITY

Record One by John & Yoko/Plastic Ono Band with Elephant's Memory and Invisible Strings

Record Two "A" Side by Plastic Ono Supergroup. Record Two "B" side by Plastic Ono Mothers

Apple SVBB 3392 – June 12, 1972

Appearing three months earlier in America than in Britain, *Sometime In New York City* entered the Billboard album chart on July 1 at No. 190, rising to No. 48 on August 12 for two weeks, and staying in the Top 100 for twelve weeks and the Top 200 for seventeen weeks. (Sleeve same as British release.)

RECORD ONE A SIDE

57a **WOMAN IS THE NIGGER OF THE WORLD**
58a **SISTERS O SISTERS**
59 **ATTICA STATE**
60 **BORN IN A PRISON**
61 **NEW YORK CITY**

B SIDE

62 **SUNDAY BLOODY SUNDAY**
63 **THE LUCK OF THE IRISH**
64 **JOHN SINCLAIR**
65 **ANGELA**
66 **WE'RE ALL WATER**

RECORD TWO

(Same as British release.)

16 (75) MIND GAMES (76) MEAT CITY

By John Lennon

Apple 1868 – October 29, 1973

Mind Games entered the Billboard chart on November 10 at No. 76, rising to No. 18 on December 29 for one week, being in the Hot Hundred for thirteen weeks, and for seven weeks in the Top 30. (Picture sleeve same as British release.)

17 MIND GAMES

By John Lennon

Apple SW 3414 – November 2, 1973

Mind Games entered the Billboard album charts on November 24 at No. 16, receiving a Gold Award from RIAA, on November 30, for sales of over one million dollars. The album rose to No. 9 for three weeks on December 8, and stayed in the Top 100 for fifteen weeks, and in the Top 200 for eighteen weeks. (Tracks and sleeve the same as British release.)

18 (87) WHATEVER GETS YOU THRU THE NIGHT (88) BEEF JERKY

By John Lennon

Apple 1874 – September 23, 1974

John's first No. 1 single in America, which entered the charts on September 28 at No. 53, rising to the top seven weeks later on November 16 for one week, and staying there for fifteen weeks. Twelve days after *Whatever Gets You Thru The Night* reached the top of the charts, John kept his promise to Elton John, that if the single got to No. 1 he would appear with Elton on stage. John performed three numbers with The Elton John Band at Madison Square Garden, New York, on November 28, 1974, which turned out to be his last concert performance.

19 WALLS AND BRIDGES

By John Lennon

Apple SW 3416 – September 26, 1974

Walls And Bridges entered the Billboard album chart on October 12 at No. 72, jumping to No. 19 the following week and qualifying for Gold Award status (one million dollars sales) by October 22. By November 1974, the album had sold one million in the States, and on November 16 rose to No. 1 for one week. It eventually stayed in the Top 100 for twenty-one weeks and the Top 200 for twenty-seven weeks. (Tracks and sleeve same as British release.)

20 (94a) No. 9 DREAM (91a) WHAT YOU GOT

By John Lennon

Apple 1878 – December 16, 1974

The second single from *Walls And Bridges, No. 9 Dream* entered the Billboard Hot Hundred chart on December 21, at No. 68, rising to No. 9 on February 22, 1975. It remained in the chart for twelve weeks and in the Top 30 for seven weeks.

21 ROCK 'N' ROLL

By John Lennon

Apple SK 3419 – February 17, 1975

Rock 'n' Roll entered the album chart on March 8 at No. 47, rising to No. 6 on April 19, and staying in the Top 100 for thirteen weeks, and in the Top 200 for fifteen weeks. (Tracks and sleeve same as British release.)

PHILADELPHIA FREEDOM I SAW HER STANDING THERE

"A" side by The Elton John Band

"B" side by The Elton John Band with John Lennon and The Muscle Shoals Horns

MCA 40364 – February 24, 1975

The "B" side of *Philadelphia Freedom, I Saw Her Standing There,* was recorded live at The Elton John Band concert at Madison Square Garden on November 28, 1974, when John Lennon made a guest appearance to fulfil a promise made to Elton John. *Philadelphia Freedom* entered the Billboard chart in April 1975, rising to No. 1 for two weeks from April 12. It then stayed in the best sellers for twenty-one weeks, receiving a Gold Award from the RIAA on April 23, 1975, and eventually selling over two million.

22 (100a) STAND BY ME (114) MOVE OVER MRS L

By John Lennon

Apple 1881 – March 10, 1975

Stand By Me entered the Billboard chart on March 15 at No. 78, rising to No. 20 for two weeks on April 26, being in the Top 30 for four weeks and the Top 100 for nine weeks. A follow up single from *Rock 'n' Roll* was scheduled in America, with promotional copies of *Slippin' And Slidin'* backed by *Ain't That A Shame* (Apple 1883) being distributed, but the release was eventually shelved.

23 SHAVED FISH

By John Lennon

Apple SW 3421 – October 24, 1975

All eleven tracks on the *Shaved Fish* album had been singles in America; whereas in Britain, three had not appeared as singles, *Mother, Woman Is The Nigger Of The World* and *Imagine* (the latter appearing as a single in America in 1972, but not receiving British single release until 1975). The album entered the Billboard charts on November 8, at No. 97, peaking at No. 12 on December 13, and staying in the charts for thirteen weeks. (Sleeve same as British release.)

A SIDE

18a **GIVE PEACE A CHANCE**

20a **COLD TURKEY**

32a **INSTANT KARMA**

45a **POWER TO THE PEOPLE**

34b **MOTHER**

57b **WOMAN IS THE NIGGER OF THE WORLD**

B SIDE

47b **IMAGINE**

87b **WHATEVER GETS YOU THRU THE NIGHT**

75b **MIND GAMES**

94b **No. 9 DREAM**

73a **HAPPY XMAS (WAR IS OVER)**

115 **GIVE PEACE A CHANCE**

24 (100b) STAND BY ME (57c) WOMAN IS THE NIGGER OF THE WORLD

By John Lennon

Capitol Star Line 6244 – April 4, 1977

With the original Apple singles of *Stand By Me* and *Woman Is The Nigger Of The World* deleted, they became eligible to appear on Capitol's subsidiary label Star Line, and were released as a double "A" side, but without chart success.

25 (116) (JUST LIKE) STARTING OVER (117) KISS KISS KISS

"A" side by John Lennon

"B" side by Yoko Ono

Geffen Records GEF–49604 – October 23, 1980

John and Yoko's come-back single entered the Billboard Hot Hundred on November 9, rising to No. 1 on December 27, after the tragic murder of Lennon. It stayed at No. 1 for five weeks, and in the chart for twenty-two weeks. (Picture sleeve same as British release.)

26 MIND GAMES

By John Lennon

Capitol SN-16068 – October, 1980

As in Britain, Capitol reissued several Beatle solo albums on their budget label, this batch consisting of George's *Dark Horse, Ringo,* and John's *Mind Games* and *Rock 'n' Roll* albums. The *Mind Games* album featured the same sleeve as the original issue. (Tracks same as the British reissue.)

27 ROCK 'N' ROLL

By John Lennon

Capitol SN-16069 – October, 1980

The second budget reissue album from John, featuring the same cover design as the original.

A SIDE TRACK TWO

100c **STAND BY ME**

(Remaining tracks same as the British reissue.)

28 DOUBLE FANTASY

By John Lennon and Yoko Ono

Geffen Records GHS–2001 – November 17, 1980

John and Yoko's first album in five years, which entered the Billboard charts on December 6, rising to No. 1 on December 27, after John was mercilessly gunned down outside his New York apartment in the Dakota Buildings. The album stayed at No. 1 for eight weeks, and was in the Top 200 for seventy-four weeks. (Tracks and sleeve same as British release.)

29 (125a) WOMAN (126a) BEAUTIFUL BOYS

"A" side by John Lennon

"B" side by Yoko Ono

Geffen Records 49644 – January 12, 1981

The second single release from the

Double Fantasy album, which entered the Billboard charts on January 17, rising to No. 2, and staying in the charts for twenty weeks. (Picture sleeve same as British release.)

30 (123a) WATCHING THE WHEELS (124a) YES I'M YOUR ANGEL

"A" side by John Lennon

"B" side by Yoko Ono

Geffen Records 49695 – March 13, 1981

The third single from the *Double Fantasy* album entered the Billboard chart on March 28, reaching No. 10, and staying in the chart for fourteen weeks. (Picture sleeve same as British release.)

31 (116b) (JUST LIKE) STARTING OVER (125b) WOMAN

By John Lennon

Geffen Records GGEF 0408 – June 5, 1981

Warner Brothers Records in America operate a policy of combining hit singles to form double "A"-sided oldies and, as they distributed Geffen Records, John's singles were in line for this treatment. This release featured the first two hits from *Double Fantasy.*

32 (123b) WATCHING THE WHEELS (122a) BEAUTIFUL BOY (DARLING BOY)

By John Lennon

Geffen Records GGEF 0415 – November 4, 1981

Having coupled the first two single "A" sides together as an oldie, only one "A" side *(Watching The Wheels)* remained. This was coupled with another Lennon song from *Double Fantasy, Beautiful Boy (Darling Boy),* and not with its original flipside of Yoko's *Yes I'm Your Angel.*

33 THE JOHN LENNON COLLECTION

By John Lennon

Geffen Records GHSP 2023 – November 10, 1982

After a year of negotiation, Geffen Records eventually gave permission for EMI to use the *Double Fantasy* recordings for this best of John Lennon album, under the proviso that Geffen released the record in the US. The album entered the Billboard charts on December 4, rising to No. 33 for four weeks, on January 8, 1983, and staying in the Top 40 for six weeks.

The American album contained two less tracks than the British release, as neither *Stand By Me* or *Happy Xmas* were hits in the United States.

A SIDE

18b **GIVE PEACE A CHANCE**

32b **INSTANT KARMA**

45b **POWER TO THE PEOPLE**

87c **WHATEVER GETS YOU THRU THE NIGHT**

94c **No. 9 DREAM**

75d **MIND GAMES**

40a **LOVE**

B SIDE

47c **IMAGINE**

49a **JEALOUS GUY**

116c **(JUST LIKE) STARTING OVER**

125c **WOMAN**

120a **I'M LOSING YOU**

122b **BEAUTIFUL BOY (DARLING BOY)**

127a **DEAR YOKO**

123c **WATCHING THE WHEELS**

34 (73b) HAPPY XMAS (WAR IS OVER) (122c) BEAUTIFUL BOY (DARLING BOY)

By John Lennon

Geffen Records 7-29855 – November 17, 1982

Although not a hit when it was originally released in the United States, Geffen reissued *Happy Xmas,* hoping to emulate its British success, but again the single failed to enter the Billboard best sellers. Geffen's reissue featured the same picture sleeve as the 1971 Capitol release, but the original "B" side coupling of *Listen The Snow Is Falling* was replaced by *Beautiful Boy (Darling Boy)* (included on *The John Lennon Collection*).

PAUL McCARTNEY

1 McCARTNEY

By Paul McCartney

Apple PCS 7102 – April 17, 1970

Although Paul McCartney had written the music to *The Family Way* film back in 1966, with an album by The George Martin Orchestra appearing in January 1967, he did not perform on the recordings, and therefore *McCartney* is his first solo recording venture. With advance sales of 19,000 in Britain, the album entered the *NME* Top 30 chart on April 22, a week after release, at No. 6, rising to No. 2 the following week where it remained for three weeks (being kept out of the No. 1 position by Simon and Garfunkel's *Bridge Over Troubled Water* album). It stayed in the Top 10 for sixteen weeks, and the Top 30 for twenty-two weeks, selling over two million worldwide.

McCartney recorded and produced the album between December 1969 and April 1970, using several recording locations – at his home using a Studer 4 track machine, at EMI's Abbey Road Studio No. 2 and at Morgan Studios, Willesden, London. Paul played all the instruments heard on the album, as well as composing all fourteen songs and singing most of the vocal parts, with Linda McCartney assisting on some songs.

The release date for the album caused some controversy between Paul and the rest of the Beatles, as he had scheduled the album to come out in April, while the "last" Beatles' album, *Let It Be,* had been scheduled at around the same time. John, George and Ringo wanted Paul to postpone the release of his album, but Paul was adamant and refused, so that eventually *Let it Be* was re-scheduled.

The twenty-three photographs contained on the gatefold sleeve were taken by Linda; the album was sent out to British DJs accompanied by a printed "question and answers" sheet, which Paul compiled as a self-interview, due to his long silence during the previous months. The insert was not included in the commercially available album.

A SIDE

1 **THE LOVELY LINDA** *(0.43)*
2 **THAT WOULD BE SOMETHING** *(2.37)*
3 **VALENTINE DAY** *(1.40)*
4 **EVERY NIGHT** *(2.29)* 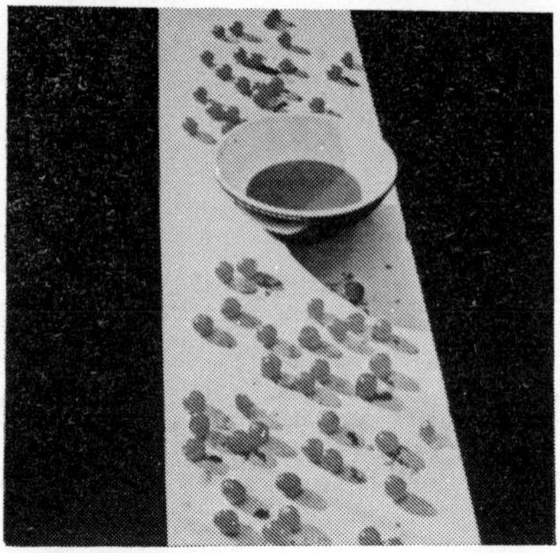
5 **HOT AS SUN** *(1.28)*
6 **GLASSES** *(0.48)*
7 **JUNK** *(1.53)*
8 **MAN WE WAS LONELY** *(2.55)*

B SIDE

9 **OO YOU** *(2.47)*
10 **MOMMA MISS AMERICA** *(4.03)*
11 **TEDDY BOY** *(2.22)*
12 **SINGALONG JUNK** *(2.34)*
13 **MAYBE I'M AMAZED** *(3.47)*
14 **KREEN-AKRORE** *(4.08)*

After Paul's new Studer 4 track recorder had been installed in his London home, he tested the machine with *The Lovely Linda*, on which he played acoustic guitar and bass, and produced percussive sounds by hand slaps on a book. Paul wrote the song in Scotland but never completed it, this recording supposedly being a trailer for the full song, which he never recorded. *That Would Be Something* was also written in Scotland, in 1969, and features Paul playing guitar, tom tom, cymbal and bass.

Paul ad libbed *Valentine Day* as he recorded it at his home, using acoustic guitar, drums, electric guitar and bass, with the final mix done at EMI. Paul completed *Every Night* while on holiday in Greece in 1969, and recorded it at EMI playing acoustic guitars, drums and bass, and double tracking his vocals in places. The song was covered by Phoebe Snow in 1979, when her version entered the *NME* Top 30 on January 20 at No. 30, rising to No. 26, but being in the chart for only two weeks.

Hot As Sun was written around 1958 or 1959, and recorded at Morgan Studios using acoustic and electric guitar, drums, organ, bass, maracas and bongos. *Glasses* features multi-tracked wine glasses, and

ANOTHER DAY*
and
OH WOMAN, OH WHY?
a great new single by
APPLE
R 5889
PAUL McCARTNEY
EMI
*Written by Mr. & Mrs. McCartney

new single
Paul and Linda McCartney
"Back seat of my car"
and
"Heart of the country"
Apple R 5914

from the album
RAM
out now
EMI
EMI Records (The Gramophone Co. Ltd) EMI House, 20 Manchester Square, London, W1A 1ES
A member of the EMI Group of Companies
International leaders in Electronics, Records and Entertainment

YOUR
EMI

an uncompleted song called "Suicide". *Junk* was started in India in 1968 and completed in London, when it was originally recorded by the Beatles during the "White Album" sessions. It was later re-recorded in March 1969 during the "Abbey Road" sessions. Paul recorded his solo version at his home using two acoustic guitars and bass, later adding percussion, a toy xylophone and harmony vocals at Morgan Studios. *Man We Was Lonely* was written during the sessions for the album; Linda joined Paul for harmony, while Paul plays guitar, bass drum, bass and "steel guitar" sound, produced by playing a Telecaster with a drum peg.

Oo You was originally recorded at Paul's home as an instrumental, with lyrics added later, and recording was completed at Morgan Studios using electric guitar, tambourine, cow bell and aerosol spray! *Momma Miss America* was also ad libbed – Paul recorded it at his home using piano, drums, acoustic and electric guitars.

Teddy Boy, another number dating back to the Beatles in India, was originally recorded in January 1969 and intended for their "Get Back" album, which was eventually scrapped. Paul completed writing the song in Scotland and London, and recorded the number at his home, and at Morgan Studios, using guitar and bass, with assistance from Linda on backing harmonies. *Singalong Junk* is the original take for *Junk*, and was recorded using guitar, piano and bass at his home; it was completed at Morgan using electric guitar, bass drum, sizzle cymbal and Mellotron (strings).

Maybe I'm Amazed, written in London, was recorded at EMI Studios, using piano, drums and guitars and with Linda joining Paul for backing vocals. The number later became a stage favourite by Rod Stewart and The Faces and was included on their 1971 album, *Long Player*.

The final song on the album was inspired by a TV film about the Kreen-Akrore Indians in the Brazilian jungle; McCartney started the recording with a drumming track, and later embellished the first half with piano, guitar and organ, and the second half with breathing, organ and two lead guitars. The recording was done at Morgan, with Robin Black engineering, and extra sound effects include a bow and arrow and an animal stampede, achieved with the aid of a guitar packing case.

2 (15) ANOTHER DAY *(3.40)*
(16) OH WOMAN OH WHY *(4.34)*

By Paul McCartney

Apple R 5889 – February 19, 1971

Paul's first solo single entered the *NME* charts on March 3, 1971, at No. 8, and went to No. 1 on March 17 for one week only, staying in the charts for ten weeks.

The single was recorded in January 1971, in New York, using the New York Philharmonic Orchestra and session men Dave Spinozza and Hugh McCracken (guitars) and Denny Seiwell (drums), with Paul producing. As with Yoko Ono's co-composing credits with John, Linda also experienced problems with her co-composition of *Another Day*, which was credited to Mr and Mrs McCartney on the label. Sir Lew Grade would not accept that she had helped write the song. *Oh Woman Oh Why* was written solely by Paul.

The single was not produced in a picture sleeve, but McCartney arranged to use the "Capitol" label in Britain in 1975, and the single was re-released on that label at that time, but using the same Parlophone catalogue number. The single has sold an estimated global million.

3 RAM

By Paul and Linda McCartney

Apple PAS 10003 – May 21, 1971

Ram entered the *NME* album charts on May 26, one week after release, at No. 10, rising to No. 2 for three weeks on June 16, when *Sticky Fingers* by The Rolling Stones was at No. 1. On July 7, *Ram* knocked *Bridge Over Troubled Water* from the No. 1 spot, for one week only, allowing the Simon and Garfunkel album to return to the top the following week by dropping to No. 2 for four weeks. The album stayed in the Top 10 for nineteen weeks, and in the Top 30 for twenty-four weeks.

The sessions for the album took place at the A and R Studios in New York, between January and March, 1971, producing twenty-one songs. The sessions were the first Paul had recorded outside London, and the first of many overseas locations which Paul would favour when recording his later albums. As well as using the New York Philharmonic Orchestra on three songs, Paul and Linda were backed by Dave Spinozza and Hugh McCracken on guitar, and Denny Seiwell on drums, with Linda supplying extra percussion and Paul guitar and bass.

The album sleeve, designed by Paul, features a collage of Linda's pictures, with Paul's drawings; the front cover, depicting Paul holding a ram by the horns, was taken on Paul's Scottish farm. On the right-hand side of the front cover, in the zigzag design, are the letters "L.I.L.Y", which possibly stands for "Linda I Love You". The back cover includes photographs of two beetles copulating, which many critics thought was Paul's dig at his former group.

A SIDE

17 **TOO MANY PEOPLE** *(4.10)*

18 **3 LEGS** *(2.43)*

19 **RAM ON** *(2.27)*

20 **DEAR BOY** *(2.11)*

21/2 **UNCLE ALBERT/ADMIRAL HALSEY** *(4.49)*

23 **SMILE AWAY** *(3.56)*

B SIDE

24 **HEART OF THE COUNTRY** *(2.21)*

25 **MONKBERRY MOON DELIGHT** *(5.23)*

26 **EAT AT HOME** *(3.20)*

27 **LONG HAIRED LADY** *(6.04)*

28 **RAM ON** *(0.53)*

29 **THE BACK SEAT OF MY CAR** *(4.25)*

Paul composed *Too Many People, 3 Legs, Ram On, Smile Away* and *The Back Seat Of My Car* alone, and Linda assisted with the remainder. Paul conducts the New York Philharmonic Orchestra on *Uncle Albert/Admiral Halsey, Long Haired Lady* and *The Back Seat Of My Car,* while on *Monkberry Moon Delight,* Heather McCartney (Linda's daughter by an earlier marriage) sings backing vocals. Two songs on the album, *Too Many People* and *Dear Boy,* supposedly provoked Lennon (who saw the songs as vindictive personal attacks) to compose *How Do You Sleep?*

4 (29a) THE BACK SEAT OF MY CAR *(4.26)* (24a) HEART OF THE COUNTRY *(2.22)*

By Paul and Linda McCartney

Apple R 5914 – August 13, 1971

Easily the best song on the *Ram* album, *The Back Seat Of My Car* was released as a single in Britain; it had no success in the *NME* chart, although it did enter the BMRB chart for five weeks, rising to No. 39.

5 WILD LIFE

By Wings

Apple PCS 7142 – December 3, 1971

The first Wings album entered the *NME* charts on December 15, 1971, at No. 13, and rose to its highest position of No. 11 during the following week. The album dropped out and re-entered the charts twice (featuring for a total of eight weeks), making it Paul's least successful album to date.

While the McCartneys were recording *Ram* in New York, Paul was yearning to perform live again as it had been five years since the Beatles last toured. To do this, he realised he needed a band, and thus started the task of forming a working unit. His first approach was to Denny Seiwell, who had drummed on the "Ram" sessions. As Seiwell was a relatively unknown session musician, he obviously jumped at the chance to play in a band with an ex-Beatle, and immediately left

Mary Had A Little Lamb

a single record from your old chums Wings

R 5949

New York to join the McCartneys on their farm in Campbelltown, Scotland. While on their farm, Paul and Linda wrote a number of new songs and, when they were ready to record, Paul decided he needed a guitarist. He immediately thought of his old friend, Denny Laine, ex-member of The Moody Blues, a group which had toured with the Beatles during December 1965.

In August 1971, Paul, with his new band "Wings", entered a London studio, and recorded most of the tracks for the album in three days, with each song being recorded in one take; the album was finished within two to three weeks. Paul later regretted recording the album in such a rush, due to the bad reviews it received in the music press. Paul and Linda produced the album with Tony Clarke, the Moody Blues producer, and Alan Parsons (who later produced the "Alan Parsons Project" series of albums) engineering. On the album, Paul plays guitar, bass and piano; Denny Laine/ guitar; Denny Seiwell/drums; and Linda/ keyboards and backing vocals.

The very simple album sleeve features a photograph, taken by Barry Lategan, of Wings (Mark One), with typography by Gordon House. As with John's solo releases, Paul adopted a special label for his own records, and the "Wild Life" labels feature a picture of Paul by Linda on the "A" side, and a picture of Linda, taken by Paul, on the "B" side.

A SIDE

30 **MUMBO** *(3.51)*

31 **BIP BOP** *(4.07)*

32 **LOVE IS STRANGE** *(4.44)*

33 **WILD LIFE** *(4.36)*

B SIDE

34 **SOME PEOPLE NEVER KNOW** *(6.35)*

35 **I AM YOUR SINGER** *(2.11)*

(Untitled track) *(0.46)*

36 **TOMORROW** *(3.21)*

37 **DEAR FRIEND** *(5.44)*

(Untitled track) *(0.44)*

All songs, except *Love Is Strange,* were written by Paul and Linda. *Mumbo* features Paul singing nonsense words, while *Bip Bop* was inspired by Paul's daughter, Mary; Paul sings lead with Linda supporting him with backing vocals. *Love Is Strange* was written by Mickey Baker and Ethel Smith, and released by Mickey and Sylvia as a single in the US in 1956, selling a million and reaching No. 13. It was later covered by the Everly Brothers in 1965, giving them a UK No. 11 hit. Paul and Linda sing this as a duet in places, with Paul singing solo at times. The song was originally scheduled as the first Wings single (R 5932), with *I Am Your Singer* as the "B" side; promotional copies were distributed, but due to the poor sales of the album Paul withdrew the release.

The title track, *Wild Life,* was Paul's comment on animal conservation; Paul sings lead with Linda and the two Dennys supplying backing vocals. *Some People Never Know* features Paul singing lead, with Linda assisting and, on *I Am Your Singer,* their roles are reversed. Before the next track, there is a short tune played on acoustic guitar which has no title. *Tomorrow* features Paul singing lead, with vocal support, while *Dear Friend* features a solo vocal from Paul, who composed the song as an answer to John's *How Do You Sleep.*

6 (38) GIVE IRELAND BACK TO THE IRISH *(3.42)*
(39) GIVE IRELAND BACK TO THE IRISH (version) *(3.45)*

By Wings

Apple R 5936 – February 25, 1972

The first single from Wings which entered the *NME* Top 30 on March 1, 1972, at No. 21, rising to No. 13 on March 15, and staying in the chart for six weeks.

In January 1972, Henry McCullough, ex-Grease Band, joined Wings as guitarist, and on February 1, 1972, the new five piece line-up of Wings (Mark Two) recorded *Give Ireland Back To The Irish.* The song was written by the McCartneys to protest about the Bloody Sunday Massacre in Ireland on January 3, 1972, (which also inspired John to write *Sunday Bloody Sunday*); it was Paul's first and only "political" song, being immediately banned by the BBC and IBA. The "B" side was an instrumental version of the "A" side.

The single, which was produced by Paul and Linda, came in a yellow sleeve, with "Wings" emblazoned upon it, while the label featured five green shamrocks on a white background.

7 (40) MARY HAD A LITTLE LAMB *(3.29)* (41) LITTLE WOMAN LOVE *(2.05)*

By Wings

Apple R 5949 – May 5, 1972

Paul's version of the nursery rhyme entered the *NME* Top 30 on May 30, 1972, at No. 28, rising to No. 6 on June 20, and staying in the chart for nine weeks.

Paul and Linda wrote *Mary Had A Little Lamb* because their daughter, Mary, liked hearing her name being sung. Their children sing along on the chorus, with Paul singing lead. The song was recorded during early 1972, with Henry McCullough playing mandolin, and Linda on piano. *Little Woman Love,* written by Paul and Linda, features Paul singing lead and, in places, Linda joins in.

The single was released in a picture sleeve with matching picture labels, and note the catalogue number, R 5949 – exactly one thousand higher than the Beatles first Parlophone single *Love Me Do* (R 4949).

8 (42) HI, HI, HI *(3.06)* (43) C MOON *(4.31)*

By Wings

Apple R 5973 – December 1, 1972

The third and last Wings single of 1972 entered the *NME* charts on December 12 at No. 20, rising to No. 3 on January 16, 1973, and staying in the charts for ten weeks.

The single, produced by Paul, was recorded in the latter half of October 1972, at Morgan Studios, London, with the Wings Mark Two line-up of Paul, Linda, Denny Laine, Henry McCullough and Denny Seiwell all playing their usual instruments on *Hi, Hi, Hi,* although on *C Moon* Paul played piano, Henry/drums, Denny Laine/bass and Denny Seiwell/trumpet. Paul sings lead on both titles.

Hi, Hi, Hi was banned by the BBC, becoming the second Wings' single to be banned in a year, the reason on this occasion being the sexually suggestive lyrics. *C Moon* therefore became the main side for radio exposure. *C Moon* was inspired by the 1965 hit by Sam The Sham and The Pharaohs, *Woolly Bully,* which includes a reference not to be "L7" or "square": so Paul made up *C Moon,* which makes a circle (the opposite of square). As with the two previous Wings singles of 1972, *Hi, Hi, Hi* did not feature the Apple logo, but a plain red label, matching the red sleeve.

9 (44) MY LOVE *(4.05)* (45) THE MESS *(4.53)*

By Paul McCartney and Wings

Apple R 5985 – March 23, 1973

Wings' fourth single, which entered the *NME* chart on April 3, 1973, at No. 26, peaked at No. 7 on May 1, and was listed in the chart for nine weeks. The single sold an estimated two million globally.

My Love was recorded during the sessions for the *Red Rose Speedway* album, which took place in March and October 1972. The song was written by Paul, who plays electric piano, and sings lead vocals, with Linda and Denny Laine supplying backing vocals. Denny Laine also plays bass, while Henry plays electric guitar and Denny Seiwell drums.

The Mess is a live recording made on August 21, at the Congresgebouw, The Hague, Holland, during Wings' July–August 1972 tour of Europe, when they played twenty-seven concerts in ten countries. During the tour, Wings played the following numbers: *Bip Bop, Smile Away, 1881, I Would Only Smile, Give Ireland Back To The Irish, Blue Moon Of Kentucky, The Mess, Best Friends, Soily, I Am Your Singer, Seaside Woman, Henry's Blues, Say You Don't Mind, Wild Life, Mary Had A Little Lamb, My Love, Maybe I'm Amazed, Hi, Hi, Hi* and *Long Tall Sally.* Several of these titles were never recorded by Wings in the studio, although a later live version of *Soily* was released on the *"Wings Over America"* triple set. The single was not released in a picture sleeve, but did have a special "Red Rose Speedway" label.

MY LOVE
and
THE MESS

PAUL McCARTNEY AND WINGS

McCartney's
Live and Let Die
the new single from
wings
R 5987

10 RED ROSE SPEEDWAY

By Paul McCartney and Wings

Apple PCTC 251 – May 3, 1973

The second Wings album performed decidedly better in the charts than the first, entering at No. 17 on May 8, 1973, rising to No. 4 twice, on May 22 and June 4, and staying in the charts for fourteen weeks.

The album, produced by Paul, was recorded in March and October 1972, at Morgan Studios, London, with the Wings line-up of Paul, Linda, Denny Laine, Henry McCullough and Denny Seiwell. The album title was inspired by Paul's housekeeper, Rose, and the album was originally intended to be a double. The credit change from "Wings" to "Paul McCartney & Wings" was due to the poor sales of the earlier album, *Wild Life*, which it was thought might have suffered because the public was unaware that it was a McCartney album.

The gatefold sleeve featured a cover photograph of Paul taken by Linda, who also supplied many of the photographs contained in the twelve page booklet insert, which included live pictures of Wings, taken by Captain Snap(?). The full colour booklet also included paintings and drawings by Alan Jones and Eduard Paolozzi, who taught Stuart Sutcliffe in Hamburg. On the back cover of the album in the top left-hand corner, there is a braille message to Stevie Wonder, which reads "We Love You".

A SIDE

46 **BIG BARN BED** *(3.49)*

44a **MY LOVE** *(4.07)*

47 **GET ON THE RIGHT THING** *(4.16)*

48 **ONE MORE KISS** *(2.28)*

49 **LITTLE LAMB DRAGONFLY** *(6.19)*

B SIDE

50 **SINGLE PIGEON** *(1.52)*

51 **WHEN THE NIGHT** *(3.36)*

52 **LOUP (1st INDIAN ON THE MOON)** *(4.23)*

MEDLEY *(11.16):*

53 **HOLD ME TIGHT** *(2.23)*

54 **LAZY DYNAMITE** *(2.49)*

55 **HANDS OF LOVE** *(2.13)*

56 **POWER CUT** *(3.51)*

All compositions on the album are credited to "McCartney". The first two lines of *Big Barn Bed* were originally used at the end of the reprise of *Ram On* on Paul and Linda's *Ram* album, although this is a different recording, featuring Paul's lead vocal, bass and piano, with Linda, Denny (Laine) and Henry supplying backing vocals and Denny Laine/acoustic guitar, Henry/electric guitar and Denny Seiwell/drums.

*Get On The Right **Thing*** was probably an out take from the "Ram" album sessions, as it features Dave Spinozza on electric guitar, while Paul plays bass, piano, electric guitar and sings lead, with Linda as backing vocalist and Denny Seiwell on drums.

Little Lamb Dragonfly was inspired by the death of one of Paul's sheep on his Scottish farm, and features Paul/bass and lead vocal; Linda/dingers and backing vocal; Denny Seiwell/drums, percussion and backing vocal; Denny Laine/backing vocal; plus Hugh McCracken/electric guitar – which suggests it may be another recording left over from the "Ram" sessions.

One More Kiss features Paul singing solo and playing acoustic guitar, while other supporting instrumentation includes Linda/electric harpsichord; Denny Laine/bass; Henry/electric guitar; and Denny Seiwell/drums. Vocals on *Single Pigeon* are by Paul and Linda; with Paul playing piano; Henry/acoustic guitar; and the two Dennys switching roles: Seiwell playing bass; and Laine/drums.

When The Night features a lead vocal and piano by Paul, with the rest of Wings supplying harmonies, and the following backing: Linda/electric bass, piano; Denny Laine and Henry/acoustic guitars; and Denny Seiwell/drums.

The neo-instrumental *Loup (1st Indian On The Moon)* features all five Wings chanting to a backing consisting of Paul/bass, guitar and Moog; Linda/ organ; Denny L and Henry/electric guitars; and Denny S/drums. The eleven minute medley features *Hold Me Tight* (not the Beatle song, by the way) with Paul/vocals, piano and bass; Linda, Henry and the Dennys/backing vocals; Denny L and Henry/electric guitars; and Denny S/drums; *Lazy Dynamite* featuring Paul/piano, bass, vocal and Mellotron; Henry/electric guitar; and Denny L/harmonica; *Hands Of Love* with Paul/acoustic guitar and vocals; Linda/vocals; Denny L/electric guitar; Henry/percussion; and Denny S/drums and percussion; and finally *Power Cut* in which the riffs from the three previous songs are repeated features: Paul/piano, celeste, Mellotron and vocals; Linda/electric piano; Denny L and Henry/electric guitars and vocals; and Denny S/drums.

11 (57) LIVE AND LET DIE *(3.09)* (58) I LIE AROUND *(4.55)*

By Wings

Apple R 5987 – June 1, 1973

Live And Let Die, Paul's theme tune for the eighth James Bond film, entered the *NME* chart on June 17, 1973, at No. 28, rising to No. 7 on July 10. It was in the charts for nine weeks, and sold over 250,000 in Britain, becoming the most successful Bond theme up to that time.

The film company approached Paul to write the song for another artist to sing in the film, but Paul only agreed to compose the song as long as Wings could perform it. After Paul had composed the song George Martin scored it for orchestra and also produced the recording, which took place in October 1972, using the Wings Mark Two line-up.

The "B" side, written by Paul, features Denny Laine singing lead for the first and only time on a Wings single.

LIVE AND LET DIE

Original Soundtrack

United Artists UAS 29475 – July 6, 1973

The soundtrack to the eighth James Bond film, *Live And Let Die*, starring Roger Moore, Yaphet Kotto and Jane Seymour, featured two versions of the title song, written by Paul and Linda: one version by Paul McCartney and Wings, which is heard over the opening credits, and the second version by Brenda J. Arnau. After he had produced the *Live And Let Die* title song for Paul, George Martin was asked to compose the score for the film, as Albert "Chubby" Broccoli and Harry Saltzman, the film producers, were impressed by George's orchestration. Martin composed twelve numbers for the film, which were performed by an orchestra under his direction.

A SIDE

57a **LIVE AND LET DIE** *(3.10)*
By Paul McCartney and Wings

JUST A CLOSER WALK WITH THEE/

NEW SECOND LINE (Milton Batiste)
By Harold A. "Duke" Dejan & The Olympia Brass Band

BOND MEETS SOLITAIRE (Martin)

WHISPER WHO DARES (Martin)

SNAKES ALIVE (Martin)

BARON SAMEDI'S DANCE OF DEATH (Martin)

SAN MONIQUE (Martin)

B SIDE

FILLET OF SOUL – NEW ORLEANS (Martin)

LIVE AND LET DIE
By Brenda J. Arnau

FILLET OF SOUL – HARLEM (Martin)

BOND DROPS IN (Martin)

IF HE FINDS IT, KILL HIM (Martin)

TRESPASSERS WILL BE EATEN (Martin)

SOLITAIRE GETS HER CARDS (Martin)

SACRIFICE (Martin)

JAMES BOND THEME (Monty Norman)

12 (59) HELEN WHEELS *(3.44)* (60) COUNTRY DREAMER *(3.07)*

By Paul McCartney and Wings

Apple R 5993 – October 26, 1973

Helen Wheels entered the *NME* Top 30 on November 6, 1973, at No. 26, and stayed in the chart for only six weeks, rising to its highest position of No. 12 on November 27.

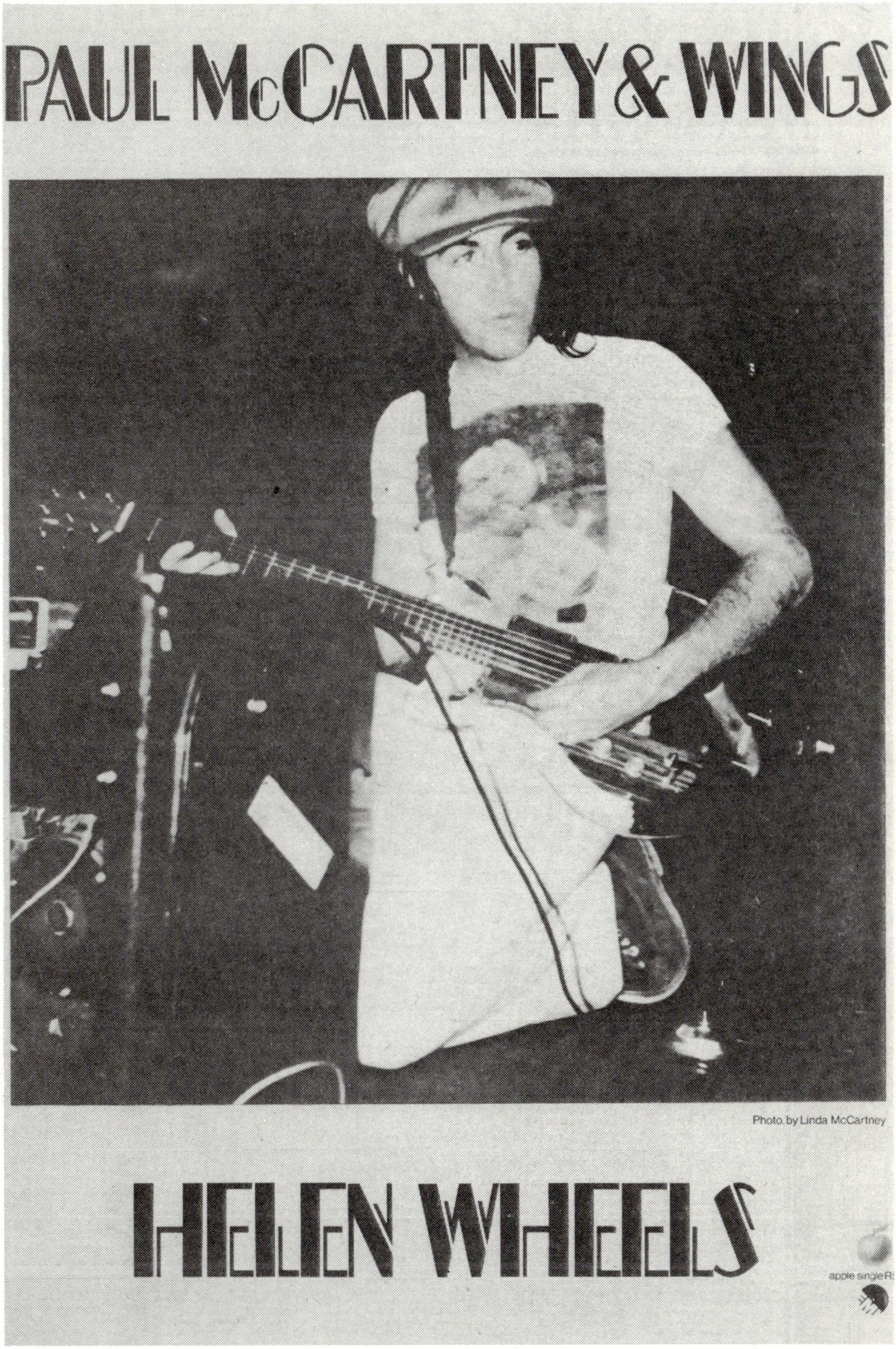

PAUL McCARTNEY & WINGS

Photo. by Linda McCartney

HELEN WHEELS

apple single R

WE'RE OVER THE MOON

To all the people who helped create, make, promote and sell
BAND ON THE RUN, and to all you people who bought the album,
and made it Number One in the U.K.

Thanks from Paul, Linda and Denny.

At the end of July 1973, Wings Mark Two came to an end; Denny Seiwell and Henry McCullough quit the group, thus leaving just Paul, Linda and Denny Laine to travel to Lagos, Nigeria, to record new material. *Helen Wheels* was recorded by the now depleted Wings line-up in September 1973, with Paul producing. *Helen Wheels* is the "name" of Paul's Land Rover and the song tells the story of a trip from Paul's Scottish farm down to London in the vehicle. The "B" side, *Country Dreamer,* was recorded in October 1972 with the Wings Mark Two line-up of Paul, Linda, Henry and the two Dennys. The single did not appear in a picture cover, but was available in the yellow "Wings" cover.

13 BAND ON THE RUN

By Paul McCartney and Wings

Apple PAS 10007 – November 30, 1973

Band On The Run remained in the *NME* Top 30 album charts for a staggering seventy-three weeks, being in the Top 10 for forty-six weeks. It entered the charts on December 11, 1973, at No. 23, hovering in the Top 5 for eight weeks until March 26, when it reached No. 2, due perhaps to the release of *Jet* as a single, which had reached No. 6 in the singles charts. The album had dropped to No. 8 by June 11 but, after the release of the title track as a single, the album went to No. 1 on July 9, staying there for ten consecutive weeks, after which it was dislodged by Mike Oldfield's *Hergest Ridge.* On April 15, 1975, the album dropped out of the Top 30 after spending sixty-nine consecutive weeks in the chart, but eleven weeks later, on June 30, it returned at No. 28 for two weeks, and returned again for single weeks on July 22 and August 12, thus making a total of seventy-three weeks (or nearly a year and a half) on the charts.

By August 1974 the album had sold two and a half million copies world-wide, and by the end of 1974, six million world-wide. It was the best-selling album in Britain for 1974, and to date ranks as the seventh best-selling album of the seventies in the UK. It was topped by:

1. *Bridge Over Troubled Water*/Simon and Garfunkel;
2. *Dark Side Of The Moon*/Pink Floyd;
3. *Tubular Bells*/Mike Oldfield;
4. *20 Golden Greats*/The Beach Boys;
5. *Simon And Garfunkel's Greatest Hits*
6. *Elvis' 40 Greatest.*

As noted above, with the departure of Denny Seiwell and Henry McCullough, Wings were down to a trio, and Paul, Linda and Denny Laine travelled to Lagos, Nigeria, to record new material. The sessions took place in Ginger Baker's ARC Studios and EMI Studios, both in Lagos; Paul played guitar, bass, drums and synthesizers and sang lead vocals; Linda/keyboards and percussion; and Denny/guitar, with Linda and Denny supplying backing vocals. Further recordings took place at Trident Studios in London, and the orchestral backing – arranged by Tony Visconti – was added at AIR Studios, London. The recordings were produced by Paul and engineered by Geoff Emerick, with most of the sessions taking place in September 1973.

The album front cover features a still taken from a short movie of a group of celebrities acting out a prison escape (the band on the run), and was used by Wings on tour as a backdrop when performing the title track. The six celebrities, chosen by Paul, are: Michael Parkinson (journalist and TV interviewer) on the left, Kenny Lynch (singer) directly behind Paul, James Coburn (actor) standing at the back, Clement Freud (Member of Parliament and TV personality), Christopher Lee (actor) behind Linda, and John Conteh (boxer) standing behind a kneeling Denny Laine. The sleeve was designed by Gordon House and Storm Thorgerson of Hipgnosis, and included a poster of polaroid photographs by Linda.

A SIDE

61 **BAND ON THE RUN** *(5.08)*

62 **JET** *(4.05)*

63 **BLUEBIRD** *(3.19)*

64 **MRS. VANDEBILT** *(4.35)*

65 **LET ME ROLL IT** *(4.45)*

B SIDE

66 **MAMUNIA** *(4.50)*

67 **NO WORDS** *(2.31)*

68 **PICASSO'S LAST WORDS (DRINK TO ME)** *(5.44)*

69 **NINETEEN HUNDRED AND EIGHTY FIVE** *(5.25)* **(Including "Band On The Run" reprise – 0.14)**

Band On The Run was inspired by a remark George Harrison made at an Apple meeting: "If we ever get out of here," with reference to the fact that everybody is a prisoner in some way. *Jet* was inspired by Paul's labrador puppy of the same name and, as with all but one track on the album, features Paul singing lead. *Jet* also features saxophone played by Howie Casey, who is also showcased with a saxophone solo on *Bluebird*, recorded at AIR Studios with Remi Kabaka playing percussion.

All songs on the album are credited to McCartney, except *No Words*, a McCartney/Laine composition, which Denny, Paul and Linda sing in unison. *Picasso's Last Words* was written at the request of Dustin Hoffman; Paul and Linda were on holiday in Jamaica, where they were staying in Montego Bay, and they heard that Dustin Hoffman and Steve McQueen were filming *Papillon* along the coast. Paul and Linda invited Dustin and his wife to dinner, during which Dustin and Paul were talking about song writing. Dustin wanted to see Paul compose a song and suggested he use Picasso's last words before he died: "Drink to me, drink to my health, you know I can't drink alone." When Paul was recording the song in Lagos, the percussive sounds during the final "Ho hey ho" fade-out were achieved with tin cans filled with gravel shaken by Ginger Baker and friends.

14 (62a) JET *(4.04)* (65a) LET ME ROLL IT *(4.44)*

By Paul McCartney and Wings

Apple R 5996 – February 18, 1974

With the release of *Jet* as a single, the *Band On The Run* album jumped back up the charts to the No. 2 position, the single entering the Top 30 on February 19, 1974, at No. 29, peaking at No. 6 for two weeks on March 19, and staying in the charts for eight weeks. The single did not appear in Britain in a picture sleeve, and the label featured the usual "Apple" logos.

15 (61a) BAND ON THE RUN *(5.08)* (70) ZOO GANG *(1.56)*

By Paul McCartney and Wings

Apple R 5997 – June 28, 1974

With the album *Band On The Run* still high in the charts, public demand forced the release of another song from the album as a single, this time the title track. *Band On The Run* entered the Top 30 on July 2 at No. 23, and rose to No. 3 twice, on July 23 and two weeks later on August 6, dropping to No. 4 in the interim. It stayed in the charts for eight weeks, becoming Wings' top-selling single to date, with an estimated global sale of two million.

The "B" side, *Zoo Gang*, was written by Paul for the television serial of the same name; the single was not released in a picture cover, appearing in the "Wings" sleeve.

WALKING IN THE PARK WITH ELOISE *(3.06)* BRIDGE OVER THE RIVER SUITE *(3.08)*

By The Country Hams

EMI EMI 2220 – October 18, 1974
(Re-released March 3, 1982)

During the spring of 1974 guitarist Jimmy McCulloch joined Wings, with Geoff Britton auditioning for the drummer's job, and beating over fifty other applicants. By May 1974, Wings were back to full strength, and flew to Nashville, USA, recording there for seven weeks in June and July. During the sessions Paul recorded *Walking In The Park With Eloise*, which his father, James McCartney, had written many years before. The recording features Chet Atkins on electric guitar and Floyd Cramer on piano, along with the Wings Mark Four line-up of Paul (playing bass and washboard), Linda, Denny, Jimmy McCulloch and Geoff Britton. The second side was written by Paul and Linda, and was also recorded during the Nashville sessions, both tracks being produced by Paul.

1. You should have seen me with the Poker man
I had a honey and I bet a grand
Just in the nick of time I looked at his hand
I was talking to an Eskimo
Said he was hoping for a fall of snow
When up popped a sea-lion ready to go

2. At the Houses of Parliament
Everybody's talking 'bout the President
We all chip in for a bag of cement
Ollie Hardy should have had more sense
He bought a gee-gee and he jumped the fence
All for the sake of a couple of pence

3. I took my bag into a grocer's store
The price is higher than the time before
Old man asked me "Why is it more?"
You should have seen me with the Poker man
I had a honey and I bet a grand
Just in the nick of time I looked at his hand

Chorus: Let's go, let's go, let's go, let's go
Down to Junior's Farm where I want to lay low
Low life, high life, let's go, let's go
Take me down to Junior's Farm
Everybody tag along
Take me down to Junior's Farm

apple single R 5999
Marketed by EMI Records
20 Manchester Square, London, W1A 1ES.

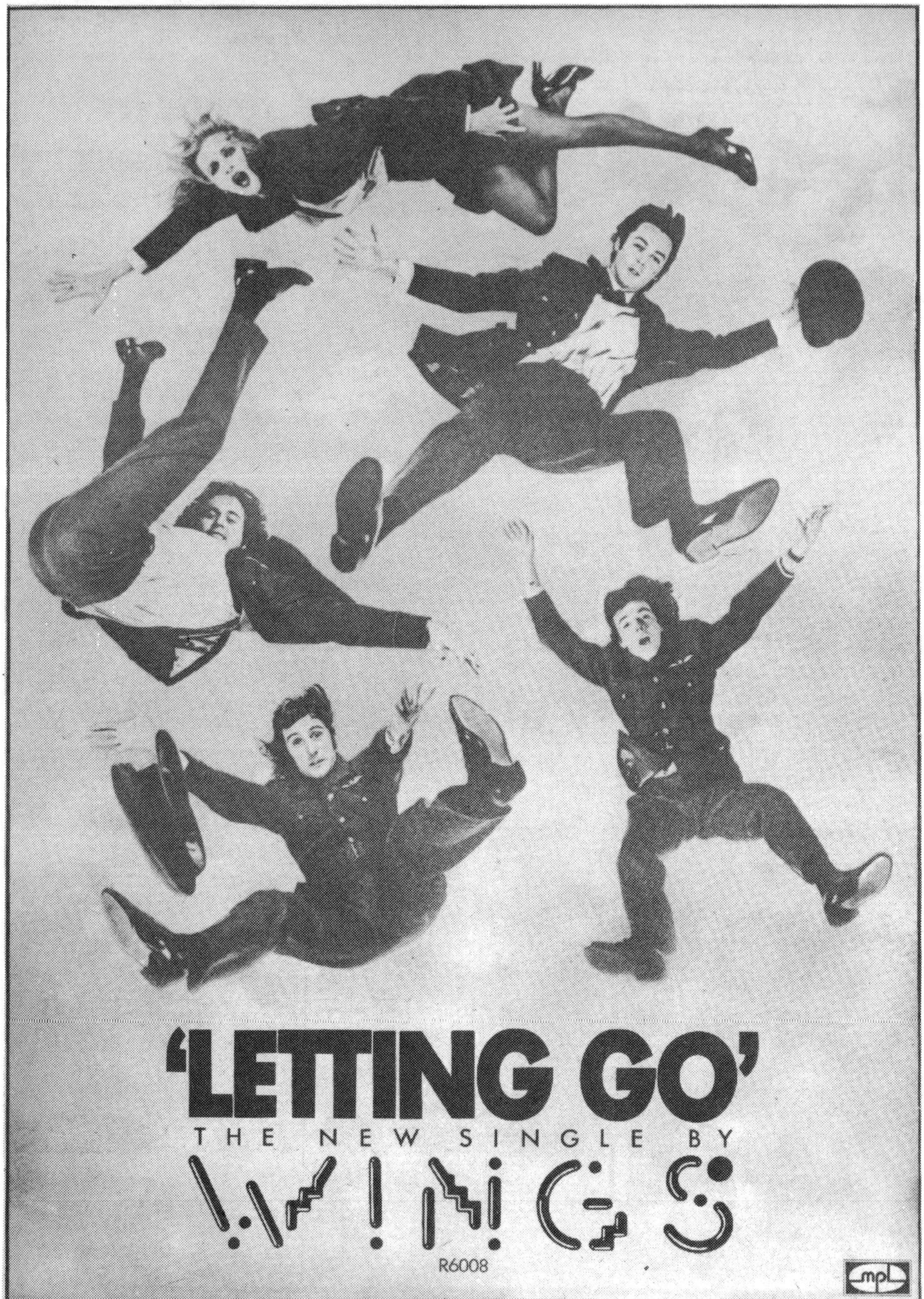

'LETTING GO'

THE NEW SINGLE BY

WINGS

R6008

As the single was not credited to Wings, very few people realised it was a McCartney record; it did not enter the charts, and was soon deleted. After Paul had listed the song as one of his choices for his "Desert Island Disc" selection on BBC Radio, EMI re-released the single on March 3, 1982, in a similar picture sleeve to the original release, although neither sleeves nor records are identical to the initial release. The original single was on the red and brown "EMI" label, while the re-release features the cream label with the small "EMI" boxed logo.

16 (71) JUNIOR'S FARM *(4.18)* (72) SALLY G *(3.37)*

By Paul McCartney and Wings

Apple R 5999 – October 25, 1974

Although *Band On The Run* was still high in the Top 10 album charts, Paul was not tempted to lift another track from it as a single, but instead released a completely new single, *Junior's Farm,* which entered the Top 30 on November 12, 1974, at No. 21, rising to No. 16 by December 3, and staying in the charts for five weeks.

Both songs, produced and written by Paul, were recorded in Nashville between June and July 1974, with Paul, Linda, Denny, Jimmy and Geoff performing on *Junior's Farm,* and being joined by Chet Atkins/electric guitar, and Floyd Cramer/piano, for *Sally G.*

Junior's Farm was written in Nashville, while the McCartneys were staying on Junior Putnam's farm, while *Sally G* refers to a country singer whom Paul met in Tennessee. Both songs feature Paul singing lead.

17 (72a) SALLY G *(3.37)* (71a) JUNIOR'S FARM *(4.18)*

By Paul McCartney and Wings

Apple R 5999 – February 7, 1975

As Wings were busy recording in New Orleans during January and February 1975, Paul decided to fill the gap by flipping the *Junior's Farm* single, making *Sally G* the "A" side, to exploit the extra sales from the song which he thought many people might not have heard. The idea did not prove fruitful in Britain – the single did not enter the charts – and one wonders why it was necessary, as Wings had been recording on and off since June 1974 in Nashville, London and New Orleans. Neither release of the single appeared in a picture sleeve, and this release was the last McCartney and Wings single to feature the Apple label.

18 (73) LISTEN TO WHAT THE MAN SAID *(3.54)* (74) LOVE IN SONG *(3.01)*

By Wings

Capitol R 6006 – May 16, 1975

Listen To What The Man Said, credited merely to Wings, entered the *NME* Top 30 on May 27, 1975, at No. 30, rising to its peak position, No. 6, on June 24, and staying for eight weeks in the charts. The song was recorded after Geoff Britton had quit the group, to be replaced by American session drummer Joe English. The session took place during February 1975 in New Orleans, and also features Tom Scott on saxophone and Dave Mason (ex Traffic) on guitar. *Love In Song* was recorded with the Wings Mark Four line-up, with Geoff Britton on drums. Both tracks, which appeared later on the *Venus And Mars* album, were written and produced by Paul.

The single appeared in a picture sleeve, while the label featured the "Capitol" logo which Paul was still contriving to use although, as with all Beatle and solo Beatle recordings at this time, it was still theoretically on the Parlophone label (note the Parlophone catalogue number). But it is the first record by one of the Beatles not to contain the legend "An Apple Record", and the first Wings' single to include the "MPL" (McCartney Productions Ltd.) logo.

19 VENUS AND MARS

By Wings

Capitol PCTC 254 – May 30, 1975

Venus And Mars entered the *NME* album charts on June 10, 1975, at No. 8, and three weeks later, on July 1, held the No. 1 spot, where it stayed for six weeks, being eventually dislodged by *The Best Of The Stylistics.* It remained in the charts for a

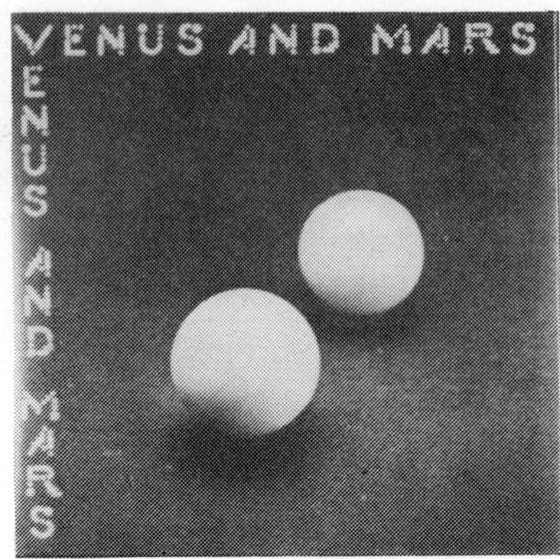

total of twenty-two weeks.

Recording sessions for the album took place between January and April 1975, firstly at the Sea Saint Studios in New Orleans, where Geoff Britton quit the group to be replaced by Joe English, and later at Wally Heider Studios in Los Angeles. Prior to these sessions, Wings Mark Four had been recording for seven weeks in June and July 1974 at Sound Shop Studios in Nashville, and in London during November 1974, but whether any of these sessions ended up as tracks on *Venus And Mars* is not possible to determine. The sessions were produced by Paul, with engineering duties taken by Alan O'Duffy and the faithful Geoff Emerick.

The majority of the album was recorded with the Wings Mark Five line-up of Paul/lead vocals, guitar and bass; Linda/piano, synthesizers, backing vocals; Denny Laine/guitar, bass, backing vocals; Jimmy McCulloch/guitar, backing vocals; and Joe English/drums; plus the addition of guest musicians on certain tracks (see below).

The album was packaged in a very elaborate sleeve, which won "Album Cover Of The Year" for 1975 from *Music Week*. The package – a gatefold sleeve, containing two posters and a "Venus And Mars Are Alright Tonight" planet sticker – was put together by Hipgnosis and George Hardie. The front cover photograph was taken by Linda, while the centre spread of Wings was shot by Po (Aubrey Powell) of Hipgnosis in a desert in North California. George Hardie provided the graphics for the cover and the inner sleeve design. As with the single from the album, *Venus And Mars* is on the Capitol label, and was the first "Beatle" album not to feature the Apple label, and the first album to contain the "MPL" logo.

A SIDE

75 **VENUS AND MARS** *(1.18)*

76 **ROCK SHOW** *(6.52)*

74a **LOVE IN SONG** *(3.02)*

77 **YOU GAVE ME THE ANSWER** *(2.13)*

78 **MAGNETO AND TITANIUM MAN** *(3.15)*

79 **LETTING GO** *(4.31)*

B SIDE

80 **VENUS AND MARS REPRISE** *(2.05)*

81 **SPIRITS OF ANCIENT EGYPT** *(3.04)*

82 **MEDICINE JAR** *(3.34)*

83 **CALL ME BACK AGAIN** *(4.50)*

73a **LISTEN TO WHAT THE MAN SAID** *(4.01)*

84 **TREAT HER GENTLY/**

85 **LONELY OLD PEOPLE** *(4.20)*

86 **CROSSROADS THEME** *(0.59)*

All compositions, except *Medicine Jar* and *Crossroads Theme*, are credited to McCartney, and feature Paul singing lead. Many supposed that *Venus And Mars* referred to Linda and Paul, who denied this, stating that the song is about an imaginary friend whose girlfriend is an astrologer.

Rock Show was written specifically as the opening number for Wings World Tour of 1975-6, and mentions three concert venues; "Concert Gebouw" in Amsterdam, Holland (where Wings performed on August 20, 1972, during their first European Tour), Madison Square Garden, New York (where Wings later performed on May 24 & 25, 1976), and the Hollywood Bowl, Los Angeles (Wings never performed here, but the Beatles did on August 23, 1964, and August 29 & 30, 1965). The track features Allen Toussaint on piano, and congas supplied by Afro.

Love In Song, Letting Go and *Medicine Jar* feature Geoff Britton on drums, and were probably recorded in London, with Geoff Emerick engineering. *Magneto And Titanium Man* was inspired by Marvel comics characters, and *Medicine Jar*, written by Jimmy McCulloch and Colin Allen, features Jimmy singing lead, thus being one of the few Wings album numbers not to feature either Paul or Linda on lead vocals. The album closes with Paul's interpretation of the "Crossroads Theme", from the long-running soap opera on Independent Television. Although Paul was criticized for using the tune on a rock album, his answer was that the mood of the music fitted in with the theme of the album. The Wings' version of the tune, composed by Tony Hatch, replaced the original version on the programme for some time, but was later dropped.

20 (79a) LETTING GO *(3.28)* (77a) YOU GAVE ME THE ANSWER *(2.10)*

By Wings

Capitol R 6008 – September 5, 1975

To try to boost sales of the album, *Letting Go* was lifted from *Venus And Mars* as Wings' second single of 1975, but did not figure in the *NME* Top 30, although it did enter the BMRB Top 50 for three weeks, rising to No. 41.

Letting Go features the Mark Four Wings line-up of Paul, Linda, Denny, Jimmy and Geoff Britton, while *You Gave Me The Answer* features Joe English on drums.

21 (75/6a) VENUS AND MARS/ROCK SHOW *(3.41)* (78a) MAGNETO AND TITANIUM MAN *(3.13)*

By Wings

Capitol R 6010 – November 28, 1975

By the beginning of November 1975, *Venus And Mars* had dropped out of the album Top 30, but this release failed either to enter the charts itself, or to further boost sales of the album.

The medley of *Venus And Mars/Rock Show* is an edited version, with *Rock Show* being abbreviated by over four minutes. As with the previous single, it did not appear in a picture sleeve.

22 WINGS AT THE SPEED OF SOUND

By Wings

Parlophone PAS 10010 – March 26, 1976

Wings At The Speed Of Sound entered the *NME* album charts on April 10, 1976, at No. 8 and rose to No. 2 on April 24 (the No. 1 position being held by *Rock Follies*), before dropping down and returning to No. 2 on May 22 (with *Greatest Hits* by Abba at No. 1). It was at No. 3 for the following three weeks, and returned to No. 2 for two weeks on June 26 (Abba still holding the No. 1 position, which it did for eight weeks). The album dropped out of the Top 10 for four weeks during July and August, but returned (probably due to the boost from the release of *Let 'Em In* as a single). The album was in the charts for

thirty weeks, being the fourth best-selling album in the UK for 1976.

Tracks for the album, the second featuring Wings Mark Five, (Paul, Linda, Denny, Jimmy and Joe), were recorded at Abbey Road Studios during January and February 1976, with Paul producing and Pete Henderson engineering. On several tracks on the album, the usual Wings line-up was augmented by the addition of a horn section, featuring Tony Dorsey, Thaddeus Richard, Steve Howard and Howie Casey.

For the first time since *Wild Life*, a lyric sheet was not included with a Wings album, and the whole package seemed rather mediocre compared to previous efforts. The album sleeve was designed by Hipgnosis and George Hardie, with back cover photographs of the band by Clive Arrowsmith. Linda provided label and inner sleeve photographs, while the inner sleeve also contained a concert picture of Wings taken by Robert Ellis, which is surrounded by a pencil and crayon drawing by Humphrey Ocean, showing Ian Dury and The Kilburns. A book, jointly published by MPL and Plexus, featuring sketches, made by Humphrey Ocean, of Wings' 1976 Tour of America, was published in 1983.

With this album, Wings dropped the Capitol logo. The record contained no noticeable label credit, although the catalogue number is that of Parlophone.

A SIDE

87 **LET 'EM IN** *(5.06)*

88 **THE NOTE YOU NEVER WROTE** *(4.17)*

89 **SHE'S MY BABY** *(3.07)*

90 **BEWARE MY LOVE** *(6.24)*

91 **WINO JUNKO** *(5.16)*

B SIDE

92 **SILLY LOVE SONGS** *(5.51)*

93 **COOK OF THE HOUSE** *(2.36)*

94 **TIME TO HIDE** *(4.49)*

95 **MUST DO SOMETHING ABOUT IT** *(3.19)*

96 **SAN FERRY ANNE** *(2.03)*

97 **WARM AND BEAUTIFUL** *(3.09)*

For the first time on a Wings album, Paul designated a song for each member of the group to sing, with Denny singing Paul's composition, *The Note You Never Wrote*, plus his own *Time To Hide*; Jimmy sings his own composition (with Colin Allen) of *Wino Junko* which, like *Medicine Jar* on the previous album, refers to drug taking. Linda and Joe are both given McCartney compositions in *Cook Of The House* and *Must Do Something About It* respectively. Paul sings lead on the remaining songs, with the opening number, *Let 'Em In*, having many references to actual people, including Sister Suzie, Brother John (Lennon), Martin Luther (King), Phil and Don (Everly), Brother Michael (McGear), Uncle Ernie and Auntie Gin (Paul's relatives). *Let 'Em In* was later covered by Billy Paul, becoming the first Wings' cover version to enter the charts, which it did on May 7, 1977, at No. 29, rising to No. 22, and staying in the charts for three weeks. Billy Paul's biggest hit was his first, *Me And Mrs Jones*, in 1973.

23 (92a) SILLY LOVE SONGS *(5.52)* (93a) COOK OF THE HOUSE *(2.36)*

By Wings

Parlophone R 6014 – April 30, 1976

Silly Love Songs entered the *NME* charts on May 22, 1976, at No. 15, and on June 19 was No. 1 to become Wings' first chart topper. The single stayed in the chart for nine weeks. In the BMRB chart, the single peaked at No. 2, being topped by the Wurzels' *Combine Harvester*. The single was not released in a picture sleeve and contained a similar *Wings At The Speed Of Sound* label, as found on the album.

24 (87a) LET 'EM IN *(5.08)* (90a) BEWARE MY LOVE *(5.59)*

By Wings

Parlophone R 6015 – July 23, 1976

With *Wings At The Speed Of Sound* dropping down the charts, another track was lifted as a single, becoming the second smash hit in Britain from the album, entering the charts on August 7, 1976, at No. 30, and rising to No. 2 on September 4, where it remained for three weeks, being kept from the No. 1 position firstly by *Don't Go Breaking My Heart* by Elton John and Kiki Dee and then by Abba's *Dancing Queen* (which held the No. 1 position for five weeks). The single stayed in the charts for ten weeks.

25 WINGS OVER AMERICA

By Wings

Parlophone PCSP 720 – December 10, 1976

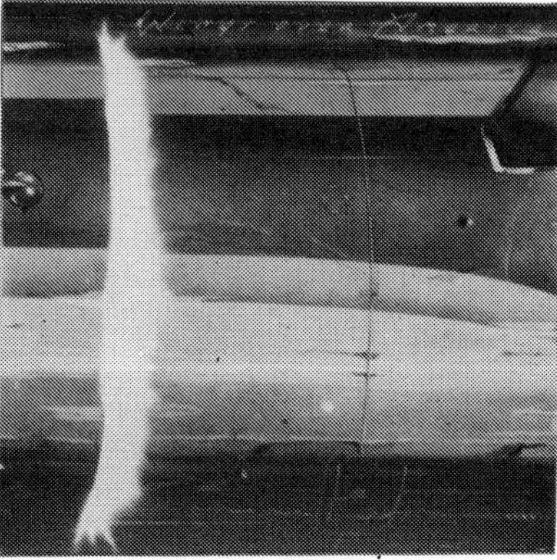

Wings' first live album, and the third triple set to be released by an ex-Beatle, entered the *NME* Top 30 on January 8, 1977, at No. 21, rising to No. 8 for two weeks from February 5, and staying in the charts for twelve weeks.

The thirty songs included on this triple set constituted Wings' complete live set as performed on the most comprehensive world tour ever undertaken up to that point in the history of rock music. The World Tour consisted of five subsidiary tours: their third British tour, which ran from September 9 to 23, 1975 (thirteen dates); an Australian tour from November 1 to 14, 1975 (nine dates); a short European tour, March 20 to 26 (five dates); a mammoth American tour from May 3 to June 23, 1976 (thirty dates); a second short European tour from September 19 to 27 (four dates) and finishing with three dates at Wembley Arena, London, on October 19 to 21, 1976. Although the concerts were basically the same throughout, slight variations occurred in terms of order of songs and the omission and addition of some songs.

Some of the statistics for the tour are mind-boggling: twelve and a half tons of equipment transported in three articulated trucks; air freight costs from London to America were over $13,000; a specially chartered BAC one-eleven plane, em-

LET 'EM IN

WINGS

NEW SINGLE RELEASED 23 JULY

R6015

Marketed by EMI Records Limited, 20, Manchester Square, London W1A 1ES.

MAYBE
I'M
AMAZED
C/W
SOILY
NEW WINGS SINGLE
FROM THE ALBUM
WINGS OVER AMERICA
R6017
mpl

blazoned with the tour motto "Wings Over America", to transport group members; a battery of instruments including thirty-seven guitars and six keyboards; and a total of sixty-four concerts played in ten countries to an estimated audience of two million.

All thirty dates on the American Tour were recorded, giving a total of ninety hours of tape; Paul and Wings listened to these during October and November 1976 at Abbey Road Studios in London. After the five best versions of each song had been established, McCartney spent six weeks selecting, mixing and producing the album, which had originally been planned for November 1976 release, but had to be delayed until December.

The sleeve design was a joint effort between MPL and Hipgnosis, with the outer cover painting by Richard Manning, and the inner spread by Jeff Cummins. The cover painting of an aeroplane door opening was a symbolic representation of McCartney arriving in America to play a gig, the door opening (or curtain rising) with the light (or music) streaming out. The idea was continued onto the inner sleeves, which depicts the door gradually opening from the front of the first sleeve to the back of the third sleeve, with spectographs showing the amount of light emitted. The six differing labels, air-brushed by Richard Evans, show aero-plane control panel instruments. The album was completed with a poster containing photographs by Robert Ellis.

RECORD ONE A SIDE

98 **VENUS AND MARS** *(1.20)*

99 **ROCK SHOW** *(4.30)*

100 **JET** *(5.25)*

101 **LET ME ROLL IT** *(3.40)*

102 **SPIRITS OF ANCIENT EGYPT** *(3.59)*

103 **MEDICINE JAR** *(3.57)*

RECORD ONE B SIDE

104 **MAYBE I'M AMAZED** *(5.10)*

105 **CALL ME BACK AGAIN** *(5.04)*

106 **LADY MADONNA** *(2.19)*

107 **THE LONG AND WINDING ROAD** *(4.13)*

108 **LIVE AND LET DIE** *(3.07)*

RECORD TWO A SIDE

109 **PICASSO'S LAST WORDS** *(1.55)/*

110 **RICHARD CORY** *(1.52)*

111 **BLUEBIRD** *(3.37)*

112 **I'VE JUST SEEN A FACE** *(1.49)*

113 **BLACKBIRD** *(2.23)*

114 **YESTERDAY** *(1.43)*

RECORD TWO B SIDE

115 **YOU GAVE ME THE ANSWER** *(1.47)*

116 **MAGNETO AND TITANIUM MAN** *(3.11)*

117 **GO NOW** *(3.27)*

118 **MY LOVE** *(4.07)*

119 **LISTEN TO WHAT THE MAN SAID** *(3.18)*

RECORD THREE A SIDE

120 **LET 'EM IN** *(4.02)*

121 **TIME TO HIDE** *(4.46)*

122 **SILLY LOVE SONGS** *(5.46)*

123 **BEWARE MY LOVE** *(4.49)*

RECORD THREE B SIDE

124 **LETTING GO** *(4.25)*

125 **BAND ON THE RUN** *(5.03)*

126 **HI, HI, HI** *(2.57)*

127 **SOILY** *(5.10)*

Of the thirty numbers featured on the album, nine were from *Venus And Mars*, five from *Band On The Run*, four from *Wings At The Speed Of Sound* and one each from *Red Rose Speedway* and *McCartney*, plus two singles and eight numbers previously never recorded by Wings. The eight new numbers included five Beatle songs, which McCartney included during the concerts to please the fans who were continually shouting for numbers by his old group. On previous tours he had refused to play any, for fear of criticism from reviewers that he was relying on past glories to make his new group a success. All five Beatle songs are credited to "McCartney-Lennon" on the record labels, and not the original "Lennon-McCartney".

The album features Wings Mark Five, with a basic instrumental line-up of: Paul/bass guitar, piano and acoustic guitar; Linda/keyboards; Denny/electric guitar, acoustic guitar, piano, bass guitar, snare drum and gob iron (harmonica); Jimmy/electric guitar, acoustic guitar and bass guitar; and Joe/drums, with the horn section of Tony Dorsey/ trombone; Howie Casey/saxophone; Steve Howard/trumpet and flugelhorn; and Thaddeus Richard/saxophone, clarinet and flute. The lead vocals are handled mainly by Paul, except on *Spirits Of Ancient Egypt* featuring Paul and Denny, *Medicine Jar* by Jimmy, and *Richard Cory*, *Go Now* and *Time To Hide* by Denny.

The concerts opened with the specially written *Venus And Mars/Rock Show* medley which was also segued into *Jet*, making it an eleven-minute opener. On *Maybe I'm Amazed* Paul sings from the piano stool, and continues with *Live And Let Die*. For the *Picasso's Last Words/ Richard Cory* medley through to *Yesterday*, Paul, Denny and Jimmy play acoustic guitars, seated stage centre, with Linda assisting all with vocal harmonies. On *Richard Cory*, written by Paul Simon, and featured on the Simon and Garfunkel 1965 album *Sounds Of Silence*, Denny re-writes the lyrics to refer to a certain John Denver.

Paul plays piano on *You Gave Me The Answer* through to *Let 'Em In*. Denny sings *Go Now*, which he originally recorded in 1964 with The Moody Blues, who took the song to No. 1 for two weeks in the UK, and to No. 10 in the US, giving them an estimated global million seller. The song was written by Larry Banks and Milton Bennett, and was originally recorded by Bessie Banks in America in 1963. The final track on the album is a McCartney original, *Soily*, performed by Wings in 1972 during their first European tour from July 9 to August 24 (from which the live version of *The Mess*, the "B" side of *My Love*, originated).

26 (104a) MAYBE I'M AMAZED *(5.17)* (127a) SOILY *(5.37)*

By Wings

Parlophone R 6017 – February 4, 1977

Seven years too late, *Maybe I'm Amazed* was released as a single, albeit the live version from *Wings Over America*, but it could still only manage two chart weeks in the *NME* Top 30, entering on March 5, 1977, at No. 27, where it remained for the following week. The single, not released in a picture sleeve, was manufactured in West Germany, and features "Wings Over America" labels.

UNCLE ALBERT/ADMIRAL HALSEY *(5.22)* EAT AT HOME *(3.28)*

By Percy "Thrills" Thrillington

Regal Zonophone EMI 2594 – April 1977

THRILLINGTON

By Percy "Thrills" Thrillington

Regal Zonophone EMC 3175 – April 29, 1977

An orchestral interpretation of Paul's *Ram* album, it features an "orchestra leader", Percy Thrillington, whom many people speculated was actually McCartney. The album was originally intended for release in 1972, but was delayed. The orchestra was arranged and conducted by Richard Hewson, and recorded at EMI Abbey Road Studios. The cover was designed by Hipgnosis, with artwork by Jeff Cummins, and a fictitious sleeve note by Clint Harrigan(?).

Neither the above single nor the album enjoyed any chart success, both becoming highly prized collectors' items.

A SIDE

TOO MANY PEOPLE *(4.29)*

3 LEGS *(3.40)*

RAM ON *(2.48)*

DEAR BOY *(2.24)*

UNCLE ALBERT/ADMIRAL HALSEY *(5.22)*

SMILE AWAY *(4.39)*

B SIDE

HEART OF THE COUNTRY *(2.28)*

MONKBERRY MOON DELIGHT *(4.38)*

EAT AT HOME *(3.28)*

LONG HAIRED LADY *(5.47)*

THE BACK SEAT OF MY CAR *(4.02)*

(Untitled piano tune – *0.48)*

The album starts with the sounds of an orchestra warming up and talking. As well as a full orchestra, some numbers include drums, bass and piano, along with a choir singing melodies. The album finishes with an uncredited piano tune.

27 (128) MULL OF KINTYRE *(4.41)* (129) GIRLS SCHOOL *(4.31)*

By Wings

Capitol R 6018 – November 11, 1977

Wings' first double "A"-sided single entered the *NME* Top 30 on November 26 at No. 11, and rose to No. 1 the following week, where it stayed for a total of eight chart weeks (nine actual weeks including Christmas week itself, when no chart was compiled). By December 10, 1977, it had sold 500,000 copies, thus initially selling over 100,000 per week. By the following week – December 17 – it had passed 800,000, thus selling 300,000 in one week, and making it EMI's fastest selling single for 1977. During the week of December 17, EMI pressed the one millionth copy of the single, which was purchased by David Ackroyd one week before Christmas and, on December 23, he was presented with a specially pressed Gold Disc. After being at No. 1 for six weeks, on January 7, 1978, the single was approaching the 1,250,000 mark, and by January 14 had sold over 1,667,000, thus becoming the biggest ever selling single in Britain, topping the previous best of 1.6 million by *She Loves You*. At this point, the single was selling 250,000 copies a week, and had topped the two million mark by the end of January, eventually selling 2.5 million in Britain.

The success of *Mull Of Kintyre* did not end in Britain, as it topped the charts in Holland, Australia, New Zealand, Belgium and Germany, being a platinum disc in Holland and becoming Australia's biggest-selling single. Although not a big hit in America, the single has still sold over six million globally, making it the fourteenth all time best-selling single world-wide.

Paul started to compose *Mull Of Kintyre* in the summer of 1976, and completed it with Denny Laine. The title of the song refers to the southern tip of the Scottish peninsular known as Kintyre. The Mull is about eleven miles from Campbelltown, the major town of Kintyre, near to which is Paul's farm. To record the song, Paul used the twenty-one bagpipers of the Campbelltown Pipe Band, who were paid the standard musicians' union rate for the session. McCartney eventually reaped the huge profits from the record. Paul was later criticised in the press when the band complained that they had been underpaid and that the huge success of the single was partly due to the authentic Scottish sound supplied by their bagpipes. McCartney later sent each member of the band a cheque for £200. By the time the single had been released, both Jimmy McCulloch and Joe English had left Wings (Jimmy in September and Joe in November 1977) so it is difficult to say whether either played on the sessions for the single, although the promotional video for the single shown on television only showed Paul, Linda and Denny and some pipers.

Girls School was written by McCartney, and was originally called *Love School*, being inspired by newspaper adverts for pornographic movies.

The single appears on the Capitol label despite a Parlophone catalogue number, and was issued in a picture sleeve with photography by Graham Hughes and was produced by Paul.

28 (130) WITH A LITTLE LUCK *(5.41)* (131-2) BACKWARDS TRAVELLER/ CUFF LINK *(3.07)*

By Wings

Parlophone R 6019 – March 23, 1978

The follow up to the biggest-selling single in the UK entered the *NME* charts on April 8, 1978, at No. 17, and rose to No. 7 for three weeks, on April 13, staying in the charts for seven weeks. The single was McCartney's fifth biggest-selling single in Britain up to 1982.

With A Little Luck was recorded in the Virgin Islands between May 1 and May 31, 1977, by Wings Mark Five (Paul, Linda, Denny, Jimmy and Joe). (See *London Town* album.) The single features the *London Town* Tower Bridge labels, and also a piece of run-out groove graffiti – on the "A" side "A NICK W CUT" with merely "NICK W" on the "B" side.

29 LONDON TOWN

By Wings

Parlophone PAS 10012 – March 31, 1978

Wings' seventh album, *London Town* entered the *NME* album charts on April 8, 1978, at No. 13, peaked at No. 4 for three

weeks on April 22, and spent ten weeks in the charts.

Rehearsals for the songs on *London Town* started in early 1977, with Wings Mark Five, consisting of Paul, Linda, Denny, Jimmy and Joe. The first recording sessions took place at EMI's Abbey Road Studios, London, between February 7 and March 31, 1977. The second sessions for the album took place between May 1 and May 31 on a motor yacht called *Fair Carol* in the Virgin Islands. The Record Plant, New York, installed a 24-track studio aboard the yacht, while three other yachts were hired as floating homes for the McCartney family (their boat was named *El Toro*) and the rest of the entourage, including other members of Wings and their families (*Samala* and *Wanderlust*). Nine tracks were recorded on the *Fair Carol*, but only seven were used on the album, the remaining two being left "in the can".

On returning to Britain, Jimmy McCulloch left the group during September 1977, and on October 25 the four-piece Wings returned to Abbey Road Studios in London. During these recordings, which lasted until December 1, Joe English also left the group, leaving Wings as a trio for the second time. On December 3, Paul, Linda and Denny moved to AIR Studios London (part owned by George Martin), where they recorded until December 14. They then took a Christmas break until January 4, 1978, when they returned to Abbey Road Studios to record through to January 23.

The album was produced by Paul, with Geoff Emerick engineering, and features the following instrumentation: Paul/vocals, bass, guitar, keyboards, drums, percussion, flageolet and recorder; Linda/vocals, keyboards and percussion; Denny/vocals, guitar, bass, flageolet, recorder and percussion; Jimmy/guitar and percussion; and Joe/vocals, drums, percussion and harmonica. On the later recordings at Abbey Road – after Joe's departure – Paul supplied the drums.

The working title of the album was "Water Wings", but this was eventually changed after the intensive recording sessions in London. Paul, Linda and Denny are credited with the cover design, collage and photographs, with assistance from Aubrey Powell (Po) and George Hardie of Hipgnosis. The labels feature no record company credit, consisting of photographs of Tower Bridge, and as can be seen from the "A" side run-out groove graffiti, the album was "MASTERED BY NICK W".

A SIDE

133 **LONDON TOWN** *(4.07)*

134 **CAFÉ ON THE LEFT BANK** *(3.24)*

135 **I'M CARRYING** *(2.42)*

131a **BACKWARDS TRAVELLER/**

132a **CUFF LINK** *(3.07)*

136 **CHILDREN CHILDREN** *(2.20)*

137 **GIRLFRIEND** *(4.39)*

138 **I'VE HAD ENOUGH** *(2.59)*

B SIDE

130a **WITH A LITTLE LUCK** *(5.44)*

139 **FAMOUS GROUPIES** *(3.34)*

140 **DELIVER YOUR CHILDREN** *(4.17)*

141 **NAME AND ADDRESS** *(3.07)*

142 **DON'T LET IT BRING YOU DOWN** *(4.34)*

143 **MOUSE MOOSE AND THE GREY GOOSE** *(6.25)*

Most of the fourteen songs on the album were written by Paul, with five being joint compositions between Paul and Denny. Paul is lead singer on most of the songs. Paul and Denny composed *London Town* partly in Perth, Australia, during the Wings World Tour, and partly in Scotland and Mexico; the track was recorded at Abbey Road with the full Wings line-up.

Café On The Left Bank, written solely by Paul, was the first number to be recorded in the Virgin Islands. Paul's *I'm Carrying*, also recorded in the Virgin Islands, and in a single take, features Paul playing the "gizmo", an instrument invented by ex 10CC members Kevin Godley and Lol Creme.

Backwards Traveller/Cuff Link was recorded in London after Jimmy and Joe had left, and features Paul on drums. *Children Children*, co-written by Paul

Backwards Traveller *just one of the fourteen tracks from*

WINGS *new album* **LONDON TOWN**

AVAILABLE ON TAPE PAS10012

and Denny, was inspired by a waterfall in Paul's garden and features Denny predominantly on lead vocals. It too was recorded in London.

Paul composed *Girlfriend* for Michael Jackson, although Jackson did not record the song until 1979, when it was included on his monster hit album, *Off The Wall.* It was then later released as a single in 1980 when it reached No. 30 for a single week on August 30. The song was composed in Scotland and recorded in London.

I've Had Enough, With A Little Luck and *Famous Groupies* were recorded in the Virgin Islands (although *With A Little Luck* was completed in London), and both *With A Little Luck* and *Famous Groupies* were written in Scotland. Paul and Denny composed *Deliver Your Children* while working on the *Venus And Mars* album in Los Angeles, and the track was recorded in London, with Denny's vocals to the fore. *Name And Address* features Paul on lead guitar and was recorded in London after Jimmy and Joe had left.

The two remaining songs were both composed jointly by Paul and Denny and were recorded in the Virgin Islands. *Don't Let It Bring You Down* features Paul and Denny playing flageolets (Irish tin whistles). *Mouse Moose And The Grey Goose* originated from a jam session on the *Fair Carol* when McCartney was experimenting with an electric piano, and was finished off in London.

30 (138a) I'VE HAD ENOUGH *(2.59)* (140a) DELIVER YOUR CHILDREN *(3.18)*

By Wings

Parlophone R 6020 – June 16, 1978

The second single release from *London Town*, which did not enter the *NME* charts, although it did rise to No. 42 in the BMRB charts, staying in the Top 75 for seven weeks. The single appeared in a picture sleeve, and the record featured the "London Town" label. The words "MASTERED AT ABBEY ROAD – NICK" are engraved on the "A" side run-out groove area.

31 (133a) LONDON TOWN *(4.08)* (135a) I'M CARRYING *(2.42)*

By Wings

Parlophone R 6021 – September 15, 1978

London Town did not enter the *NME* Top 30, managing only to rise to No. 60 in the BMRB chart during a four week run. The single features the "London Town" label as well as the engraved legends "MASTERED AT ABBEY ROAD" on the "A" side and "NICK" on the "B" side.

32 WINGS GREATEST

By Wings

Parlophone PCTC 256 – December 1, 1978

Paul's greatest hits album entered the *NME* Top 30 album chart on December 23, 1978, at No. 23, peaking at No. 3 on January 27, 1979, and staying in the chart for thirteen weeks until March 21. The album re-entered the Top 30 on May 3 for one week at No. 24.

During 1978, Paul again expanded the Wings line-up with the addition of Steve Holly and Lawrence Juber. As no new album was ready, due to the need for rehearsals with the new line-up, Paul put together an album of his hit singles for the Christmas market. Although titled *Wings Greatest*, two of the included songs, namely *Another Day* and *Uncle Albert/Admiral Halsey*, were not originally recorded by Wings. Moreover, the latter had not even been a hit in Britain, although it was a No. 1 in America.

Of the other ten tracks, all had reached the Top 20 in Britain, with nine reaching the Top 10, and two (plus *Another Day*) had reached No. 1 in the *NME* charts. Up to December 1978, Wings had had fifteen Top 30 hits; thus five were omitted from the album – *Give Ireland Back To The Irish, Mary Had A Little Lamb, Helen Wheels, Listen To What The Man Said* and *Maybe I'm Amazed.* These were possibly being saved for a "Wings Greatest Volume 2" (although at the time of writing Wings as a group no longer exists and no such album appears to be in the pipeline).

The sleeve design, which cost over £4,000, was by Paul and Linda, with assistance from Hipgnosis stalwarts Aubrey Powell and George Hardie, with photography by Angus Forbes. The album included a double-sided poster, featuring a group photograph by Clive Arrowsmith.

A SIDE

15a **ANOTHER DAY** *(3.39)*

92b **SILLY LOVE SONGS** *(5.50)*

57b **LIVE AND LET DIE** *(3.09)*

71b **JUNIOR'S FARM** *(4.18)*

130b **WITH A LITTLE LUCK** *(5.42)*

61b **BAND ON THE RUN** *(5.08)*

B SIDE

21/2a **UNCLE ALBERT/ADMIRAL HALSEY** *(4.38)*

42a **HI, HI, HI** *(3.05)*

87b **LET 'EM IN** *(5.06)*

44b **MY LOVE** *(4.05)*

62b **JET** *(4.04)*

128a **MULL OF KINTYRE** *(4.40)*

33 (144) GOODNIGHT TONIGHT *(4.15)* (145) DAYTIME NIGHTIME SUFFERING *(3.18)*

By Wings

Parlophone R 6023 – March 23, 1979

34 (144a) GOODNIGHT TONIGHT *(7.14)* (145a) DAYTIME NIGHTIME SUFFERING *(3.18)* (12-inch single)

By Wings

Parlophone 12Y R 6023 – March 23, 1979

Goodnight Tonight entered the *NME* charts on April 14 at No. 14, rising to No. 6 on May 12 for one week, staying in the chart for seven weeks, and becoming

McCartney's third best-selling single in Britain up to 1982.

The two songs were the first release by the Wings Mark Seven line-up, featuring Paul, Linda, Denny and newcomers Lawrence Juber/guitar and Steve Holly/drums. The single was the first McCartney release to feature the "Parlophone" label, although all Wings and other ex-Beatle releases with the "R" prefix catalogue number were theoretically released on the Parlophone label. However, *Goodnight Tonight* was the first Wings single to feature the Parlophone logo. The seven-inch single features a scribbled message on the run-out groove area – "HELLO TOM 1979". Another first for a McCartney release was the twelve-inch version of the single, released in a full colour picture sleeve, with a special printed cardboard inner sleeve featuring an extended disco version of *Goodnight Tonight,* written and produced by Paul. The "B" side, *Daytime Nightime Suffering* was composed by Paul, but produced by Paul and Chris Thomas.

35 (146) OLD SIAM SIR *(4.09)* (147) SPIN IT ON *(2.11)*

By Wings

Parlophone R 6026 – June 1, 1979

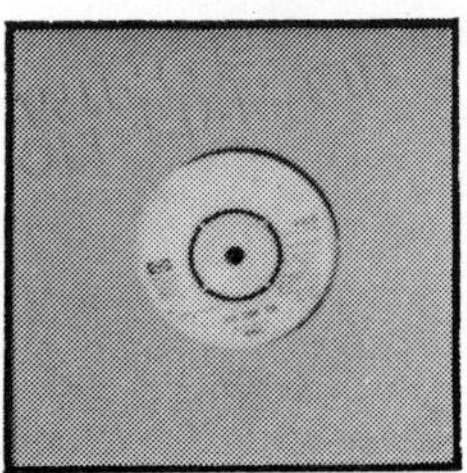

After the success of *Goodnight Tonight,* the follow-up performed very poorly in the *NME* charts; it entered at its highest

position of No. 27 on June 30, after which it dropped to No. 29 for two weeks, and thus remained in the charts for only three weeks. It was the last Wings single to enter the *NME* charts to date.

Both songs were written by Paul and were taken from the forthcoming album, *Back To The Egg*, the single featured the "fried egg" label and the MPL logo, and appeared in a colour sleeve.

36 BACK TO THE EGG

By Wings

Parlophone/MPL PCTC 257 – June 8, 1979

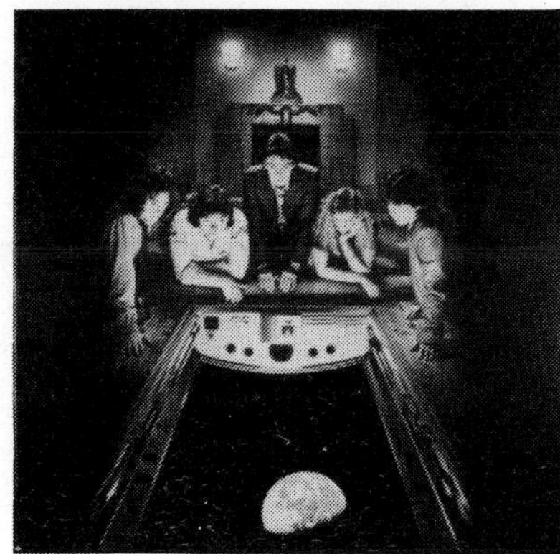

The first (and last) album from Wings Mark Seven, and the last Wings album to date, entered the *NME* album charts on June 30 at No. 15, rising to No. 4 – its highest position – the following week, but staying in the chart for only eight weeks.

Unlike previous sessions, Paul limited his recording locations to Britain, and all of *Back To The Egg* was recorded in either Scotland or England. Four locations were used: Spirit of Ranachan Studio, previously called Rude Studios, built on Paul's farm in Scotland; Lympne Castle, near Canterbury, Kent; Replica Studio, an exact duplicate of EMI Studio No. 2 at Abbey Road, which McCartney had built in the basement of his MPL headquarters in London in 1978; and EMI Studios, Abbey Road, London. The album was recorded over several months in 1978 and 1979, and featured the final Wings line-up: Paul/vocals, bass, guitar and keyboards; Linda/vocals, and keyboards; Denny/vocals, guitar, and bass; Lawrence Juber/guitar and vocals; and Steve Holly/drums and percussion. The album was produced by Paul and Chris Thomas.

The album sleeve, designed by Hipgnosis, features a still taken from a promotional video made for the album.

A SIDE

148 **RECEPTION** *(1.04)*

149 **GETTING CLOSER** *(3.21)*

150 **WE'RE OPEN TONIGHT** *(1.27)*

147a **SPIN IT ON** *(2.12)*

151 **AGAIN AND AGAIN AND AGAIN** *(3.33)*

146a **OLD SIAM SIR** *(4.09)*

152 **ARROW THROUGH ME** *(3.34)*

B SIDE

153 **ROCKESTRA THEME** *(2.34)*

154 **TO YOU** *(3.12)*

155 **AFTER THE BALL** *(2.31)/*

156 **MILLION MILES** *(1.27)*

157 **WINTER ROSE** *(2.03)/*

158 **LOVE AWAKE** *(2.53)*

159 **THE BROADCAST** *(1.29)*

160 **SO GLAD TO SEE YOU HERE** *(3.18)*

161 **BABY'S REQUEST** *(2.48)*

All sixteen songs on the album were written by McCartney, except *Again And Again And Again* which was written and sung by Denny. *Reception* features a Norwegian commuter by the name of Ourind Anderson. *Arrow Through Me* was recorded without guitars, the backing being supplied by Moog synthesizers and brass. Two numbers on the album, *Rockestra Theme* and *So Glad To See You Here*, were recorded by Paul on October 3, 1978, at Abbey Road Studios, using what he called the Rockestra line-up. Paul had composed a tune which he thought needed a large instrumental sound to do it justice, so he invited a galaxy of stars to assist in the recordings, which were also filmed. The "Rockestra" line-up features: Denny Laine, Lawrence Juber, Dave Gilmour (Pink Floyd), Hank Marvin (The Shadows) and Pete Townshend (The Who) on guitars; Steve Holly, John Bonham (Led Zeppelin) and Kenny Jones (The Who) on drums; John Paul Jones (Led Zeppelin), Ronnie Lane (ex-Small Faces but by this time a solo artist) and Bruce Thomas (Elvis Costello's group, The Attractions) on bass guitars; Paul, Gary Brooker (ex Procol Harum), John Paul Jones (Led Zeppelin) on pianos; Linda and Tony Ashton on keyboards; Speedy Acquaye, Tony Carr, Ray Cooper and Morris Pert on percussion and Howie Casey, Tony Dorsey, Steve Howard and Thaddeus Richard on horns.

Paul plays concertina on *Million Miles,* while *Winter Rose* and *Love Awake* feature the Black Dyke Mills Band, a brass band which recorded Paul's *Thingumybob* theme music as an Apple single in 1968. *The Broadcast* features two poems (*The Sport Of Kings* by Ian Hay and *The Little Man* by John Galsworthy) recited by Mr Margery, the owner of Lympne Castle, where the number was recorded.

37 (149a) GETTING CLOSER *(3.20)* (161a) BABY'S REQUEST *(2.48)*

By Wings

Parlophone R 6027 – August 10, 1979

The last Wings single, a double "A" sider, failed to enter the *NME* charts, although it did manage a three week run in the BMRB charts, peaking at No. 60 after entering on September 1, 1979.

Both tracks were taken from the *Back To The Egg* album, which was dropping down the charts. The single was no doubt released to boost sales of the album, but without success. The single was released in a picture sleeve featuring a photograph of the band taken from the promotional film for *Baby's Request* on the back cover, while the front featured a picture by Hipgnosis which originally appeared in their excellent book *The Work Of Hipgnosis – Walk Away Renée* (1978), and was listed under "Unsold Ideas".

SEASIDE WOMAN *(3.41)* B SIDE TO SEASIDE *(2.37)* (yellow vinyl)

By Suzy And The Red Stripes

A&M AMS 7461 – August 1979

SEASIDE WOMAN *(3.41)* B SIDE TO SEASIDE *(2.37)* (Box set – yellow vinyl)

By Suzy And The Red Stripes

A&M AMSP 7461 – August 1979

Linda McCartney and Wings recorded Linda's composition under the pseudonym of Suzy And The Red Stripes in late 1973, with the plan for an album to follow. The single didn't see the light of day until 1977, when it was released in the US, but it was delayed until 1979 in the UK, and the proposed album still hasn't materialised. When released in August 1979 in the UK, the single appeared in yellow vinyl, and also in a limited edition box set containing a button badge and ten miniature postcards depicting saucy seaside-type cartoon jokes. The single, released by A&M Records, featured a red and yellow concentric circular striped label.

Even though the single was produced by Paul, it had no commercial success, failing even to enter the BMRB Top 75 singles charts.

38 (162) WONDERFUL CHRISTMASTIME *(3.44)* (163) RUDOLPH THE RED NOSED REGGAE *(1.44)*

By Paul McCartney

Parlophone R 6029 – November 16, 1979

WINGS

Wings' New Single is a Double 'A' Side.
Baby's Request/Getting Closer.

Baby's Request

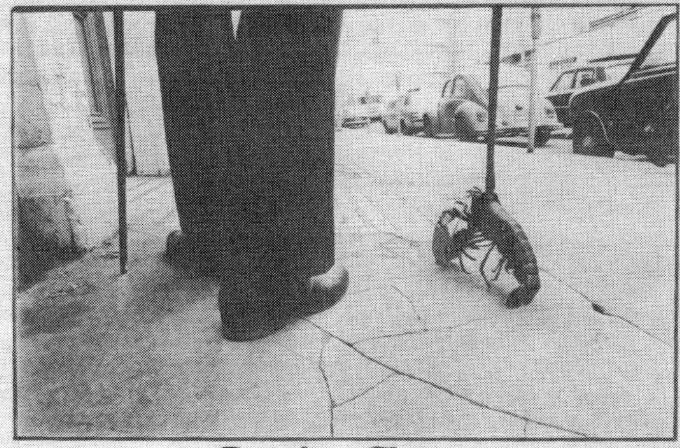

Getting Closer

"A double 'A' side from Wings? If you think we've done it because we couldn't make up our minds – you'd be dead right. We believe in both.

Listen to them and you'll see what we mean."

R6027

From the Album 'Back to the Egg'

McCartney's first solo single since 1971 entered the *NME* charts on December 15, 1979, at No. 24, rising to its highest position, No. 16, in its last week in the chart on January 12, 1980. The single appeared in three *NME* weekly charts between December 15 and January 12 and, as no charts were published over the Christmas period, the single was a hit for five weeks.

Wonderful Christmastime was written by Paul and although it was the first festive song he had recorded as a solo artist, it was not his first Christmas composition, as he had previously composed two Christmas songs for the Beatles 1968 and 1969 Christmas Records. The song was recorded in July 1969, during a solo session in which Paul laid down over twenty tracks. *Rudolph The Red Nosed Reggae*, written by Johnny Marks and originally titled *Rudolph The Red Nosed Reindeer*, was recorded in 1976 and features a mystery violinist, who actually delivered a violin which Paul had ordered while Paul was rehearsing the song.

The single, produced by Paul, was released in a picture sleeve, and features the silver and black Parlophone label. Two Christmas messages are engraved on the run-out groove areas: "To lift a glass...Xmas 79" on the "A" side and "Love from Rudi! Xmas 79" on the "B" side.

THE SUMMIT

By Various Artists

K-tel NE 1067 – January 1, 1980

The Summit was the first various artists compilation to feature a Wings track. It entered the *NME* album charts on February 2, 1980, at No. 23, rising to No. 19, its highest position, the following week, and staying in the chart for three weeks.

The album was a TV advertised charity compilation, with proceeds going to "The Year Of The Child" to help sick and handicapped children. The album featured some of the greatest names in British rock (who donated their services free) and was compiled by Nigel Mason, Richard Stanley and Phil Carson, with special assistance from the members of Led Zeppelin. The sleeve, designed by Spiral Graphics, featured photographs of each act appearing on the album.

A SIDE

SHINE A LITTLE LOVE
By The Electric Light Orchestra

62c **JET** *(4.07)*
By Wings

BAKER STREET
By Gerry Rafferty

SULTANS OF SWING
By Dire Straits

LET IT GROW
By Eric Clapton

SORRY SEEMS TO BE THE HARDEST WORD
By Elton John

DEVIL WOMAN
By Cliff Richard

B SIDE

GIVE A LITTLE LOVE
By Supertramp

BOYS ARE BACK IN TOWN
By Thin Lizzy

DON'T KILL THE WHALE
By Yes

WELCOME TO THE MACHINE
By Pink Floyd

ROCK AND ROLL FANTASY
By Bad Company

CANDY STORE ROCK
By Led Zeppelin

39 (164) COMING UP *(3.47)* (165) COMING UP (LIVE AT GLASGOW) *(3.48)* (166) LUNCHBOX/ODD SOX *(3.47)*

"A" side by Paul McCartney
"B" side by Paul McCartney and Wings

Parlophone R 6035 – April 11, 1980

Coming Up entered the *NME* charts on April 26 at No. 26, rising to No. 2 for one week on May 10, and staying in the chart for six weeks. The single was released in a picture sleeve on the black and silver Parlophone label.

The "A" side *Coming Up* was recorded during the solo sessions that produced *Wonderful Christmastime* in July 1979, with Paul singing and playing bass, synthesizers, piano, guitar and drums. The live version of the song on the "B" side was recorded at the Glasgow Apollo on December 17, 1979, during Wings' first British tour for over four years. The Wings line-up for the tour was Paul, Linda, Denny, Steve Holly and Lawrence Juber, plus the horn section featuring Tony Dorsey, Howie Casey, Steve Howard and Thaddeus Richard. The second track on the "B" side, a medley of *Lunchbox/Odd Sox*, was recorded in Los Angeles in February 1975, during the *Venus And Mars* sessions, and features Wings Mark Five, with Joe English/drums and Jimmy McCulloch/guitar. (cover illustration)

To promote the single on television, Paul made a special video in which he portrayed ten different "rock stars", who all appeared on stage at the same time to perform the song. The trick was achieved by film-maker Keef McMillan, using a new computerised lighting desk. This allowed McCartney to imitate Buddy Holly, Frank Zappa, Ron Mael, Andy Mackay and a 1964 Beatle version of himself (playing his famous violin bass) – plus five others – to form the band, which Paul dubbed "The Plastic Macs".

40 McCARTNEY II

By Paul McCartney

Parlophone PCTC 258 – May 16, 1980

Paul's belated follow-up to his first solo album, which entered the *NME* charts on May 31, 1980, at No. 16, jumping to No. 1 the following week, for two weeks. The album stayed in the Top 30 for fifteen weeks.

As with the *McCartney* album from 1970, Paul recorded *McCartney II* completely solo (with the exception of Linda's assistance on vocals on the last track) during the summer of 1979. This solo enterprise stretched to composing, engineering and producing the whole venture, with technical assistance from Eddie Klein. As the sessions (held at McCartney's farmhouse) produced over twenty songs, the album was originally intended to be a double, but was later edited down to a single album.

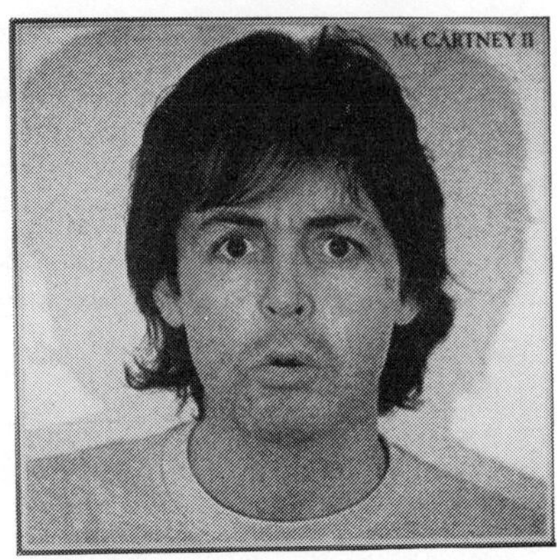

The cover photographs were taken by Linda and the record features the black and silver Parlophone label.

A SIDE

164a **COMING UP** *(3.51)*

167 **TEMPORARY SECRETARY** *(3.13)*

168 **ON THE WAY** *(3.35)*

169 **WATERFALLS** *(4.40)*

170 **NOBODY KNOWS** *(2.50)*

B SIDE

171 **FRONT PARLOUR** *(3.30)*

172 **SUMMERS DAY SONG** *(3.23)*

173 **FROZEN JAP** *(3.38)*

174 **BOGEY MUSIC** *(3.26)*

175 **DARKROOM** *(2.18)*

176 **ONE OF THESE DAYS** *(3.34)*

The album was recorded without a mixing console, the microphones being plugged directly into the tape machines. For most of the songs on the album, Paul initially laid down drums, guitars and bass to create a backing track, to which vocals were added later.

Coming Up features Paul's vocals electronically distorted using a vari-speed machine. *Temporary Secretary* is a song in the form of a letter to the Alfred Marks Bureau, the employment agency, who later asked McCartney for permission to use the song for advertising purposes, but were turned down.

After recording the drum and bass backing tracks for *On The Way*, Paul left it for a week, when he later returned to it, making it a bluesy number after being influenced by seeing Alexis Korner on a BBC TV programme about the blues. Unlike many of the tracks on the album, *Waterfalls* was written in advance of recording, many tracks being ad libbed in the studio. (Paul's house in Kent is also called "Waterfalls".) *Nobody Knows* was also influenced by Alexis Korner's TV programme.

Front Parlour, an instrumental, was so named because most of the track was recorded in the empty front parlour of Paul's farmhouse. *Bogey Music* was inspired by Raymond Briggs' book *Fungus The Bogeyman*. *Darkroom* was ad libbed in the studio, but nearly didn't make it onto the album. It was *not* inspired by Linda's photographic interests. The last track, *One Of These Days*, features Linda on backing vocals.

41 (169a) WATERFALLS *(4.40)*
(177) CHECK MY MACHINE *(4.45)*

By Paul McCartney

Parlophone R 6037 – June 14, 1980

The second single release from the *McCartney II* album, *Waterfalls* entered the *NME* charts at No. 9 on July 5, rising to No. 7 on July 19, and staying in the chart for five weeks. The single was released in a picture sleeve, featuring a painting by Christian Broutin and a photograph of Paul, taken by Linda.

The "B" side, *Check My Machine*, written by Paul, was a previously unreleased song from the summer 1979 solo sessions.

SEASIDE WOMAN *(3.41)*
B SIDE TO SEASIDE *(2.37)*

By Linda McCartney alias Suzy And The Red Stripes

A&M AMS 7548 – July 18, 1980

SEASIDE WOMAN *(3.41)*
B SIDE TO SEASIDE *(2.37)* **(12-inch single)**

By Linda McCartney alias Suzy And The Red Stripes

A&M AMSP 7548 – July 18, 1980

In May 1980, a three and a half minute cartoon based upon Linda's *Seaside Woman* was entered in the Short Film Competition at the Cannes Film Festival. The film – made by Oscar Grillo – won first prize in the competition, and to celebrate this event A&M reissued the single of *Seaside Woman* (which had originally appeared in 1979 in the UK). The single, released in a new picture sleeve and with the usual brown and grey A&M label, was credited to Linda McCartney, in an attempt to generate more sales than the original "Suzy And The Red Stripes" alias. Unfortunately neither this, nor the limited edition twelve-inch single release, could boost it into the charts. Both seven-inch and twelve-inch picture sleeves featured illustrations from the film: two appeared on the seven-inch, and five on the twelve-inch version.

42 (167a) TEMPORARY SECRETARY *(3.13)*
(178) SECRET FRIEND *(10.24)* **(Limited edition 12-inch single)**

By Paul McCartney

Parlophone 12 R 6039 – September 15, 1980

Released as a twelve-inch single only (limited edition of 25,000), *Temporary Secretary* was lifted from the *McCartney II* album, which had dropped out of the Top 30. This release failed either to enter the singles charts, or to generate more sales for the album.

The "B" side, *Secret Friend* – written by Paul – is the longest song he has ever recorded, clocking in at nearly ten and a half minutes long. Previously unreleased, the song was recorded during the *McCartney II* sessions, with Paul producing. The front cover of the picture sleeve features a drawing of McCartney by Jeff Cummins (a painter with Hipgnosis) with additional "artwork" by Paul. The "B" side photograph of McCartney was taken by David Thorpe.

43 THE McCARTNEY INTERVIEW

By Paul McCartney and Vic Garbarini

Parlophone CHAT 1 – February 23, 1981

The interview was recorded in the summer of 1980 for *Musician: Player and Listener* magazine, originally appearing in the August 1980 issue. Vic Garbarini conducted the interview in McCartney's MPL London office. Columbia (CBS), McCartney's record company in America, originally released the recording as a promotional album for radio stations in America, and it immediately became a collector's item. Due to public demand for the record, it was decided to release it officially, but in Britain it appeared on the Parlophone label on February 23, 1981, and was immediately deleted – only a few hours after first going on sale. Although only supposedly available for one day, the album entered the *NME* charts three weeks later at No. 25 for one week on March 14, 1981. The sleeve features two photographs of Paul, taken by Linda, and a sleeve note by Vic Garbarini, a contributor to *Musician; Player and Listener* magazine.

A SIDE (29.38)

PAUL DISCUSSES:

1. McCartney II
2. Negative criticism of Beatles & Wings
3. His influences
4. *Venus & Mars/Wild Life*
5. *Band On The Run*
6. Musical direction/Ringo/George/*Hey Jude*
7. *The White Album*/Tension/*Helter Skelter*
8. *Abbey Road*
9. Musical Background/Trumpet, guitar, piano/Learning bass in Hamburg
10. Early Beatles mixes/Motown & Stax influences
11. The Sgt. Pepper Story/The Beach Boys' *Pet Sounds*
12. *Rubber Soul/Revolver*
13. Fame & success/Paul's & John's reactions
14. Stage fright during The Beatles & Wings
15. How Wings started
16. New Wave/Early Beatles
17. Creating The Beatles' sound/*Love Me Do*/& early songs

B SIDE (24.35)

PAUL DISCUSSES:

1. The Beatles' conquest of America
2. Beatles' haircuts and image
3. Paying dues in Hamburg & Liverpool/Early tours
4. Weathering pressures/The break-up
5. Video of *Coming Up*/Reliving The Beatle image
6. Playing bass

7. Lennon-McCartney songwriting/Dislike of formulas

8. Beatles' imitators

9. *I Am The Walrus/The Black Carnation/Sgt. Pepper* LP Cover

10. New Wave/Bowie, Ferry, Elvis

11. Pop music & radio

12. Getting married/Changing perspective/ *Waterfalls*

13. *Give Ireland Back To The Irish/Hi, Hi, Hi*/Banned songs/Children's songs/*Mary Had A Little Lamb*

CONCERTS FOR THE PEOPLE OF KAMPUCHEA

By Various Artists

Atlantic K 60153 – April 3, 1981

During 1979, the whole world became aware of the terrible plight of the people of Kampuchea. Millions were faced with starvation after four years of war, followed by four years of dictatorship rule by the Khmer Rouge Government – headed by Premier Pol Pot.

Relief and charity organisations quickly swung into operation to feed these starving Kampucheans; UNICEF (United Nation's Children's Fund) became the major United Nation's agency for the operation.

The shows to assist in the relief operation started with the UN Secretary General Kurt Waldheim making contact with Paul McCartney, and from there invitations were issued to various acts. December 26, 27, 28 and 29, 1979, were booked for the evening concerts at the Hammersmith Odeon, London. The four shows arguably constituted the greatest gathering of British rock talent ever assembled, with all the musicians, roadies, technicians, etc., donating their services free to the charitable cause. The artists appearing at the concerts were as follows:

December 26 –Queen (who gave a solo performance).
December 27 –Ian Dury and The Blockheads, The Clash and Matumbi.
December 28 –The Pretenders, The Specials and The Who (who played a marathon three-hour set).
December 29 –Elvis Costello & The Attractions, Rockpile with Dave Edmunds and Nick Lowe, featuring a guest appearance by Robert Plant (Led Zeppelin), Paul McCartney & Wings and lastly Billy Connolly introducing the Rockestra (see below).

All four nights were filmed and recorded, although both the film and album were delayed by over a year. The film was eventually screened on television on January 4, 1981, a few months before the album was released. The sound recording was made on the RAK and Island Mobiles, with Chris Thomas producing.

8 *RECORD ONE A SIDE*

BABA O'RILEY

SISTER DISCO

BEHIND BLUE EYES

SEE ME, FEEL ME
By The Who

RECORD ONE B SIDE

THE WAIT

PRECIOUS

TATTOOED LOVE BOYS
By The Pretenders

THE IMPOSTER
By Elvis Costello & The Attractions

CRAWLING FROM THE WRECKAGE
By Rockpile

LITTLE SISTER
By Rockpile with Robert Plant

RECORD TWO A SIDE

NOW I'M HERE
By Queen

ARMAGIDEON TIME
By The Clash

HIT ME WITH YOUR RHYTHM STICK
By Ian Dury & The Blockheads

MONKEY MAN
By The Specials

RECORD TWO B SIDE

179 **GOT TO GET YOU INTO MY LIFE** *(2.57)*

180 **EVERY NIGHT** *(4.17)*

181 **COMING UP** *(4.03)*
By Paul McCartney & Wings

182 **LUCILLE** *(3.00)*

183 **LET IT BE** *(3.00)*

184 **ROCKESTRA THEME** *(2.28)*
By Rockestra

The three numbers performed by Paul McCartney and Wings feature: Paul/vocals and bass; Linda/keyboards; Denny/guitar; Lawrence Juber/guitar; and Steve Holly/drums; plus the horn section of Howie Casey, Tony Dorsey, Steve Howard and Thaddeus Richard. For the final three songs, McCartney and Wings were joined by eleven guests to form the Rockestra, the greatest "supergroup" ever assembled on a British stage. Rockestra featured twenty musicians: the nine members of Wings, plus three members from Led Zeppelin, two from The Who, two from Rockpile, one Pretender, one Attraction, an ex-member of the Small Faces/The Faces and an ex-member of Procol Harum. The full line-up reads: guitarists/Billy Bremner (Rockpile), Dave Edmunds (Rockpile), James Honeyman-Scott (The Pretenders, Lawrence Juber, Denny Laine, and Peter Townshend (The Who); bass guitarists/John Paul Jones (Led Zeppelin); Ronnie Lane (ex-Small Faces) and Bruce Thomas (The Attractions); drummers/John Bonham (Led Zeppelin), Steve Holly and Kenny Jones (The Who); keyboard players/Gary Brooker (ex-Procol Harum), Linda and Paul (on piano); vocalists/Robert Plant (Led Zeppelin) and Paul; and the Wings Horn section (see above).

JAMES BOND GREATEST HITS

By Various Artists

Liberty EMTV 007 – March 8, 1982

This TV advertised compilation album entered the *NME* charts on April 3 at No. 26, selling 100,000 copies in less than a month; it peaked at No. 6 on April 24, and stayed in the charts for seven weeks.

The album, devised and compiled by Iain McLay, features nineteen tracks from the twelve "James Bond" films produced up to 1981, including nine title songs which became charts hits (BMRB highest chart positions given in brackets below). The album sleeve was designed by Cream.

A SIDE

JAMES BOND THEME

KINGSTON CALYPSO

UNDER THE MANGO TREE
(All above from the Original Soundtrack of *Dr. No*, 1962)

FROM RUSSIA WITH LOVE
By Matt Monro (No. 20 – 1963)

GOLDFINGER
By Shirley Bassey (No. 21 – 1964)

007
(From the Original Soundtrack of *Thunderball*, 1965)

YOU ONLY LIVE TWICE
By Nancy Sinatra (No. 11 – 1967)

ON HER MAJESTY'S SECRET SERVICE

WE HAVE ALL THE TIME IN THE WORLD
By Louis Armstrong

(Above two from the Original Soundtrack of *On Her Majesty's Secret Service*, 1969)

B SIDE

DIAMONDS ARE FOREVER
By Shirley Bassey (No. 38 – 1971)

57c **LIVE AND LET DIE** *(3.10)*
By Paul McCartney & Wings (No. 9 – 1973)

JUST A CLOSER WALK WITH THEE/ NEW SOUND LINE
By Harold A. "Duke" Dejan and The Olympia Brass Band

BOND MEETS SOLITAIRE
(Above three from the Original Soundtrack of *Live And Let Die*, 1973)

THE MAN WITH THE GOLDEN GUN
By Lulu (1974)

NOBODY DOES IT BETTER
By Carly Simon (No. 7 – 1977)

BOND '77
(Above two titles from the Original Soundtrack of *The Spy Who Loved Me*, 1977)

MOONRAKER
By Shirley Bassey (1979)

FOR YOUR EYES ONLY
By Sheena Easton (No. 8 – 1981)

JAMES BOND THEME (reprise)

The *James Bond Theme* was a hit for John Barry (No. 13) in November 1962, but the version on this album is that from the Original Soundtrack album. *Live And Let Die* was the first Bond single to break into the Top 10, the previous highest placing being *You Only Live Twice* (a double "A"-sided hit with *Jackson*) by Nancy Sinatra. The 1977 and 1981 Bond singles improved on Wings' highest position, by reaching No's 7 and 8 respectively.

44 (185) EBONY AND IVORY *(3.41)* (186) RAINCLOUDS *(3.07)*

"A" side by Paul McCartney with additional vocals by Stevie Wonder

"B" side by Paul McCartney

Parlophone R 6054 – March 29, 1982

45 (185a) EBONY AND IVORY *(3.41)* (186a) RAINCLOUDS *(3.07)*/(187) EBONY AND IVORY (solo version) *(3.41) (12-inch single)*

"A" side by Paul McCartney with additional vocals by Stevie Wonder

"B" side by Paul McCartney

Parlophone 12 R 6054 – March 29, 1982

Paul's duet with Stevie Wonder entered the charts on April 17 at No. 9, rising to No. 2 the following week, by which time it had sold over 250,000 in Britain. On May 1, it rose to No. 1 for two weeks, dropping to No. 3 on May 15, and passing the 500,000 mark. The single was in the charts for seven weeks, and gave Stevie Wonder his first British No. 1, albeit as part of a duo.

The single was released in seven-inch and twelve-inch forms in Britain, both

featuring the same picture sleeve, although the twelve-inch version contained an extra track. The two releases feature the first appearance of the new MPL logo of a figure juggling with three planets. A promotional video of *Ebony And Ivory* was produced, showing Paul and Stevie apparently performing the song together. However, both parties shot their sequences separately – Paul in Britain and Stevie in America – and the two films were very cleverly edited together.

Ebony And Ivory was written by Paul, and the "B" side, *Rainclouds*, was jointly composed by Paul and Denny Laine. The twelve-inch credits only Paul as composer of *Rainclouds*, but this is incorrect. The songs were recorded during the *Tug Of War* album sessions – which lasted over a year, between October 1980 and January 1982. *Rainclouds* was recorded in early 1981, with Denny Laine present. For the first time since *Live And Let Die* in 1973, Paul did not produce his own recording sessions, allowing George Martin to perform this duty.

46 TUG OF WAR

By Paul McCartney

Parlophone PCTC 259 – April 26, 1982

Almost two years after *McCartney II*, Paul's follow-up solo album was released. It entered the *NME* Top 30 album charts on May 9 at No. 11, rising to No. 1 for one week on May 15. It sold around 20,000 within two weeks, and went Gold (100,000 sales) by July 31, staying in the charts for eighteen weeks.

The production of the album spanned a year and a half, starting in October 1980 and ending in March 1982. In October 1980 it was reported by *Beatles Monthly* that Wings were recording their follow-up to the *Back To The Egg* album, with later reports stating that George Martin was producing. In February 1981, Wings were in Montseratt, West Indies, recording at George Martin's AIR Studios, with Paul and George Martin producing jointly. During this period rumours spread that both Ringo and George (Harrison) were to join Paul in Montserrat to record a tribute album to John Lennon. On April 27, 1981, it was officially announced that Wings had disbanded following the departure of Denny Laine (both Juber and Holly had left unannounced several months previously).

Then, in the July issue of *Beatles Monthly*, it was reported that Paul's new album had been over-dubbed and mixed in London during the first week of June – with George Martin producing and Geoff Emerick engineering, and with Stevie Wonder and Michael Jackson adding backing vocals to certain tracks. In September 1981, *Beatles Monthly* reported that Paul's recently completed album was scheduled for a November release, but in early September, McCartney returned to the studio for further recordings. Having assisted Paul several months previously, Michael Jackson re-joined Paul in the studio at the end of November 1981 for further recordings in London.

The first definite release date for the *Tug Of War* album was set for February 15, 1982, but because of further re-mixing it was delayed and a new date – March 12 – set. It was again re-scheduled for April 19, but put back again after Paul noticed a flaw in the cover artwork (which he ordered to be redesigned) during March. After being re-scheduled about five times, the album eventually appeared on April 26, 1982.

The sleeve was designed by Hipgnosis and Sinc, with artwork by Brian Clarke and photographs by Linda.

A SIDE

188 TUG OF WAR *(4.21)*

189 TAKE IT AWAY *(4.13)*

190 SOMEBODY WHO CARES *(3.18)*

191 WHAT'S THAT YOU'RE DOING *(6.19)*

192 HERE TODAY *(2.24)*

B SIDE

193 BALLROOM DANCING *(4.06)*

194 THE POUND IS SINKING *(2.53)*

195 WANDERLUST *(3.49)*

196 GET IT *(2.30)*

197 BE WHAT YOU SEE (link) *(0.32)*

198 DRESS ME UP AS A ROBBER *(5.43)*

185b EBONY AND IVORY *(3.41)*

Paul used over a dozen well-known musicians to record *Tug Of War*, the line-up reading as follows: Denny Laine/electric guitar (*Tug Of War*, *Ballroom Dancing* and *Dress Me Up As A Robber*), guitar synthesizer (*Somebody Who Cares*) and synthesizer *(Dress Me Up As A Robber*); Campbell Maloney/military snares (*Tug Of War*); Eric Stewart (of 10CC)/electric guitar (*Tug Of War*); Steve Gadd/drums (*Take It Away*, *Somebody Who Cares*), percussion (*Somebody Who Cares*); Ringo Starr/drums (*Take It Away*); George Martin/electric piano (*Take It Away* and *Dress Me Up As A Robber*); Stanley Clarke/bass (*Somebody Who Cares* and *The Pound Is Sinking*); Adrian Brett/pan pipes (*Somebody Who Cares*); Stevie Wonder/synthesizers (*What's That You're Doing* and *Ebony And Ivory*), electric piano, drums and percussion (*Ebony And Ivory*); Jack Brymer/clarinet gliss (*Ballroom Dancing*); Adrian Sheppard/drums and percussion (*Wanderlust*); Carl Perkins/electric guitar (*Get It*) and Dave Mattacks/drums and percussion (*Dress Me Up As A Robber*).

Paul played the following instruments: acoustic, electric and Spanish guitars, bass, piano, synthesizers, drums, percussion and vocoder. Vocal backing on all but five tracks (*Here Today*, *Get It*, *Be What You See*, *Dress Me Up As A Robber* and *Ebony and Ivory*) was supplied by Paul, Linda and Eric Stewart.

All the songs on the album were written by McCartney, with the exception of *What's That You're Doing*. This song was co-written with Stevie Wonder and originated out of a jam session in the studio (with both Paul and Stevie on lead vocals).

Here Today, Paul's tribute to John, features Paul singing to his own acoustic guitar accompaniment, plus a quartet of strings, supplied by Jack Rothstein/violin, Bernard Partridge/violin, Ian Jewel/viola and Keith Harvey/cello, with no other musicians being heard.

Ballroom Dancing features narration by Peter Marshall, while *Wanderlust* (the name of one of the yachts used by Wings whilst recording *London Town* in the Virgin Islands) features the Philip Jones Brass Ensemble.

Get It features only Paul and Carl Perkins, who plays electric guitar and sings. At the end of the number Carl is heard laughing; this was due to a rather saucy joke told to him by Paul, but the joke was removed from the recording since it was considered too rude for the public's ears.

The link track, *Be What You See*, features only Paul on guitar and vocoder. *Ebony And Ivory* has just Paul and Stevie playing all the instruments, as well as singing lead and backing vocals.

47 (189a) TAKE IT AWAY *(4.00)*
(199) I'LL GIVE YOU A RING *(3.04)*

By Paul McCartney

Parlophone R 6056 – June 21, 1982

48 (189b) TAKE IT AWAY *(4.00)*
(199a) I'LL GIVE YOU A RING *(3.04)*/**(198a) DRESS ME UP AS A ROBBER** *(2.38)* **(12-inch single)**

By Paul McCartney

Parlophone 12 R 6056 – July 5, 1982

With *Tug Of War* dropping out of the album charts, *Take It Away* was released as a second single. It entered the singles chart at No. 26 on July 17 and rose to No. 14 on August 21. During its seven week run in the charts, it boosted sales of the album, which jumped back up the LP charts to No. 12 on August 7.

Both the seven-inch and twelve-inch versions were released in matching picture sleeves; these showed McCartney together with various musicians on the reverse (Eric Stewart and Linda top left, Ringo and Steve Gadd top and bottom right and George Martin bottom left). Photographs were taken by Linda, with the sleeve design by Hipgnosis.

The non-*Tug Of War* "B" side, *I'll Give You A Ring*, was recorded during the sessions, with McCartney playing all instruments except clarinet (which was supplied by Tony Coe). Paul, Linda and Eric Stewart supplied backing vocals on this song written by Paul and produced by George Martin.

49 (188a) TUG OF WAR *(4.01)*
(196a) GET IT *(2.29)*

"A" side by Paul McCartney

"B" side by Paul McCartney and Carl Perkins

Parlophone R 6057 – September 20, 1982

Both tracks on this single were lifted from the *Tug Of War* album, which had dropped out of the Top 30 album charts at the beginning of September. The single, which failed to reach the charts, was released in a picture sleeve designed by MTI, London, and showing a photograph by Linda.

THE GIRL IS MINE *(3.40)*
CAN'T GET OUT OF THE RAIN *(4.03)*

"A" side by Michael Jackson/Paul McCartney

"B" side by Michael Jackson

Epic EPC A2729 – November 29, 1982

THE GIRL IS MINE *(3.40)*
CAN'T GET OUT OF THE RAIN *(4.03)*
(Picture disc)

"A" side by Michael Jackson/Paul McCartney

"B" side by Michael Jackson

Epic EPC A 11-2729 – November, 1982

The Jackson/McCartney duet entered the *NME* Top 30 charts on November 13 at No. 15, rising to No. 4 the following week, and staying in the charts for four weeks.

During May and June 1982, Paul was busy recording the follow up to *Tug Of War*. Whilst in Los Angeles he assisted Michael Jackson in recording the latter's new album, *Thriller*, as he had promised when Michael assisted Paul with his recordings the previous year. Although George Martin was present at the session, Quincy Jones produced the resulting recording of Michael Jackson's composition, *The Girl Is Mine*, with Michael and Paul sharing lead vocals. The "B" side does not feature Paul.

The single was released in a picture sleeve, using a photograph taken by Linda, and it also appeared as a picture disc.

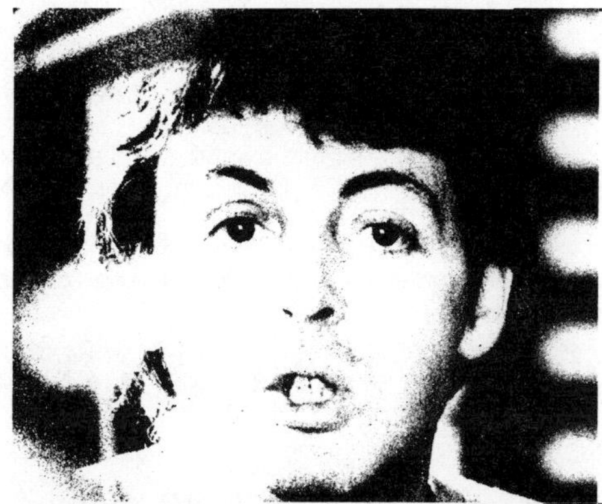

PAUL – US SECTION

1 McCARTNEY

By Paul McCartney

Apple STAO 3363 – April 20, 1970

Paul's first solo album entered the American Billboard album charts at No. 14 on May 9, rising to No. 1 on May 23 where it remained for three weeks. Advance orders amounted to two million copies and it sold a million in its first month on release, receiving an R.I.A.A. Gold Award on April 30, 1970. The album stayed in the Top 10 for thirteen weeks, the Top 30 for twenty weeks, the Top 100 for thirty-two weeks, and the Top 200 for forty-seven weeks. (Tracks and cover same as British release.)

2 (15) ANOTHER DAY (16) OH WOMAN OH WHY

By Paul McCartney

Apple 1829 – February 22, 1971

Another Day entered the Billboard Hot Hundred at No. 55 on March 6, peaking at No. 5 for two weeks from April 17. The single stayed in the Top 30 for nine weeks, and in the Top 100 for eleven weeks. As in Britain, the single was released in a plain Apple sleeve.

3 RAM

By Paul and Linda McCartney

Apple SMAS 3375 – May 17, 1971

Ram entered the Billboard album charts three weeks after release at No. 6 on June 6, rising to No. 2 for two weeks from August 21 (*Tapestry* by Carole King being at No. 1). The album was in the Top 10 for twenty-four weeks, was awarded an R.I.A.A. Gold Award on June 9, 1971, and eventually sold a million in America, staying in the Top 100 for thirty-four weeks and the Top 200 for thirty-seven weeks. (Tracks and cover same as British release.)

4 (21-2a) UNCLE ALBERT/ADMIRAL HALSEY/ (17a) TOO MANY PEOPLE

By Paul and Linda McCartney

Apple 1837 – August 2, 1971

Not released as a single in Britain, *Uncle Albert/Admiral Halsey* entered the Billboard charts on August 14 at No. 65, topping the chart on September 4 for one week, selling a million by September 21, 1971, and receiving an R.I.A.A. Gold Award. The single stayed in the Top 30 for twelve weeks, and McCartney received a Grammy Award for Best Arrangement-Accompanying Vocalists for the song. The single was not released in a picture sleeve.

5 WILD LIFE

By Wings

Apple SW 3386 – December 7, 1971

Although not a great success in Britain, *Wild Life* fared better in the American charts, entering on December 25, 1971, at No. 25, and peaking at No. 10 for two weeks on January 22, 1972. On January 13, 1972, it was awarded a Gold Disc, having reached the million dollar sales mark. The song stayed in the Top 30 for nine weeks, the Top 100 for sixteen weeks, and the Top 200 for eighteen weeks. (Tracks and cover same as British release.)

6 (38) GIVE IRELAND BACK TO THE IRISH (39) GIVE IRELAND BACK TO THE IRISH (version)

By Wings

Apple 1847 – February 28, 1972

As in Britain, *Give Ireland Back To The Irish* enjoyed comparatively little success in the charts, rising only to No. 21 on April 8, after entering on March 11 at No. 78. The single was in the charts for a mere eight weeks, and features the same shamrock style label as the British release. However, the song lyrics were reproduced on the sleeve.

7 (40) MARY HAD A LITTLE LAMB (41) LITTLE WOMAN LOVE

By Wings

Apple 1851 – May 29, 1972

Despite being issued in a picture sleeve (identical to the British release) *Mary Had A Little Lamb* was unable to improve on the success of the first Wings single, only breaking into the Top 30 for two weeks, with a highest position of No. 28 on July 22. The single entered the Hot Hundred on June 17 at No. 85, staying in the chart for seven weeks.

8 (42) HI, HI, HI (43) C MOON

By Wings

Apple 1857 – December 4, 1972

McCartney eventually managed to break into the US Top 10 with a Wings single, when *Hi, Hi, Hi* reached No. 10 for one week on February 3, 1973. The single entered the Billboard chart on December 16 at No. 100, and remained in the Top 30 for eight weeks, and in the Top 100 for eleven weeks.

9 (44) MY LOVE (45) THE MESS

By Paul McCartney and Wings

Apple 1861 – April 9, 1973

After three comparatively unsuccessful singles, Paul and Wings scored a smash No. 1 American hit. *My Love* entered the Top 100 on April 14 at No. 73, rising to No. 1 by June 2 for two weeks, and passing the million sales mark by July 6, 1973. The single stayed in the Top 30 for twelve weeks, and in the Top 100 for eighteen weeks.

10 RED ROSE SPEEDWAY

By Paul McCartney and Wings

Apple SMAL 3409 – April 30, 1973

Red Rose Speedway entered the Top 200 on May 12 at No. 127, and four weeks later – on June 2 – rose to No. 1 for three weeks, passing the million dollar sales mark on May 25. The album stayed in the Top 30 for thirteen weeks, the Top 100 for twenty-four weeks and the Top 200 for thirty-one weeks. (Tracks and cover same as British release.)

11 (57) LIVE AND LET DIE (58) I LIE AROUND

By Wings

Apple 1863 – June 18, 1973

Paul's *James Bond* movie theme entered the Billboard chart on July 7 at No. 69, and rose to No. 2 for three weeks on August 11 The single stayed in the Top 30 for eleven weeks and in the Top 100 for fourteen weeks, selling over a million units and receiving an R.I.A.A. Gold Award on August 31, 1973. George Martin received a Grammy Award for Best Arrangement-Accompanying Vocalist.

LIVE AND LET DIE

Original Soundtrack by Various Artists

United Artists LA 100-G – July 2, 1973

The soundtrack album of the "James Bond" film, featuring the title track by Wings, entered the Billboard Top 100 on July 28 at No. 93, rising to No. 17 on September 1, 1973, and staying in the chart for twelve weeks. (Track listing and cover same as British release.)

12 (59) HELEN WHEELS (60) COUNTRY DREAMER

By Paul McCartney and Wings

Apple 1869 – November 12, 1973

Helen Wheels entered the charts on November 24 at No. 66, rising to No. 10 on January 12, 1974; it remained in the Top 30 for eight weeks, and the Top 100 for fourteen weeks.

13 BAND ON THE RUN

By Paul McCartney and Wings

Apple SO 3415 – December 5, 1973

Band On The Run, Wings' biggest-selling album in America, entered the Billboard chart at No. 33 on December 22, having achieved over a million dollars worth of sales on December 7, 1973. After entering the Top 10 on January 19, 1974, it hovered around the lower part of the Top 10 until *Jet* was lifted from the album as a single. This was done at the suggestion of Al Coury, of Capitol, who persuaded Paul that it would boost sales of the album. After sixteen weeks in the chart, the album rose to No. 1 for one week on April 13, 1974, passing the million units mark by the end of April.

With *Jet* still in the Hot Hundred, *Band On The Run* was released as a single. This boosted sales of the album, which recaptured the No. 1 position – the first time this had happened in the American record industry's history. The album returned to No. 1 on June 8, the same date as the *Band On The Run* single captured the No. 1 position in the singles chart. The LP stayed at the top for two weeks, dropping to No. 2 for two weeks, and returning yet again to No. 1 on July 6 for one week.

The album was at No. 1 for a total of four weeks, in the Top 10 for thirty-two weeks, the Top 30 for thirty-eight weeks, the Top 100 for forty-six weeks and the Top 200 for seventy-four weeks. By the end of August 1974, the album had sold over two million copies in the United States, and this total increased to over five million by 1976. It won two Grammy Awards for Best Engineered (Non-Classical) Recording and Best Pop Vocals Performance by a Duo, Group or Chorus (1974).

The American album included *Helen Wheels*; Capitol insisted it should be included to encourage sales resulting from the previous hit single. (Cover same as British release.)

A SIDE

61 **BAND ON THE RUN**

62 **JET**

63 **BLUEBIRD**

64 **MRS. VANDEBILT**

65 **LET ME ROLL IT**

B SIDE

66 **MAMUNIA**

67 **NO WORDS**

59a **HELEN WHEELS**

68 **PICASSO'S LAST WORDS (DRINK TO ME)**

69 **NINETEEN HUNDRED AND EIGHTY FIVE**

14 (62a) JET (66a) MAMUNIA

By Paul McCartney and Wings

Apple 1871 – January 28, 1974

15 (62b) JET (65a) LET ME ROLL IT

By Paul McCartney and Wings

Apple 1871 – February 18, 1974

Capitol initially released *Jet* with *Mamunia* as the "B" side, but changed the coupling (following EMI's "B" side selection in the rest of the world) to *Let Me Roll It*, although the two singles have the same catalogue number.

Jet entered the Hot Hundred singles charts on February 9 at No. 69, rising to No. 7 on March 30, and staying in the Top 30 for nine weeks, and in the Top 100 for fourteen weeks. The release of the single – suggested by Al Coury – assisted sales of the *Band On The Run* album to the point where it reached the No. 1 position.

16 (61a) BAND ON THE RUN (69a) NINETEEN HUNDRED AND EIGHTY FIVE

By Paul McCartney and Wings

Apple 1873 – April 8, 1974

After the success of *Jet*, Al Coury again persuaded Paul to release another single from the *Band On The Run* album, this time plumping for the title track. The single entered the charts on April 20, at No. 68, making the Top 10 after four weeks, and rising to No. 1 on June 8, which coincided with the album hitting the Top spot in the album charts. The single sold a million by June 4, 1974, staying in the Top 30 for twelve weeks and the Top 100 for eighteen weeks. The song won a Grammy Award for Best Pop Vocal Performance by a Group, 1974.

17 (71) JUNIOR'S FARM (72) SALLY G

By Paul McCartney and Wings

Apple 1875 – November 4, 1974

Junior's Farm entered the Billboard Hot Hundred on November 9 (a week after release) at No. 59, rising to No. 3 on January 11, 1975. The single was in the Top 30 for ten weeks and the Top 100 for twelve weeks.

WALKING IN THE PARK WITH ELOISE
BRIDGE OVER THE RIVER SUITE

By The Country Hams

EMI 3977 – December 2, 1974

As with the British release, this single – by Wings under a pseudonym – did not enter the charts, but was released in an identical picture sleeve.

18 (72a) SALLY G
(71a) JUNIOR'S FARM

By Paul McCartney and Wings

Apple 1875 – January 20, 1975

With *Junior's Farm* still registering in the Top 30 at No. 7 on January 18, the "A" and "B" sides of the single were flipped to promote *Sally G* as the "A" side. *Sally G* entered the Hot Hundred on February 1 at No. 66, rising to No. 39 on February 22, and featuring in the chart for five weeks. As in Britain, this was the last Wings' single to appear on the Apple label.

19 (73) LISTEN TO WHAT THE MAN SAID
(74) LOVE IN SONG

By Wings

Capitol 4091 – May 23, 1975

The first Wings' single to appear on the Capitol label entered the Hot Hundred on May 31 at No. 65, rising to No. 1 for one week on July 19, and staying in the charts for fourteen weeks, seven of which were spent in the Top 10. After dropping out of the charts at the end of August, the single passed the million sales mark in the United States, receiving a Gold Disc on September 5, 1975. The single was released in the same picture sleeve as the British release.

20 VENUS AND MARS

By Wings

Capitol SMAS 11419 – May 27, 1975

With advance orders of 1,500,000, *Venus And Mars* received an R.I.A.A. Gold Disc immediately after release on June 2, 1975, entering the album charts on June 14 at No. 25. It jumped to No. 2 the following week for four weeks, then held the No. 1 spot on July 19 for one week, eventually selling well over a million copies. By October 4, 1975, the album had dropped to No. 99, but with the release of the title track as a single, the album rose back up the charts to No. 32 on December 13. It eventually stayed in the Top 100 for thirty-six weeks, thirteen of them in the Top 30, and seventy-seven weeks in the Top 200. (Tracks and cover same as the British release.)

21 (79a) LETTING GO
(77a) YOU GAVE ME THE ANSWER

By Wings

Capitol 4145 – September 29, 1975

As in Britain, *Letting Go* failed to enter the American Top 30. It peaked at only No. 39 for two weeks on October 25 during a six week stay in the charts – after entering on October 4 at No. 74.

22 (76-6a) VENUS AND MARS/ROCK SHOW
(78a) MAGNETO AND TITANIUM MAN

By Wings

Capitol 4175 – October 27, 1975

This medley from the *Venus And Mars* album gave Wings another Top 30 hit, after entering the Top 100 on November 1 at No. 82 and rising to No. 12 on December 13. It was listed in the Top 30 for four weeks, and in the Top 100 for nine weeks.

23 WINGS AT THE SPEED OF SOUND

By Wings

Capitol SW 11525 – March 25, 1976

Wings At The Speed Of Sound entered the Billboard charts on April 10, and reached No. 1 on April 24th, staying there for seven weeks. The album sold a million in the United States, staying in the Top 200 for fifty-one weeks and becoming the third best-selling album in the Billboard charts table for 1976. (Track listing and sleeve same as British release.)

24 (92a) SILLY LOVE SONGS
(93a) COOK OF THE HOUSE

By Wings

Capitol 4256 – April 1, 1976

Silly Love Songs became Wings' fourth No. 1 American single (and McCartney's fifth), after entering the Billboard charts on April 10, and rising to No. 1 on May 22, where it stayed for five weeks. The single was in the Top 100 for nineteen weeks, becoming an American million seller and Billboard's Top Single of 1976.

25 (87a) LET 'EM IN (90a) BEWARE MY LOVE

By Wings

Capitol 4293 – June 28, 1976

The second singles release from *Wings At The Speed Of Sound* entered the Billboard charts on July 4, reaching No. 3 and staying in the chart for sixteen weeks. It sold a million copies in the United States.

26 WINGS OVER AMERICA

By Wings

Capitol SWCO 11593 – December 11, 1976

The live *Wings Over America* triple set entered the Billboard album chart on December 25, reaching No. 1 on January 22, 1977, for a single week, and becoming a million seller. It featured in the chart for eighty-six weeks. (Tracks and sleeve same as British release.)

27 (104a) MAYBE I'M AMAZED (127a) SOILY

By Wings

Capitol 4385 – February 7, 1977

Wings' first live single in America entered the Top 100 on February 12, reaching No. 10 and staying in the chart for thirteen weeks.

SEASIDE WOMAN B SIDE TO SEASIDE

By Suzy And The Red Stripes

Epic 8-50403 – May 31, 1977

Appearing in America two years before its British release, this Linda McCartney single made a brief appearance in the Billboard Top 100, reaching No. 59, and staying in the chart for five weeks after entering during July.

28 (128) MULL OF KINTYRE (129) GIRLS' SCHOOL

By Wings

Capitol 4504 – November 14, 1977

Although becoming the biggest-selling single of all time in Britain, *Mull Of Kintyre/Girls' School* failed to enter the Top 30 of the Billboard charts. It peaked at No. 33, staying in the chart for eleven weeks. Although a double "A"-sided hit, *Mull Of Kintyre* received maximum airplay in Britain, while in America *Girls' School* was promoted as the main side. (Picture sleeve same as British release.)

29 (130) WITH A LITTLE LUCK (131-2) BACKWARDS TRAVELLER/ CUFF LINK

By Wings

Capitol 4559 – March 20, 1978

The fifth Wings' single to reach No. 1 in the Billboard charts, which it entered during May 1978. The single went to No. 1 on May 20 for two weeks, staying in the charts for eighteen weeks altogether.

30 LONDON TOWN

By Wings

Capitol SW 11777 – March 31, 1978

Although not a big hit in Britain, *London Town* rose to No. 2 in the Billboard album charts; it remained there for twenty-eight weeks, after entering on April 15th. (Tracks and sleeve same as the British release.)

31 (138a) I'VE HAD ENOUGH (140a) DELIVER YOUR CHILDREN

By Wings

Capitol 4594 – June 12, 1978

Although not making the Top 30 in Britain, *I've Had Enough* rose to No. 25 in the Billboard charts. It entered during August 1978, staying in the chart for eleven weeks.

32 (133a) LONDON TOWN (135a) I'M CARRYING

By Wings

Capitol 4625 – August 21, 1978

The last Wings' single on the Capitol label, as McCartney transferred his contract to Columbia Records for the American market. The single failed to enter the Top 30, rising to only No. 39. It stayed in the Top 100 for eight weeks after entering during October 1978.

33 WINGS GREATEST

By Wings

Capitol SOO 11905 – November 22, 1978

Although boasting five number one singles, along with six other Top Ten singles, *Wings Greatest* only rose to No. 29 in the Billboard album charts, staying in the best sellers for eighteen weeks. Of the twelve singles on the album, only *Mull Of Kintyre* had failed to enter the Top 30 (it reached No. 33), while *Uncle Albert/ Admiral Halsey, My Love, Band On The Run, Silly Love Songs* and *With A Little Luck* had all reached No. 1 in the Billboard singles chart. One other Wings' single reached the coveted No. 1 position in America – *Listen To What The Man Said.* (Sleeve same as British release.)

A SIDE

(Same as British release)

B SIDE

21-2b **UNCLE ALBERT/ADMIRAL HALSEY**

42a **HI, HI, HI**

87b **LET 'EM IN**

44b **MY LOVE**

62c **JET**

128a **MULL OF KINTYRE**

34 BAND ON THE RUN (Picture disc)

By Wings

Capitol SEAX 11901 – December 1978

As a companion to the Beatles picture disc releases of *Sgt. Pepper* and *Abbey Road*, Capitol released *Band On The Run* in picture disc form in a limited edition of 150,000. (Tracks same as original release.)

35 (144) GOODNIGHT TONIGHT (145) DAYTIME NIGHTIME SUFFERING

By Wings

Colombia 3-10939 – March 15, 1979

36 (144a) GOODNIGHT TONIGHT (145a) DAYTIME NIGHTIME SUFFERING (Special 12-inch single)

By Wings

Columbia 23-10940 – March 15, 1979

After two comparatively unsuccessful singles, Wings scored a Top 5 hit with this disco single *Goodnight Tonight*, which entered the charts on March 31, reaching No. 5, and staying in the charts for sixteen weeks. As in Britain, the single appeared in both seven-inch and twelve-inch pressings, the latter being an extended disco version of the "A" side. The record was the first Wings' single to appear on the Columbia label, and appeared in a picture sleeve. (Sleeve same as British release.)

37 BACK TO THE EGG

By Wings

Columbia FC-36057 – May 24, 1979

The first Wings' album on the Columbia label, which entered the Billboard charts on June 30, reaching No. 8, and staying in the chart for twenty-four weeks. It achieved platinum status in the US. (Tracks and sleeve same as the British release.)

38 (149a) GETTING CLOSER (147a) SPIN IT ON

By Wings

Columbia 3-11020 – June 5, 1979

For the first time (with the exception of the premature release of the *Jet/Mamunia* single) the US release of a Wings' single was different from the equivalent British release. In Britain, *Old Siam Sir* was released as the first single from the *Back To The Egg* album. In America, Columbia picked *Getting Closer*, which gave Wings a No. 20 chart hit. The single entered the Billboard charts on June 16, staying in the Top 100 for ten weeks.

39 (152a) ARROW THROUGH ME (146a) OLD SIAM SIR

By Wings

Columbia 1-11070 – August 14, 1979

For the second singles release from *Back To The Egg*, Columbia selected *Arrow Through Me*; this was not released in Britain as a 45, although the US coupling, *Old Siam Sir*, had already appeared as a British seven-inch. *Arrow Through Me* only reached No. 29 in the Billboard charts, in which it was listed for ten weeks, after entering on August 25.

40 (162) WONDERFUL CHRISTMASTIME (163) RUDOLPH THE RED NOSED REGGAE

By Paul McCartney

Columbia 1-11162 – November 20, 1979

As with the Christmas singles of John and Yoko and George in America, Paul had little success with his festive single (it failed to enter any of the three major American charts). (Picture sleeve same as British release.)

41 (164) COMING UP (165) COMING UP (LIVE AT GLASGOW) (166) LUNCHBOX/ ODD SOX

"A" side by Paul McCartney

"B" side by Paul McCartney and Wings

Columbia 1-11263 – April 15, 1980

In the United States, radio station programmers preferred the live version of *Coming Up*, and it was this version which received airplay. It therefore charted, since the American charts are partially based on radio plays. It was the last Wings' single to chart in America, reaching No. 1 for three weeks, after entering on April 26. The single went to No. 1 on June 28 and stayed in the charts for twenty-one weeks. (Picture sleeve same as British release.)

42 McCARTNEY II

By Paul McCartney

Columbia FC-36511 – May 21, 1980

After the success of the *Coming Up* single, *McCartney II* followed suit and entered the charts on June 14, reaching No. 3, and staying in the Top 200 album charts for nineteen weeks. (Tracks and sleeve same as British release.)

43 McCARTNEY

By Paul McCartney

Columbia FC-36478 – May 22, 1980

44 RAM

By Paul and Linda McCartney

Columbia FC-36479 – May 22, 1980

45 WILD LIFE

By Wings

Columbia FC-36480 – May 22, 1980

46 RED ROSE SPEEDWAY

By Paul McCartney and Wings

Columbia FC-36481 – May 22, 1980

47 BAND ON THE RUN

By Paul McCartney and Wings

Columbia FC-36482 – May 22, 1980

As all Paul McCartney's albums were leased to Capitol on a five year basis, when his Capitol contract expired and he moved to Columbia, he took his contractual rights to each record with him. Thus each of his earlier albums was made available for Columbia to reissue. The above five albums were the first batch under these terms, each being identical to the original releases.

48 (169a) WATERFALLS (177) CHECK MY MACHINE

Columbia 1-11335 – July 22, 1980

One of Paul's least successful singles ever, *Waterfalls* failed to enter the Top 100, managing only to rise to No. 106 in the singles just outside the chart. (Picture sleeve same as British release.)

49 VENUS AND MARS

By Wings

Columbia FC-36801 – September 25, 1980

The sixth re-release of a McCartney album on Columbia. (Tracks and sleeve same as original release.)

50 THE McCARTNEY INTERVIEW

By Paul McCartney and Vic Garbarini

Columbia PC-36987 – December 4, 1980

After Columbia released a special promotional double album of the McCartney interview by *Musician, Player and Listener,* public demand for the records prompted them to release the album officially. This limited edition release reached No. 158 in the Top 200 album charts after entering on January 31, staying for a mere three weeks in the chart. (Cover and tracks same as British release.)

51 (149b) GETTING CLOSER (144b) GOODNIGHT TONIGHT

By Wings

Columbia Hall Of Fame 13-33405 – December 4, 1980

52 (44c) MY LOVE (13a) MAYBE I'M AMAZED

"A" side by Paul McCartney and Wings

"B" side by Paul McCartney

Columbia Hall Of Fame 13-33407 – December 4, 1980

53 (21-2c) UNCLE ALBERT/ADMIRAL HALSEY (62d) JET

"A" side by Paul and Linda McCartney

"B" side by Paul McCartney and Wings

Columbia Hall Of Fame 13-33408 – December 4, 1980

54 (61c) BAND ON THE RUN (59b) HELEN WHEELS

By Paul McCartney and Wings

Columbia Hall Of Fame 13-33409 – December 4, 1980

As with his Capitol albums, McCartney's singles were deleted five years after release and replaced with the above Columbia singles, on their Hall of Fame label. Both sides of each single were originally "A" sides of earlier Capitol singles, except *Maybe I'm Amazed* – which features the original *McCartney* studio version, rather than the live version which appeared on the 1979 single. Other singles elegible to be reissued in the series (but that were not in fact used) were *Another Day, Give Ireland Back To The Irish, Mary Had A Little Lamb, Hi, Hi, Hi, Live And Let Die, Junior's Farm, Listen To What The Man Said, Letting Go* and *Venus And Mars/Rock Show.*

CONCERTS FOR KAMPUCHEA

By Various Artists

Atlantic SD 2 7005 – March 30, 1981

The only new material from McCartney in 1981 appeared on this various artists charity album to help the starving people of Kampuchea. The album entered the Billboard charts on April 18, reaching No. 36 and staying in the chart for twelve weeks. (Tracks and sleeve same as British release.)

55 BAND ON THE RUN (Half-speed master)

By Paul McCartney and Wings

Columbia HC 46482 – April 24, 1981

The third reappearance of *Band On The Run* after the picture disc and Columbia reissue, this high quality pressing appeared on Columbia in conjunction with Half-Speed Master Audiophile Recordings. (Tracks and sleeve as original release.)

56 (92c) SILLY LOVE SONGS (93b) COOK OF THE HOUSE

Columbia 18-02171 – June 12, 1981

Unlike the original Hall Of Fame series of reissues of McCartney singles, *Silly Love Songs* was reissued on Columbia's normal singles series, with its original "B" side (although it failed to make the charts.)

57 WINGS AT THE SPEED OF SOUND

By Wings

Columbia FC-37409 – July 13, 1981

Five years after its Capitol release, *Wings At The Speed Of Sound* was reissued by Columbia. (Tracks and sleeve same as original release.)

58 (185) EBONY AND IVORY (186) RAINCLOUDS

"A" side by Paul McCartney with Stevie Wonder

"B" side by Paul McCartney

Columbia 18-02860 – April 2, 1982

59 (185a) EBONY AND IVORY (186a) RAINCLOUDS/(187) EBONY AND IVORY (solo version; 12-inch single)

"A" side by Paul McCartney with Stevie Wonder

"B" side by Paul McCartney

Columbia 44-02878 – April 16, 1982

Ebony And Ivory entered the Billboard Hot Hundred on April 10, at No. 29 – the highest new entry position since John Lennon's *Imagine* entered at No. 20 in 1971. On May 15, it rose to No. 1 for seven weeks, eventually staying in the Top 100 for nineteen weeks. As in Britain, the single appeared in a picture sleeve, and as a twelve-inch release, with the solo version of *Ebony And Ivory* on the "B" side.

60 TUG OF WAR

By Paul McCartney

Columbia TC 37462 – April 26, 1982

Tug Of War entered the Billboard charts on May 15 at No. 15, rising to No. 1 for three weeks on May 29. It had remained in the Top 200 for twenty-nine weeks by the end of 1982. (Tracks and sleeve same as British release.)

61 (189a) TAKE IT AWAY
(199) I'LL GIVE YOU A RING

By Paul McCartney

Columbia 18-03018 – June 29, 1982

62 (189b) TAKE IT AWAY
(199a) I'LL GIVE YOU A RING/(198a) DRESS ME UP AS A ROBBER
(12-inch single)

Columbia 44-03019 – July 16, 1982

The second singles release from *Tug Of War*, which appeared in both seven-inch and twelve-inch forms, entered the Billboard chart on July 10, rising to No. 10 on August 21 and staying in the chart for sixteen weeks.

63 (188a) TUG OF WAR
(196a) GET IT

"A" side by Paul McCartney

"B" side by Paul McCartney and Carl Perkins

Columbia 38-03235 – September 14, 1982

The third release from the *Tug Of War* album, the title track entered the Billboard charts on October 2, peaking at No. 55 on October 23, and remaining in the chart for eight weeks.

THE GIRL IS MINE
CAN'T GET OUT OF THE RAIN

"A" side by Michael Jackson/Paul McCartney

"B" side by Michael Jackson

Epic 34-03288 – October 3, 1982

McCartney's first collaboration with Michael Jackson entered the Billboard chart on November 6 at No. 45; it rose to No. 2 for three weeks from January 8, 1983, and remained in the Top 40 for fourteen weeks.

George Harrison's Wonderwall Music.
An Apple LP. (Apcor 1 Mono Sapcor 1 Stereo)

GEORGE HARRISON

1 WONDERWALL MUSIC

Apple SAPCOR 1 – November 1, 1968

The first solo release by a Beatle, *Wonderwall Music* was the soundtrack album to Joe Mussot's film, *Wonderwall* (1969), starring Jack MacGowran, Jane Birkin, Irene Handl, Richard Wattis, Beatrix Lehmann and Iain Quarrier. The album did not enter the British album charts, and was one of the first Beatle solo albums to be deleted in Britain.

The album was recorded in London in December 1967 (English titles) and at EMI Studios, Bombay, India, between June 9 and 15, 1968, (Indian titles) – during the same sessions which produced the Beatles' *The Inner Light*.

For the London sessions, George used the following musicians: John Barham/piano and flugelhorn; Tommy Reilly/harmonica; Colin Manley/guitar and steel guitar; Edward Antony (Tony) Ashton/jangle piano and organ; Philip Rogers/bass; and Roy Dyke/drums. Reports state that both Ringo and Eric Clapton also assisted with the recordings. Four of the musicians – Colin Manley, Tony Ashton, Roy Dyke and Philip Rogers – comprised the Liverpool group, The Remo Four.

George used the following Indian musicians for the Bombay sessions: Ashish Khan/sarod; Mahapurush Misra/tabla and pakavaj; Sharad and Hanuman Jadev/shanhais; Shambu-Das, Indril Bhattacharya and Shankar Ghosh/sitars; Chandra Shakher/surbahar; Shiv Kumar Shermar/santoor; S. R. Kenkare/flute; Vinaik Vora/thar-shanhai and Rij Ram Desad/harmonium and tablatarang.

The album sleeve was designed by Bob Gill, John Kelly and Alan Aldridge, with the front cover illustration by Bob Gill. The album featured a printed insert credit sheet, and the record catalogue number was originally scheduled as STAP 1 (this number is engraved, but crossed out, on the run-out groove area).

A SIDE

1 **MICROBES** *(3.39)**

2 **RED LADY TOO** *(1.54)*

3 **TABLA AND PAKAVAJ** *(1.04)**

4 **IN THE PARK** *(4.05)**

5 **DRILLING A HOME** *(3.07)*

6 **GURU VANDANA** *(1.03)**

7 **GREASY LEGS** *(1.27)*

8 **SKI-ING** *(1.50)*

9 **GAT KIRWANI** *(1.15)**

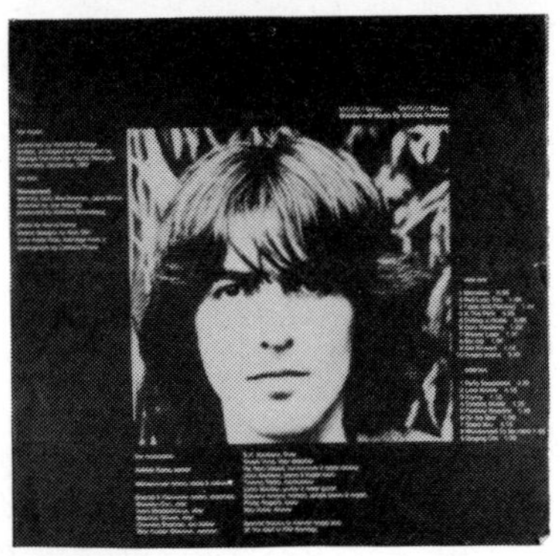

10 **DREAM SCENE** *(5.26)**

B SIDE

11 **PARTY SECOMBE** *(4.32)*

12 **LOVE SCENE** *(4.14)**

13 **CRYING** *(1.12)**

14 **COWBOY MUSIC** *(1.26)*

15 **FANTASY SEQUINS** *(1.48)**

16 **ON THE BED** *(2.17)*

17 **GLASS BOX** *(1.04)**

18 **WONDERWALL TO BE HERE** *(1.22)*

19 **SINGING OM** *(1.52)**

(Titles marked * recorded in India, although *Dream Scene* contains Western instruments.)

The film's director, Joe Massot, a personal friend of George's, invited him to compose the soundtrack for the film. George composed all the music after viewing an unfinished version of the film. He arranged each tune and made home recordings of each theme as an outline for the actual recordings, which he produced using session musicians. However, many of the themes were made up in the studio, with George using the skills of the musicians to develop certain pieces.

2 ELECTRONIC SOUND

Zapple ZAPPLE 02 – May 9, 1969.

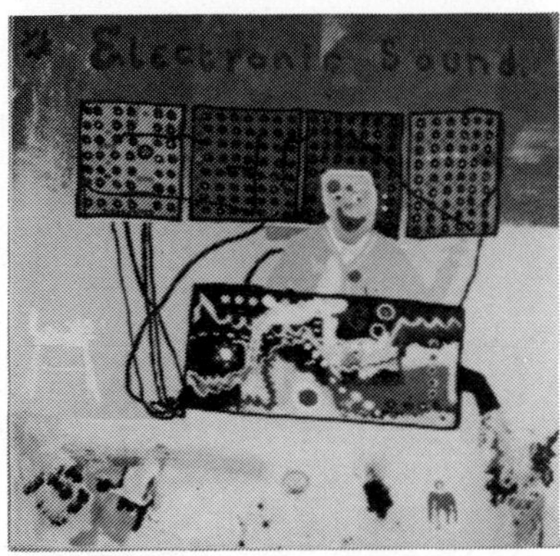

George's second solo album also failed to enter the British charts, being the second (and final) release on Apple's subsidiary label, Zapple. The album featured George playing his newly acquired Moog Synthesizer, and is probably the very first album to contain solely synthesized sounds. The first side was recorded in George's home studio at Esher, in February 1969, while the second side was recorded in California, in November 1968 – supposedly with Bernie Krause assisting. Krause later claimed in print that he had made the recordings, and that George had appropriated them for his album.

The sleeve featured two paintings by George, who is also credited with the sleeve design and production of the album. As with many early Apple records, the inner sleeve contains the album credits, including a quote by a certain Arthur Wax: "There are a lot of people around, making a lot of noise, here's some more." As the album features a collage of synthesized "noise", with no discernible music, this quote seemed very appropriate.

A SIDE

20 **UNDER THE MERSEY WALL** *(18.37)*

B SIDE

21 **NO TIME OR SPACE** *(25.03)*

3 ALL THINGS MUST PASS

Apple STCH 639 – November 27, 1970

George's third solo release and his first to enter the *NME* album charts, which it did on December 23 at No. 11. It rose to No. 1 on January 27, 1971 (by which time sales were approaching 60,000 in Britain). The triple LP, which stayed at No. 1 for seven weeks, was the first three record set to hold the No. 1 spot in Britain, selling for £4 19s 6d (£4.98), which was more than double the price of a normal album at this time. The album stayed in the *NME* Top 30 for twenty-three weeks, selling well over three million globally.

George recorded the album between May and August 1970, mostly at Trident Studios, London, though some sessions took place at EMI Studios, Abbey Road, with George and Phil Spector producing. The album features a star-studded cast of top musicians as follows: drums and percussion/Ringo Starr, Jim Gordon, Alan White and Ginger Baker; bass guitar/Klaus Voorman and Carl Radle; keyboards/Gary Wright, Bobby Whitlock, Billy Preston and Gary Brooker; pedal steel guitar/Pete Drake; guitars/George Harrison, Eric Clapton and Dave Mason; tenor saxophone/Bobby Keyes; trumpet/Jim Price; rhythm guitars and percussion/Badfinger – Tom Evans, Pete Ham, Joey Molland and Mike Gibbons; and tambourine/Mal Evans. As well as singing all lead vocals, George multi-tracked his own voice to provide all backing vocals, dubbing the resultant "choir" the George O'Hara-Smith Singers. Orchestral arrangements were supplied by John Barham.

An interesting side issue is that *All Things Must Pass* saw the recorded debut of Eric Clapton's group, Derek and the Dominoes (Clapton, Whitlock, Radle and Gordon). During the sessions for

George's album, Derek and the Dominoes experimented with the use of Phil Spector as their producer, although very little resulted.

The album package cost around £36,000 to produce, as the inner sleeves and poster were printed in the USA and imported. During late December 1970 and early January 1971, stocks of the album began to dwindle. 250,000 imported sleeves had been impounded by import officials at Heathrow Airport (due to certain printed paper restrictions) and further production of the album was delayed.

The album design and photography was by Tom Wilkes and Barry Feinstein for Camouflage Productions, with the cover photographs of George being taken at his Henley-on-Thames estate. The first and second albums featured a new orange Apple, as opposed to the usual green colour, while the *Apple Jam* third album featured a special label showing an apple jam pot. The inner sleeves for each record, containing song lyrics and credits, were made in purple, grey and green cartridge paper.

RECORD ONE A SIDE

22 **I'D HAVE YOU ANYTIME** *(2.54)*

23 **MY SWEET LORD** *(4.37)*

24 **WAH-WAH** *(5.33)*

25 **ISN'T IT A PITY (version one)** *(7.07)*

RECORD ONE B SIDE

26 **WHAT IS LIFE** *(4.20)*

27 **IF NOT FOR YOU** *(3.27)*

28 **BEHIND THAT LOCKED DOOR** *(3.03)*

29 **LET IT DOWN** *(4.53)*

30 **RUN OF THE MILL** *(2.48)*

RECORD TWO A SIDE

31 **BEWARE OF DARKNESS** *(3.46)*

32 **APPLE SCRUFFS** *(3.02)*

33 **BALLAD OF SIR FRANKIE CRISP (LET IT ROLL)** *(3.45)*

34 **AWAITING ON YOU ALL** *(2.43)*

35 **ALL THINGS MUST PASS** *(3.43)*

RECORD TWO B SIDE

36 **I DIG LOVE** *(4.54)*

37 **ART OF DYING** *(3.35)*

38 **ISN'T IT A PITY (version two)** *(4.43)*

39 **HEAR ME LORD** *(5.43)*

RECORD THREE "APPLE JAM" A SIDE

40 **OUT OF THE BLUE** *(11.12)*

41 **IT'S JOHNNY'S BIRTHDAY** *(0.49)*

42 **PLUG ME IN** *(3.17)*

RECORD THREE B SIDE

43 **I REMEMBER JEEP** *(8.04)*

44 **THANKS FOR THE PEPPERONI** *(5.28)*

Of the eighteen songs on Records One and Two, George composed sixteen, mostly during 1969. *I'd Have You Anytime* was written jointly with Bob Dylan at his home in Woodstock, New York, during November 1968; *If Not For You* was a Bob Dylan composition from 1968, which George first heard when visiting Dylan. *My Sweet Lord* was inspired by *Oh Happy Day* from the Edwin Hawkins Singers, and was composed during the Delaney and Bonnie tour (on which George guested) of December 1969. George gave *My Sweet Lord* and *All Things Must Pass* to Billy Preston for his *Encouraging Words* album, which George produced and recorded between April and June 1970, before he started to record the songs himself. At one time, *My Sweet Lord* was to be Preston's third Apple single (APPLE 29), for release on September 4, 1969, but was withdrawn, possibly as a result of George recording the number himself.

Wah-Wah was written in January 1969, during the *Let It Be* rehearsal sessions, when George walked out after a disagreement with Paul. *What Is Life* was written for Billy Preston on the way to Olympic Studios, London, when George was producing his album, *Encouraging Words;* Preston never recorded the song, however, as George later realised it was not suited to Billy's style. The song was later recorded by Olivia Newton-John, becoming her third Top 30 hit and entering the *NME* charts on March 15, 1972, at No. 25. It rose to No. 14 on March 29 and stayed in the chart for seven weeks. (Olivia Newton-John's first hit single was *If Not For You*, which she recorded after George had covered it on *All Things Must Pass*; she took it to No. 6 on April 14, 1971, after it entered on March 17, at No. 26 – the start of a stay in the charts lasting nine weeks.)

Apple Scruffs is George's affectionate tribute to the legendary fans who daily congregated outside any building that housed a Beatle. Whenever the Beatles were busy recording at Abbey Road – or any other studio – a horde of die-hard fans would collect outside the studio day

'Z' is for Zapple.

Introducing Zapple, a new label from Apple Records.

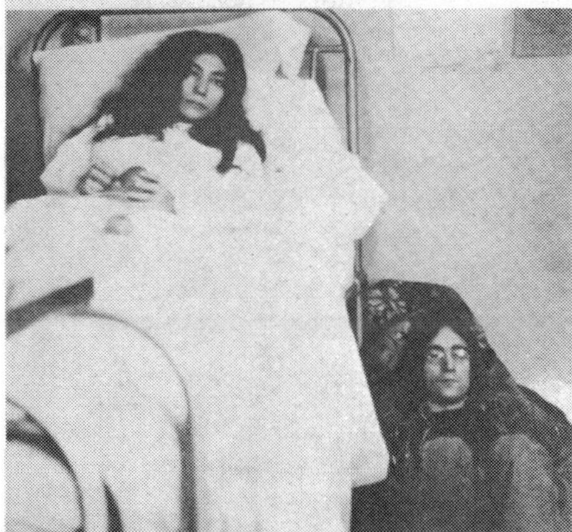

John Lennon/Yoko Ono: (Zapple 01) 'Life with the Lions: Unfinished Music No. 2.'

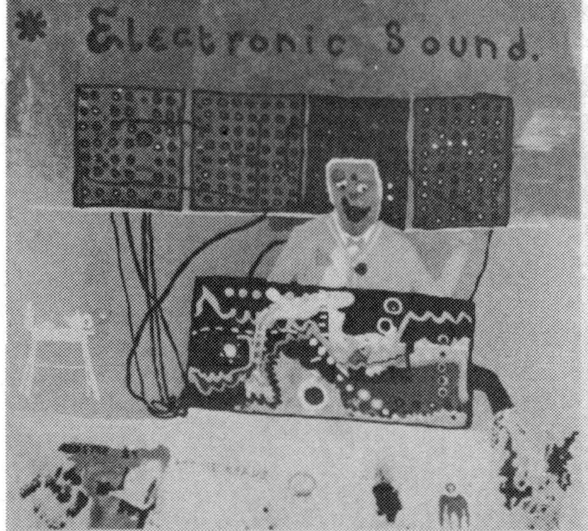

George Harrison: (Zapple 02) 'Electronic Sounds.'

I'm interested in 'Zapple'. I'd like to know where my nearest stockist is. Also, could you please let me know what you'll be up to next before you get up to it.

Name...

Address..

....

....

Send this coupon to JACK OLIVER (ZAPPLE) APPLE RECORDS 3 SAVILE ROW, LONDON W.1.

NME

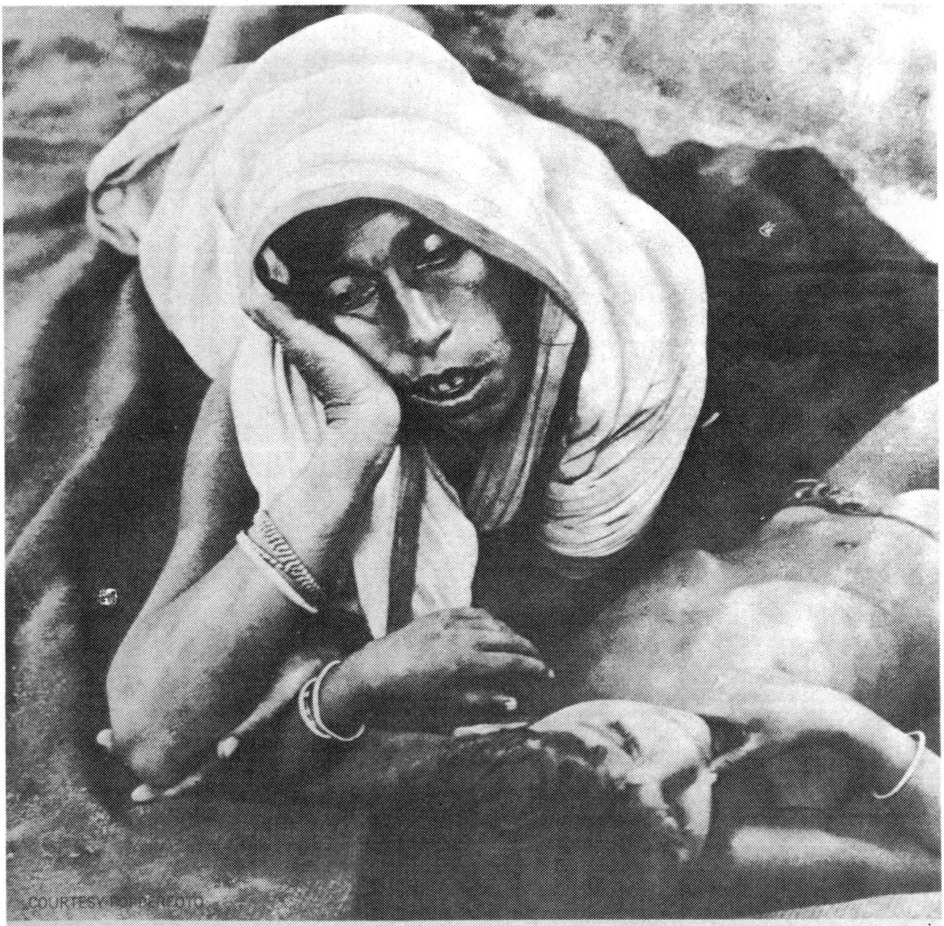

COURTESY POPPERFOTO

Contributions for the benefit of the Homeless Children of Bangla-Desh can be sent to:
The George Harrison-Ravi Shankar Special Emergency Relief Fund for Displaced People of Bangla-Desh.
c/o UNICEF, United Nations, N.Y. City

(we've got to relieve)

BANGLA DESH

george harrison

and night, waiting for their idols to emerge. The main meeting point was outside the Apple Offices in Savile Row, in the centre of London's West End, and therefore an easy target for visiting Beatles' fans. After George had recorded the song, he invited the waiting Apple Scruffs into the studio for a special preview hearing.

Sir Frankie Crisp was a Victorian architect and lawyer, who originally designed and built George's castle in Henley. *All Things Must Pass* was written in 1968; it was originally recorded by the Beatles during the *Let It Be* rehearsals, though the recording was never finished (being only a rough demo version). George wrote *The Art Of Dying* in 1966, but never considered it for the Beatles as he thought the theme too "way-out".

The third album of the set features five tracks recorded during the sessions for the first two records, each tune being improvised by the musicians present. *It's Johnny's Birthday*, however, uses the tune of *Congratulations*, by Bill Martin and Phil Coulter, who later claimed royalties (and received them). Each tune is credited to the musicians playing on each number: *Out Of The Blue* features Jim Gordon/drums; Carl Radle/bass; Bobby Whitlock/piano; Eric Clapton/guitar; Gary Wright/organ; George Harrison/guitar; Jim Price/trumpet; Bobby Keyes/saxophone; and journalist Al Aronowitz/?. *It's Johnny's Birthday* features George, Mal Evans and Eddie Klein.

Both *Plug Me In* and *Thanks For The Pepperoni* feature Jim Gordon/drums; Carl Radle/bass; Bobby Whitlock/piano; and three electric guitars played by Eric Clapton, Dave Mason and George. *I Remember Jeep* features a slightly different line-up from that used on the other "jam" tracks: Ginger Baker/drums; Klaus Voorman/bass; Billy Preston/piano; Eric Clapton/guitar; and George/Moog Synthesizer. "Jeep" was in fact a dog belonging to Eric Clapton; the dog was apparently stolen around this time.

4 (23a) MY SWEET LORD *(4.37)* (26a) WHAT IS LIFE *(4.20)*

Apple R 5884 – January 15, 1971

George's first solo single entered the *NME* Top 30 on January 20 at No. 14, rising to No. 1 the following week on January 27. By January 30, after two weeks on sale, the single had sold 250,000 in Britain alone, and by February 9 had passed the half million mark (556,485 to be exact) – keeping it at No. 1 for six

weeks. By the end of February it had sold over 700,000, becoming the top-selling single in Britain in 1971. The record is the third best-selling single by an ex-Beatle, being topped by *Mull Of Kintyre* and *Imagine* in Britain, with sales approaching the million mark.

World sales of the single by February 9, 1971, were between three and four million (being estimated at over five million to date). As well as becoming a chart topper in Britain and America, the single also reached No. 1 in Australia, Austria, Brazil, France, Germany, Mexico, Norway, Singapore, Spain, Sweden and Switzerland.

The release of the single was originally announced by Harrison on October 23, 1970, for November, but three days later George changed his mind, and the single was withdrawn. George stated that he didn't want the single to detract from the impact of the *All Things Must Pass* album. After the release of the album, disc jockeys were continually playing *My Sweet Lord*, and public demand forced the single to be finally released on January 15, 1971, in Britain.

In March 1971, the American publisher of *He's So Fine* instituted legal action against Harrison and Apple, on the basis that *My Sweet Lord* was an unauthorised plagiarism of their single by The Chiffons. This was the start of a long and tortuous court battle between Harrison and Bright Tunes (the American publishers), which was finally resolved in 1976 when Harrison lost the case, and paid compensation of $587,000 to Bright Tunes, somewhat ironically then owned by Allen Klein.

My Sweet Lord features Ringo/drums; Klaus Voorman/bass; Gary Wright/piano; Badfinger and George/guitars; and steel guitar by Pete Drake, who was flown over from the States at a cost of $10,000 to play on the *All Things Must Pass* album.

5 (45) BANGLA DESH *(3.55)* (46) DEEP BLUE *(3.40)*

Apple R 5912 – July 30, 1971

George's song for the people of Bangla Desh, which entered the *NME* charts on

August 18 at No. 16, rising to No. 10 for two weeks on August 23, and staying in the chart for seven weeks.

George composed *Bangla Desh* after Ravi Shankar had approached him to aid the starving refugees of his homeland by organising a charity concert. The song was written as a prelude to the concerts and was recorded during July 1971. The "B" side of the single, which does not appear on any other Harrison record, was written by George after his mother died of a terminal disease during the recording of *All Things Must Pass*. Both tracks were produced by Phil Spector and George.

6 THE CONCERT FOR BANGLA DESH

Apple STCX 3385 – January 7, 1972

George's second triple boxed set entered the *NME* album charts on January 19 at No. 6, rising to No. 4 the following week where it remained for two weeks. It stayed in the charts altogether for ten weeks.

With millions starving and suffering from disease in his home country, Ravi Shankar approached George Harrison to assist him in organising a benefit concert to aid UNICEF in their relief of refugee children in Bangla Desh. In a matter of five or six weeks, George had invited several top stars to donate their services, including John, Paul and Ringo. Only Ringo accepted the offer. Paul refused because he didn't consider the time right for a Beatles reunion; John initially agreed but later declined when he realised that the invitation did not extend to Yoko. The concert was staged on August 1, 1971, at Madison Square Gardens, New York, with an afternoon and evening show. The concerts were recorded via forty-four microphones, using a Wally Heider sixteen-track machine from the Record Plant, controlled by Phil Spector. The resultant tape was mixed by Spector and produced by Harrison and Spector.

The concerts raised $243,418.50 for the charity. A cheque for that sum was sent by Madison Square Gardens Center Inc. to UNICEF on August 12, 1971, with total proceeds from the concerts, film and album raising over fifteen million dollars. Unfortunately only a small amount of this figure ever got to Bangla Desh, as legal problems with various record companies and US revenue tied the money up for years. Ravi Shankar and George received *The Child Is The Father Of Man* award from UNICEF on June 5, 1972.

The album design was by Barry Feinstein and Tom Wilkes for Camouflage Productions, with photography by Barry Feinstein, Tom Wilkes and Alan Pariser. The brown box included a sixty-four page full colour booklet, featuring pictures taken at the concerts, printed in the USA. With an elaborate package, the album retailed for £5.50, which George thought was too high.

RECORD ONE A SIDE

Introductions by George Harrison and Ravi Shankar

BANGLA DHUN *(16.27)*

RECORD ONE B SIDE

47 **WAH-WAH** *(3.19)*

48 **MY SWEET LORD** *(4.19)*

49 **AWAITING ON YOU ALL** *(2.36)*

THAT'S THE WAY GOD PLANNED IT *(4.06)*

RECORD TWO A SIDE

IT DON'T COME EASY *(2.38)*

50

BEWARE OF DARKNESS *(3.26)*

Introduction of band by George

51 **WHILE MY GUITAR GENTLY WEEPS** *(4.38)*

RECORD TWO B SIDE

JUMPIN' JACK FLASH/YOUNGBLOOD *(9.08)*

52 **HERE COMES THE SUN** *(2.50)*

RECORD THREE A SIDE

A HARD RAIN'S GONNA FALL *(5.14)*

IT TAKES A LOT TO LAUGH/IT TAKES A TRAIN TO CRY *(2.53)*

BLOWIN' IN THE WIND *(3.34)*

MR. TAMBOURINE MAN *(4.10)*

GIVE ME LOVE
(Give Me Peace On Earth)

George Harrison.

Apple
R.5988 EMI

JUST LIKE A WOMAN *(4.35)*

RECORD THREE B SIDE

53 **SOMETHING** *(3.03)*

54 **BANGLA DESH** *(4.26)*

The concert started with an introduction from George – who received a standing ovation from the 20,000 concert-goers – followed by Ravi Shankar introducing his Indian music section. This featured a long raga written by Shankar, called Bangla Dhun. The piece was performed by Ravi Shankar/sitar; Ali Akbar Khan/sarod; Alla Rakha/tabla; and Kamala Chakravarty/tamboura.

For the second part of the concert, George was backed by a twenty-five piece back-up band, constituting the "Greatest Rock Spectacle of the Decade" (*NME*: August 7, 1971). The Bangla Desh band consisted of: George, Eric Clapton and Jesse Ed Davis/ guitars; Pete Ham, Tom Evans and Joey Molland/acoustic guitars; Mike Gibbons/percussion; Billy Preston/organ; Leon Russell/piano; Jim Horn, Chuck Findley, and Ollie Mitchell/horns; Carl Radle and Klaus Voorman/bass; Ringo Starr and Jim Keltner/drums; with backing vocals supplied by a chorus line of Alan Beutler, Marlin Greene, Jeanie Greene, Jo Green, Dolores Hall, Jackie Kelso, Claudia Lennear, Lou McCreary, Don Nix and Don Preston.

George takes the vocal spotlight on the first three numbers, while on *That's The Way God Planned It* Billy Preston sings his 1969 Apple hit. *It Don't Come Easy* features Ringo singing, although at times he forgets his own lyrics and mumbles through the song. On *Beware Of Darkness* George sings lead, with Leon Russell soloing on one verse, and Jim Horn supplying the saxophone.

While My Guitar Gently Weeps features the twin guitars of George and Eric, with George singing. For the *Jumpin' Jack Flash/Youngblood* medley Leon Russell sings solo lead vocal on the former song, being joined by Don Preston on the latter. *Jumpin' Jack Flash* also features Carl Radle on bass, and Don Preston on lead guitar.

Here Comes The Sun features the acoustic guitars of George and Badfinger's Pete Ham, with vocals by George. For Bob Dylan's five tracks, only four artists performed on stage: Dylan playing harmonica and acoustic guitar, Leon Russell on bass, George on electric guitar and Ringo on tambourine. For the last Dylan song, *Just Like A Woman*, Leon and George assisted on vocals. The last two songs – both sung by George – featured the full band, with Jim Horn supplying saxophone on *Bangla Desh*.

7 (55) GIVE ME LOVE (GIVE ME PEACE ON EARTH) *(3.32)* (56) MISS O'DELL *(2.26)*

Apple R 5988 – May 25, 1973

George's first single for nearly two years entered the *NME* charts on June 5 at No. 17, rising to No. 8 on July 3, and staying in the chart for eight weeks. It was George's last hit single (according to the *NME* chart) for eight years – until 1981 and *All Those Years Ago*. *Give Me Love* was from the *Living In The Material World* album, recorded between January and April 1973. *Miss O'Dell* was written by George in Los Angeles in April 1971 about Chris O'Dell, who worked for Apple. The song was recorded several times and George picked the most humorous version for the single, which does not appear on any other Harrison record. The single was produced by George and did not appear in a picture sleeve.

8 LIVING IN THE MATERIAL WORLD

Apple PAS 10006 – June 21, 1973

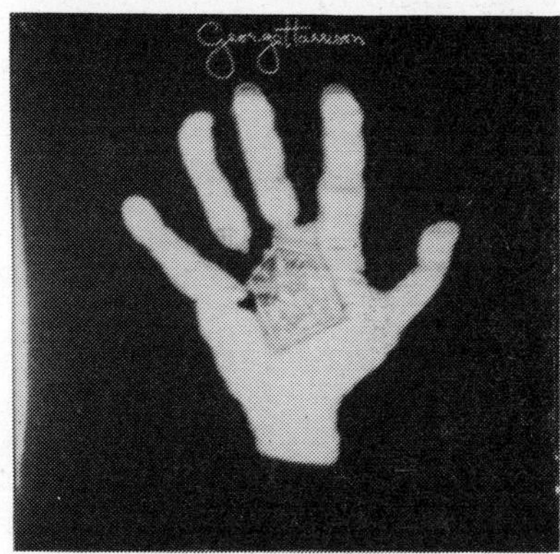

Living In The Material World entered the *NME* album charts on June 26 at No. 8, rising to No. 3 on July 24 and staying in the chart for eight weeks. The album has sold over three million globally.

The album was mostly recorded between January and April 1973 at the Apple Studios, 3 Savile Row, London, with George producing. The backing track for *Try Some, Buy Some* was recorded in late February 1971, with George and Phil Spector producing. The album was recorded with the following musicians: Nicky Hopkins and Gary Wright/keyboards; Klaus Voorman/bass; Jim Keltner and Ringo Starr/drums (Jim Gordon on *Try*

Some Buy Some); George/guitar; Jim Horn/saxophone and flutes; Zakir Hussein/tabla; with John Barham supplying strings.

The elaborately packaged album featured a gatefold sleeve, with design by Wilkes & Braun Inc., and included a four-page insert of song lyrics. The front cover photograph was taken at George's Henley home by Ken Marcus and features George toasting the musicians heard on the album: (left to right) Gary Wright, Jim Horn, Klaus Voorman, Nicky Hopkins, Jim Keltner and Ringo. The record label does not feature the usual green apple; there are two extracts from photographs on the sleeve, and the run-out groove area features two messages: "HARE KRSNA" and "HARE RAMA".

A SIDE

55a **GIVE ME LOVE (GIVE ME PEACE ON EARTH)** *(3.32)*

57 **SUE ME SUE YOU BLUES** *(4.38)*

58 **THE LIGHT THAT HAS LIGHTED THE WORLD** *(3.26)*

59 **DON'T LET ME WAIT TOO LONG** *(2.52)*

60 **WHO CAN SEE IT** *(3.48)*

61 **LIVING IN THE MATERIAL WORLD** *(5.26)*

B SIDE

62 **THE LORD LOVES THE ONE (THAT LOVES THE LORD)***(4.30)*

63 **BE HERE NOW** *(4.04)*

64 **TRY SOME BUY SOME** *(4.02)*

65 **THE DAY THE WORLD GETS 'ROUND** *(2.48)*

66 **THAT IS ALL** *(3.38)*

All songs on the album were written and sung by George, with *Sue Me Sue You Blues* being written during the period at Apple when Paul was suing the other Beatles. *The Light That Has Lighted The World* originally started as the "B" side to Cilla Black's record, *When Every Song Is Sung*, which was never completed. *Living In The Material World* includes references to John, Paul and Ringo. *Be Here Now* was written in Nichols Canyon, Los Angeles, in April 1971. *Try Some Buy Some* was originally written for Ronnie Spector, Phil's wife. It was recorded in February 1971, with Spector producing and resulted in a single which unfortunately flopped. George liked the song so much that he removed Ronnie's vocals from the recording, slowed the tempo down, and overdubbed his own vocals onto the instrumental track. *The Day The World Gets 'Round* was written the day after the Bangla Desh concert, on August 2, 1971. The majority of the songs were inspired by George's religious beliefs.

9 (67) DING DONG *(3.36)* (68) I DON'T CARE ANYMORE *(2.36)*

Apple R 6002 – December 6, 1974

George's fourth single, and the first not to enter the *NME* Top 30 (although it did manage five weeks in the BMRB chart, rising to No. 38 after entering on December 21, 1974). *Ding Dong* was recorded between September and October 1974, and was inspired by engravings on the walls of George's Henley home – built by Sir Frankie Crisp. The "B" side, *I Don't Care Anymore*, probably refers to George's troubles with the *He's So Fine/My Sweet Lord* lawsuit, and does not appear on any other Harrison release.

10 DARK HORSE

Apple PAS 10008 – December 20, 1974

As with the single, *Ding Dong*, the album *Dark Horse* failed to enter the *NME* charts. The album was recorded and produced by George at F.P.S.H.O.T. Studios in England and A&M Studios, Los Angeles, during September and October 1974. F.P.S.H.O.T. stands for "Friars Park Studio Henley-On-Thames" – George's home recording studio. The album was hurriedly recorded for completion before George's first solo Tour of America during November and December 1974; as he was suffering from laryngitis at that point, the vocals at times sound strained.

To record the album, George used over twenty musicians including: guitars/Robben Ford (*Hari's On Tour, Simply Shady* & *Dark Horse*), Eric Clapton (*Bye Bye Love*), Mick Jones (*Ding Dong*), Alvin

LIVING IN THE MATERIAL WORLD

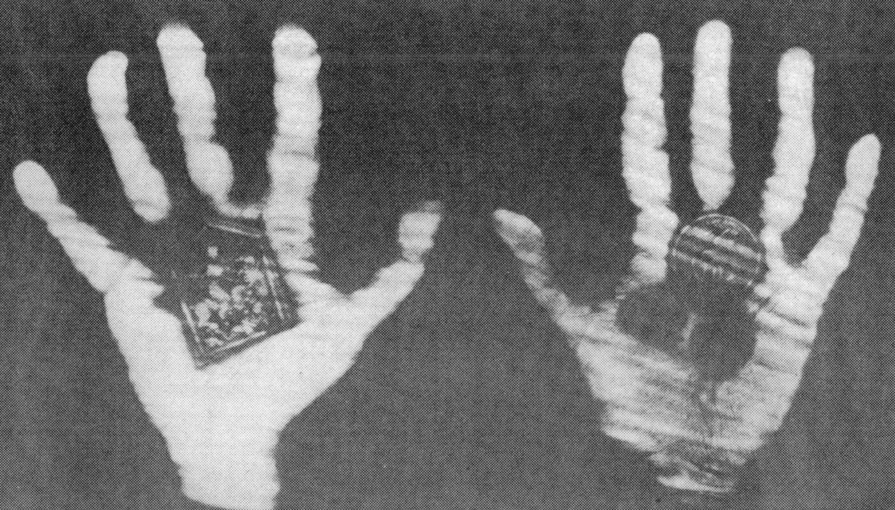

George Harrison

APPLE ALBUM PAS 10006
Also available on cassette and cartridge

Lee (*Ding Dong*) and Ron Wood (*Ding Dong*); bass/Max Bennett (*Hari's On Tour* & *Simply Shady*), Willie Weeks (*So Sad, Maya Love, Dark Horse, Far East Man* & *It Is He*) and Klaus Voorman (*Ding Dong*); drums/John Guerin (*Hari's On Tour* & *Simply Shady*), Ringo Starr (*So Sad* & *Ding Dong*), Jim Keltner (*So Sad, Ding Dong* & hi hat on *Dark Horse*) and Andy Newmark (*Maya Love, Dark Horse, Far East Man* & *It Is He*); piano/Roger Kennaway (*Hari's On Tour* & *Simply Shady*), Nicky Hopkins (*So Sad*) and Billy Preston (*It Is He*); electric piano/Billy Preston (*Maya Love, Dark Horse* and *Far East Man*); horns/Tom Scott (*Hari's On Tour, Maya Love, Ding Dong* & *Far East Man*); flutes/Chuck Findley, Jim Horn and Tom Scott (*Dark Horse* & *It Is He*) and Emil Richards (wobble board on *It Is He* and crochet on *Dark Horse*); while backing vocals were supplied by Patti Clapton on *Bye Bye Love* and by Lon and Derrek Van Eaton on *Dark Horse*.

The album appeared in a gatefold sleeve, with design by Tom Wilkes and photography by Terry Doran, George's assistant. The label photographs of George and Olivia Arias (who later became George's second wife) were taken by Henry Grossman. The front cover shows George's school photograph, while the inner and back cover pictures were taken in the gardens of George's Friar Park estate (the inner picture supposedly shows George walking with the late Peter Sellers). The album inner sleeve included song credits, while a single leaf insert contained the song lyrics. For the British release, EMI must have used the American master (as the American catalogue number, SMAS 1 – 3418, is engraved on the run-out groove area of the record).

A SIDE

69 **HARI'S ON TOUR (EXPRESS)** *(4.40)*

70 **SIMPLY SHADY** *(4.35)*

71 **SO SAD** *(4.57)*

72 **BYE BYE LOVE** *(4.02)*

73 **MAYA LOVE** *(4.19)*

B SIDE

67a **DING DONG DING DONG** *(3.38)*

74 **DARK HORSE** *(3.52)*

75 **FAR EAST MAN** *(5.48)*

76 **IT IS "HE"** *(4.43)*

George composed all the songs, except *Bye Bye Love* – written by Felice and Boudleaux Bryant, with amended lyrics by George – and *Far East Man*, with words by George and music by George and Ron Wood. *Simply Shady* was written in Bombay, India, about George's split with his first wife, Patti, who sings backing vocals on the next song, *Bye Bye Love*, with amended lyrics to refer to Patti's elopement with Eric Clapton, who plays lead guitar on the track. George's re-written lyrics to the song mention both Patti ("our lady") and Clapton ("old 'Clapper"). During 1974, George decided he needed a name for his publishing and record companies. His business manager, Dennis O'Brien, suggested that he use one of his song titles – George had just written *Dark Horse*, which he had recorded "live" in America, using his backing band, during rehearsals for his American tour. *Far East Man* was written for Ronnie Wood's album, *I've Got My Own Album To Do*, and was inspired by a T-shirt worn by Ronnie after the Faces Far East Tour. George later altered the lyrics and arrangement for his own album. *It Is "He"* was inspired by George's experiences at Brindabin in India.

11 **(74a) DARK HORSE** *(3.51)* **(69a) HARI'S ON TOUR (EXPRESS)** *(4.40)*

Apple R 6001 – February 28, 1975

Although appearing in a printed sleeve – showing the song lyrics – *Dark Horse* failed to enter the *NME* charts or the BMRB Top 75. This single and *Ding Dong* were released out of sequence, as *Dark*

Horse has a lower Parlophone catalogue number than the former single.

12 (77) YOU *(3.39)* (78) WORLD OF STONE *(4.37)*

Apple R 6007 – September 12, 1975

Released in a full colour picture sleeve, *You* did not enter the *NME* Top 30, but it did reach No. 38 in the BMRB charts, where it was listed for five weeks after entering on October 11, 1975. The single was lifted from the forthcoming album, *Extra Texture*, and features an "Extra Texture" label, including the "Apple core" logo. The run-out groove areas of the record feature two "messages" from George Peckham, the notable cutting engineer, with "A PORKY PRIME CUT" on the "A" side, and "PECKO" on the "B" side.

13 EXTRA TEXTURE (Read All About It)

Apple PAS 10009 – September 9, 1975

George's last album for Apple, which entered the *NME* charts for two separate weeks on October 14 at No. 25, and October 25 at No. 22. Most of the album was recorded at A&M Studios, Los Angeles, between May and June 1975, with George producing, and Norman Kinney engineering. A host of well-known musicians helped George to record the album, including: drums/Jim Gordon (*You*), Andy Newmark (*His Name Is Legs*) and Jim Keltner (all tracks except *Legs*); percussion/Jim Keltner (*Tired Of Midnight Blue*), Norman Kinney (*The Answer's At The End*); bass/Carl Radle (*You*), Paul Stallworth (*The Answer's At The End, Tired Of Midnight Blue*, also backing vocals on *Can't Stop Thinking About You*), Klaus Voorman (*Ooh Baby, World Of Stone* & *Can't Stop Thinking About You*) and Willie Weeks (*His Name Is Legs*); keyboards/Leon Russell (piano/*You* and *Tired Of Midnight Blue*), David Foster (piano/*The Answer's At The End, This Guitar Can't Keep From Crying, World Of Stone, Grey Cloudy Lies* & *His Name Is Legs*, electric piano/*Can't Stop Thinking About You*, organ/*You* and string arrangements/*The Answer's At The End, This Guitar, World Of Stone* and *Can't Stop Thinking About You*), Nicky Hopkins (piano/*Can't Stop Thinking About You*), Billy Preston (piano/*His Name Is Legs*) and Gary Wright (electric piano/*You* & *Ooh Baby*, organ/*The Answer's At The End* & *World Of Stone* & ARP Strings/*This Guitar* & *Can't Stop Thinking About You*); saxophone/Jim Horn (*You*); horns/Jim Horn & Chuck Findley (*Ooh Baby* & *His Name Is Legs*); guitars/Jesse Ed Davis (*This Guitar, Ooh Baby, World Of Stone, Can't Stop Thinking About You* & *Grey Cloudy Lies*). George himself played a variety of instruments including guitar (all tracks), acoustic guitar (*This Guitar*), ARP Bass (*This Guitar*), ARP (*Grey Cloudy Lies*), Bass Moog (*Grey Cloudy Lies*) and piano (*His Name Is Legs*).

After the elaborate packaging of his previous albums, *Extra Texture* (the title was suggested by bass player, Paul Stallworth) was relatively sombre, boasting only a "blocked" textured finish, and a printed inner sleeve containing the legend "OHNOTHIMAGEN" (Oh no not him again). This referred to George's many production credits – he had been producing a host of artists over the past years and his name seemed to appear on nearly every other album released. The album was designed by Roy Kohara, with photographs by Henry Grossman. The special "Extra Texture" label features the partly eaten apple core, signifying the end of Apple. George Peckham mastered the album, leaving his trademark behind – on the "A" side run-out groove area appears "A PORKY/TONE PRIME CUT" with a message to George H. from George P. on the "B" side: "OOH GEORGE, YOU'RE SUCH A DARK HORSE LUV GEORGE".

George Harrison

a new single

"YOU" R 6007

from his forthcoming album

EXTRA TEXTURE

(Read All About It)

George Harrison

EXTRA TEXTURE

DAVID HAMILTON'S RECORD OF THE WEEK RADIO 1 This Week

... OHNOTHIMAGEN ...

Marketed by EMI Records Limited, 20, Manchester Square, London W1A 1ES.

A SIDE

77a **YOU** *(3.38)*

79 **THE ANSWER'S AT THE END** *(5.29)*

80 **THIS GUITAR (CAN'T KEEP FROM CRYING)** *(4.04)*

81 **OOH BABY (YOU KNOW THAT I LOVE YOU)** *(3.58)*

78a **WORLD OF STONE** *(4.38)*

B SIDE

82 **A BIT MORE OF YOU** *(0.45)*

83 **CAN'T STOP THINKING ABOUT YOU** *(4.29)*

84 **TIRED OF MIDNIGHT BLUE** *(4.51)*

85 **GREY CLOUDY LIES** *(3.39)*

86 **HIS NAME IS LEGS (LADIES AND GENTLEMEN)** *(5.44)*

George composed all ten songs on the album, and sings all lead vocals. *You* was another track left over from the Ronnie Spector sessions of February 1971, although Ronnie never added her vocals to the instrumental track, which George used for this album. *The Answer's At The End* was inspired by Sir Frankie Crisp's writing on the walls of George's Henley estate. *This Guitar* – the continuation of *While My Guitar Gently Weeps* – was written while George was on holiday in Hawaii. George wrote *Tired Of Midnight Blue* after visiting a seedy Los Angeles club. *His Name Is Legs* was written about "Legs" Larry Smith, ex of the Bonzo Dog Band, who is featured as guest vocalist.

14 (80a) THIS GUITAR (CAN'T KEEP FROM CRYING) *(3.45)* (73a) MAYA LOVE *(4.19)*

Apple R 6012 – February 6, 1976

George's last single on the Apple label, and also the last Beatles solo record to be released on Apple (disregarding the reissue of *My Sweet Lord*), did not enjoy any chart success in Britain. *This Guitar* was lifted from *Extra Texture*, while *Maya Love* was taken from the *Dark Horse* album. The single did not appear in a picture sleeve. George Peckham mastered the record leaving the legend "A PORKY PRIME CUT" on the "A" side run-out groove, and on the "B" side another message to George: "ONOTHIMAGEN YERRITIZ LA!"

15 (87) THIS SONG *(3.50)* (88) LEARNING HOW TO LOVE YOU *(4.10)*

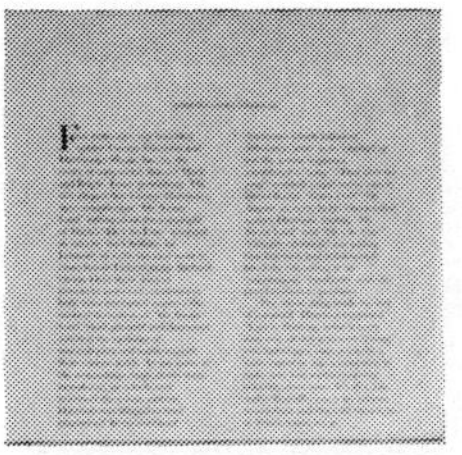

Dark Horse K 16856 – November 19, 1976

George's first single for his own Dark Horse label was released simultaneously with the album on which it was included, *Thirty Three & ⅓*, and again George had no chart success. *This Song* was George's "tongue in cheek" statement about the *My Sweet Lord/He's So Fine* copyright suit, filed in 1971 by the estate of Ronald Mack and Bright Tunes Publishing against George and Harrisongs Music Inc. The protracted case made George so cautious that he was afraid of writing any more songs. He composed *This Song* to explain his fears:

"This song has nothing tricky about it,
This song ain't black or white as far as I know,
Don't infringe on anyone's copyright so..."

George also managed to include a reference to Bright Tunes, the publishers of *He's So Fine*:

"This tune has nothing Bright about it..."

(Copyright © 1976 Ganga Publishing B.V. All Rights Reserved. Use by Permission. International copyright secured.)

The talking in the middle of the song was courtesy of George's Monty Python friend, Eric Idle.

The single was released in a "picture" sleeve, which reprinted the lyrics and the story behind George's reason for writing the song. The single was mastered by George Peckham, having "A PORKY PRIME CUT" on the "A" side run-out groove, and "PECKO" on the "B" side.

16 THIRTY THREE & ⅓

Dark Horse K 56319 – November 19, 1976

George's first album for his own Dark Horse label, which entered the *NME* charts for one week only at No. 25, on January 8, 1977. When George started his Dark Horse Records company in 1974, the distribution deal with A&M Records included an agreement that Harrison's

first Dark Horse album would be completed ready to be released as soon as his Apple contract expired in June 1976. During the spring of 1976, George was seriously ill with hepatitis and was unable to complete the required album, which A&M had scheduled for June 25, 1976 (this date being George's 33⅓ birthday). After recovering from his illness, George found himself being sued by A&M Records to the tune of ten million dollars for failing to deliver the proposed album. Many people realised that A&M were using the opportunity to drop their option on an artist and label which seemed commercially viable no longer. Harrison's record sales had been surprisingly low over the last few years compared to his fellow ex-Beatles, and none of the Dark Horse artists – Splinter, Jiva, Attitudes, Stairsteps, Henry McCullough and Ravi Shankar – had established any lasting commercial success. After the case was settled, George looked for another label, and found Warner Brothers only too willing to distribute his label. George completed the album, which was recorded at his home studio, F.P.S.H.O.T., during the summer of 1976, and it was released through Warner Brothers on November 19, 1976.

The album was produced by George with Tom Scott assisting, using the following musicians: Tom Scott/saxophones, flute and lyricon; Willie Weeks/bass; Alvin Taylor/drums; Gary Wright/keyboards; Richard Tee/piano, organ and Fender Rhodes; Billy Preston/piano, organ and synthesizer (*Beautiful Girl*, *This Song* and *See Yourself*); David Foster/Fender Rhodes and clavinet; Emil Richards/marimba; and George/guitar, synthesizers and percussion, with George supplying all vocals.

The gatefold album sleeve was designed by Bob Cato, who also took the photographs of George and the other musicians in George's Friar Park grounds. The album was deleted in late 1979, but re-released by Warners on January 23, 1981, with the same catalogue number.

A SIDE

89 **WOMAN DON'T YOU CRY FOR ME** *(3.15)*

90 **DEAR ONE** *(5.08)*

91 **BEAUTIFUL GIRL** *(3.38)*

87a **THIS SONG** *(4.11)*

92 **SEE YOURSELF** *(2.47)*

B SIDE

93 **IT'S WHAT YOU VALUE** *(5.06)*

94 **TRUE LOVE** *(2.43)*

95 **PURE SMOKEY** *(3.50)*

96 **CRACKERBOX PALACE** *(3.55)*

88a **LEARNING HOW TO LOVE YOU** *(4.12)*

George composed all the songs on the album, except *True Love*, a Cole Porter composition from the 1956 film, *High Society*. It was sung by Bing Crosby and Grace Kelly, who had a million-selling hit with the song, reaching No. 4 in both the US and the UK. *Woman Don't You Cry For Me* was written in December 1969, while George was touring with Delaney and Bonnie and Eric Clapton, in Gothenburg, Sweden. George wrote *Dear One* while in the Virgin Islands in 1976; *Beautiful Girl* was started in 1969, when George was producing Doris Troy's album, with Stephen Stills. George wrote the first verse to the song on a twelve string guitar that Stills had loaned him, and completed the song in 1976.

It's What You Value was written during George's 1974 American Tour, when Jim Keltner required payment of a Mercedes 450SL, instead of money, for his drumming work. *Pure Smokey* was apparently written about Smokey Robinson, and named after one of his albums. *Crackerbox Palace* is the name of the house owned by Lord Buckley in Los Angeles; George wrote the song in 1975 after talking to George Grief, who George likened to Buckley. *Learning How To Love You* was written for Herb Alpert, but George recorded the song himself.

17 THE BEST OF GEORGE HARRISON

Parlophone PAS 10011 – November 20, 1976

Now that George's Apple/Parlophone contract had expired, EMI were left

Read All About It

THE NEW ALBUM BY

George Harrison

INCLUDING HIS LATEST SINGLE **'YOU'** R 6007

PAS 10009
TC-PAS 10009
8X-PAS 10009

Marketed by EMI Records Limited, 20 Manchester Square, London W1A 1ES

with the option to recycle his earlier solo material. Having already released compilations of John's and Ringo's singles material, EMI put together this half group/half solo compilation, without George's involvement. George was very annoyed that EMI had used his earlier Beatles material, rather than drawing from his solo catalogue, seeing the move as an insinuation that his solo material had not yielded sufficient hits. George had suggested a title, as well as song selection for the release, but EMI ignored him. So he disowned the record, which didn't sell anyway (never even entering the charts).

The album sleeve was designed by Cream, with a front cover photograph by Bob Cato, and an inner sleeve photograph by Michael Putland. The record appeared on the black and silver Parlophone label, the first Beatle solo album to do so, and the record contains the inner groove engravings – "A NICKY CUT" on the "A" side and "NICKY W" on the "B" side.

A SIDE (THE BEATLES)

SOMETHING

IF I NEEDED SOMEONE

HERE COMES THE SUN

TAXMAN

THINK FOR YOURSELF

FOR YOU BLUE

WHILE MY GUITAR GENTLY WEEPS

B SIDE (GEORGE HARRISON)

23b MY SWEET LORD *(4.38)*

55b GIVE ME LOVE (GIVE ME PEACE ON EARTH) *(3.32)*

77b YOU *(3.40)*

45a BANGLA DESH *(3.56)*

74b DARK HORSE *(3.51)*

26b WHAT IS LIFE *(5.20)*

18 (23c) MY SWEET LORD *(4.37)*
(26c) WHAT IS LIFE *(4.18)*

Apple R 5884 – December, 1976

To create interest in the *Best Of George Harrison* compilation, EMI re-released *My Sweet Lord* in a new picture sleeve, using the same catalogue number as the original. A new matrix was cut for the "A" side, which is noticeably tracked differently and also features the word "BLAIR" engraved on the run-out groove area. The song publishing credits also differ from the original release, which was "Harrisongs, Essex Int MCPS Briteco NCB"; the re-release simply states "Harrisongs". The single did not re-enter the charts and seemingly failed to generate any interest in the Harrison compilation.

19 (94a) TRUE LOVE *(2.41)*
(95a) PURE SMOKEY *(3.44)*

Dark Horse K 16896 – February 18, 1977

George's second Dark Horse single, and the second release from *Thirty Three & ⅓*, did not enter the singles charts. The single was not available in a picture sleeve, but did appear in the "Dark Horse Records" sleeve.

20 (93a) IT'S WHAT YOU VALUE *(3.49)*
(89a) WOMAN DON'T YOU CRY FOR ME *(3.14)*

Dark Horse K 16967 – June 10, 1977

The third singles release from *Thirty Three & ⅓* did not dent the singles charts, and did not appear in a picture sleeve.

21 GEORGE HARRISON

Dark Horse K 56562 – February 23, 1979

George's first album release in two years, which did not enjoy any chart success. The reason for the delay between albums was that George felt he needed a break from the music business; in 1977 he travelled the world enjoying his new pursuit of Grand Prix motor racing and motor cycling. He also took a break from song writing, though it was his motor racing friends who persuaded him to start writing again when they asked him if he was going to compose a song about their sport.

The album was recorded during 1978 at F.P.S.H.O.T., and produced by George and Russ Titelman, using the following musicians: Andy Newmark/drums; Willie Weeks/bass; Neil Larson/keyboards, mini Moog; Ray Cooper/percussion; Steve Winwood/polymoog, harmonium, mini Moog and backing vocals; Emil Richards/marimba; Gayle Levant/harp; Eric Clapton/guitar intro (*Love Comes To Everyone*); Gary Wright/Oberheim (*If You Believe*) with Del Newman/strings and horn arrangements, and George/guitar, bass (*Faster*), dobro (*Soft-Hearted Hana*) and all vocals and backing vocals. The strings were recorded at AIR Studios, London.

Mike Salisbury designed the album sleeve, and took the cover shots of George, while the inner sleeve, featuring song lyrics, includes a photograph taken by Jeff Bloxham of George with Jackie Stewart.

A SIDE

97 **LOVE COMES TO EVERYONE** *(4.30)*

98 **NOT GUILTY** *(3.28)*

99 **HERE COMES THE MOON** *(4.39)*

100 **SOFT-HEARTED HANA** *(3.59)*

101 **BLOW AWAY** *(3.54)*

B SIDE

102 **FASTER** *(4.39)*

103 **DARK SWEET LADY** *(3.22)*

104 **YOUR LOVE IS FOREVER** *(3.43)*

105 **SOFT TOUCH** *(3.57)*

106 **IF YOU BELIEVE** *(2.50)*

George composed nine of the ten songs on the album and co-wrote the tenth. The music to *Love Comes To Everyone* was composed in 1977, George adding the lyrics in Hawaii in February 1978. *Not Guilty* was written in 1968 (it was recorded by the Beatles during the *White Album* sessions, but never released). *Here Comes The Moon*, the "follow-up" to *Here Comes The Sun*, was written by George whilst in Hawaii, and was inspired by the Hawaiian sunset (or moonrise). *Soft-Hearted Hana* was started in Los Angeles, the lyrics written during February 1978, and was partly recorded in a pub in Henley.

Blow Away was the song George composed for his motor racing friends, who had asked him to write a song for them, and was his first composition after his 1977 break. *Faster* was inspired by Jackie Stewart's book of the same name, and by Niki Lauda's fight to overcome his injuries after a motor racing crash. The racing cars heard at the start of the song were recorded at the beginning of the British Grand Prix in 1978. *Dark Sweet Lady* was written in Hawaii for Olivia Arias, George's second wife. George composed *Soft Touch* whilst in the Virgin Islands, about his son, Dhani. *If You Believe* was co-written by George and Gary Wright on New Year's Day 1978 in England, and finished in Hawaii.

22 (101a) BLOW AWAY *(3.56)* (105a) SOFT TOUCH *(3.50)*

Dark Horse K 17327 – March 2, 1979

George's first singles chart success since October 1975, *Blow Away* entered the BMRB charts on March 10, rising to No. 51 during its five weeks in the lists. The single did not enter the *NME* Top 30, and appeared in a picture sleeve, the tracks being taken from the *George Harrison* album.

23 (97a) LOVE COMES TO EVERYONE *(3.31)*
(100a) SOFT-HEARTED HANA *(3.56)*

Dark Horse K 17284 – May, 1979

The second singles release from *George Harrison*, which did not enter the *NME* charts, nor the BMRB charts, and was not released in a picture sleeve.

A MONUMENT TO BRITISH ROCK
Volume One
(20 Rock/Pop Classics From EMI)

By Various Artists

Harvest EMTV 17 – May 4, 1979

George's first appearance on a compilation album, *A Monument to British Rock* was released in EMI's TV advertised series, and features an edited version of *My Sweet Lord*. (The album also features the Beatles' *Get Back*; see the Beatles British section in *The Long and Winding Road*, page 103, for complete track listing.)

A SIDE TRACK TWO:

23d **MY SWEET LORD** *(3.49)*

24 (102a) FASTER *(4.43)*
(104a) YOUR LOVE IS FOREVER *(3.43)*

Dark Horse K 17423 – July 20, 1979

25 (102b) FASTER *(4.43)*
(104b) YOUR LOVE IS FOREVER *(3.43)*
(Picture disc)

Dark Horse K 17423P – July, 1979

The third single from the *George Harrison* album, and George's first picture disc release, and also the first such release from an ex-Beatle. The single was released to raise money for the Gunnar Nilsson Cancer Fund, George donating all his royalties from the sale of the record to the fund. Unfortunately, this worthy charity could not have benefited greatly from the record, as it failed to enter either the *NME* Top 30 or the BMRB Top 75. (Gunnar Nilsson was a Swedish motor racing ace who died of cancer.)

The picture disc featured a "John Player Special" motor car on the "B" side,

while the "A" side featured pictures of nine motor racing drivers: Juan-Manuel Fangio, Jackie Stewart, Niki Lauda, Jochen Rindt, Jim Clark, Graham Hill, Jody Scheckter, Emerson Fittipaldi and Stirling Moss. The two singles, pressed from the same matrix, were mastered at Strawberry Studio, as were the previous two singles and the *George Harrison* album, all featuring the word "STRAWBERRY" engraved on the run-out groove areas.

26 DARK HORSE

Music For Pleasure MFP 50510 – November 27, 1980

The first re-release of George's material on a budget label, *Dark Horse* appeared with four other "Beatles" releases, *Rock 'n' Roll Music Volumes 1 & 2, Ringo* and *Mind Games.* Since the original album had been deleted for some years, *Dark Horse* was reissued on EMI's budget label, Music For Pleasure, using a re-designed sleeve that utilised the original back cover photograph from the album for the front cover. The musician credits were reproduced on the back cover.

A SIDE

69b **HARI'S ON TOUR (EXPRESS)** *(4.40)*

70a **SIMPLY SHADY** *(4.35)*

71a **SO SAD** *(4.57)*

72a **BYE BYE LOVE** *(4.02)*

73b **MAYA LOVE** *(4.19)*

B SIDE

67b **DING DONG DING DONG** *(3.38)*

74c **DARK HORSE** *(3.52)*

75a **FAR EAST MAN** *(5.48)*

76 **IT IS "HE"** *(4.43)*

THE GUINNESS ALBUM – HITS OF THE 70's

By Various Artists

CBS S CBS 10020 – December 5, 1980

The second compilation album to feature George's best-selling single, *My Sweet Lord.* The double album was released to coincide with the publication of *The Guinness Book Of Hits Of The Seventies* by Jo and Tim Rice, Paul Gambaccini and Mike Read, and features thirty No. 1 and five No. 2 hits, based on the BMRB charts.

RECORD ONE A SIDE

MAGGIE MAY
Rod Stewart

ALL RIGHT NOW
Free

GET IT ON
T. Rex

GONNA MAKE YOU A STAR
David Essex

IN THE SUMMERTIME
Mungo Jerry

I HEAR YOU KNOCKING
Dave Edmunds

CUM ON FEEL THE NOIZE
Slade

BYE BYE BABY
Bay City Rollers

23e **MY SWEET LORD** *(4.34)*
George Harrison

RECORD ONE B SIDE

I'M NOT IN LOVE
10CC

WHEN I NEED YOU
Leo Sayer

THE AIR THAT I BREATHE
The Hollies

SYLVIA'S MOTHER
Dr Hook and The Medicine Show

VINCENT
Don McLean

CLAIRE
Gilbert O'Sullivan

I'D LIKE TO TEACH THE WORLD TO SING (IN PERFECT HARMONY)
The New Seekers

WITHOUT YOU
Nilsson

LOVE ME FOR A REASON
The Osmonds

RECORD TWO A SIDE

NIGHT FEVER
The Bee Gees

YOU'RE THE ONE THAT I WANT
John Travolta and Olivia Newton-John

HIT ME WITH YOUR RHYTHM STICK
Ian Dury and The Blockheads

DANCE AWAY
Roxy Music

DON'T GIVE UP ON US
David Soul

WE DON'T TALK ANYMORE
Cliff Richard

DON'T GO BREAKING MY HEART
Elton John and Kiki Dee

WUTHERING HEIGHTS
Kate Bush

I DON'T LIKE MONDAYS
The Boomtown Rats

RECORD TWO B SIDE

DANCING QUEEN
Abba

SHOW YOU THE WAY TO GO
The Jacksons

ROCK YOUR BABY
George McCrae

BAND OF GOLD
Freda Payne

TEARS ON MY PILLOW
Johnny Nash

WHEN WILL I SEE YOU AGAIN
The Three Degrees

FREE
Deniece Williams

YOU MAKE ME FEEL BRAND NEW
The Stylistics

27 (107) ALL THOSE YEARS AGO *(3.42)* (108) WRITING'S ON THE WALL *(3.55)*

Dark Horse K 17807 – May 15, 1981

All Those Years Ago, George's tribute to John, became his first Top 30 hit for eight years. It entered the *NME* charts on May 30 at No. 26, rose to No. 9 the following week, and stayed in the chart for four weeks.

George originally wrote the song for Ringo's album, *Can't Fight Lightning* (later released in amended form, as *Stop And Smell The Roses*) and Ringo recorded it, with different lyrics, during the July 1980 sessions for that album in Paris. Ringo eventually decided against using the recording, which featured George. Following John's murder in December 1980, George rewrote the lyrics to the song, and during January 1981 recorded his own vocal track to use on the original recording. Later Paul, Linda and Denny Laine dropped into George's home studio to put backing vocals on to the track, which already featured Ringo. Therefore, although *All Those Years Ago* is the first post-Beatles song to feature Paul, George and Ringo, they were not all reunited in the studio at the same time. The single appeared in a picture sleeve, with the song lyrics printed on the reverse.

28 SOMEWHERE IN ENGLAND

Dark Horse K 56870 – June 5, 1981

Following the success of the single, *Somewhere In England* entered the *NME* album charts on June 13 at No. 28, rising to No. 13 the following week, but stayed for only three weeks in the charts.

Somewhere In England was originally scheduled to appear in October 1980, but when George presented the completed album to Warner Brothers, they disliked both the album cover (showing George's face superimposed onto a map of England) and the recorded material. They asked George to re-mix the album, and to write some new material to replace four songs of which they disapproved.

The recordings were produced by George and percussionist Ray Cooper, using the following musicians: drums/Ray Cooper, Jim Keltner, Ringo Starr and Dave Mattacks; bass/Willie Weeks and Herbie Flowers; keyboards & synthesizers/Neil Larson, Gary Brooker, Al Kooper, Mike Moran, George and Ray Cooper; lyricon and horn/Tom Scott; tuba/Herbie Flowers; tabla/Alla Rakha; percussion/Ray Cooper; and guitars and vocals/George.

The cover was photographed by Caroline Irwin, and shows George sitting in front of "Holland Park Avenue Study", a three dimensional painting by Mark Boyle made in 1967, and presently housed in the Tate Gallery, London. The inner sleeve features the song lyrics, plus a dedication to John Lennon.

A SIDE

109 **BLOOD FROM A CLONE** *(3.58)*

110 **UNCONSCIOUSNESS RULES** *(3.03)*

111 **LIFE ITSELF** *(4.23)*

107a **ALL THOSE YEARS AGO** *(3.43)*

112 **BALTIMORE ORIOLE** *(3.56)*

B SIDE

113 **TEARDROPS** *(4.06)*

114 **THAT WHICH I HAVE LOST** *(3.43)*

108a **WRITING'S ON THE WALL** *(3.58)*

115 **HONG KONG BLUES** *(2.53)*

116 **SAVE THE WORLD** *(4.54)*

George composed all songs except *Hong Kong Blues* and *Baltimore Oriole. Hong Kong Blues* was written by Hoagy Carmichael in 1938, and was originally recorded by the composer in that year. Carmichael re-recorded the song several more times during his life, and it was also released on record by Pearl Bailey, Kenny Ball, Frank Ifield and George Melly, among others. Hoagy Carmichael also composed the music to *Baltimore Oriole* with lyrics by Paul Francis Webster, in 1944; it was originally recorded by Frances Langford, accompanied by Carmichael himself whistling. It was later recorded by the Four Freshmen and Maynard Ferguson among others. *All Those Years Ago, Teardrops, Blood From A Clone* and *That Which I Have Lost* replaced the four numbers that Warners disliked, these tracks being: *Tears Of The World, Lay His Head, Flying Hour* and *Sat Singing*. At the end of the last track – *Save The World* – there is a very short excerpt of *Crying* from George's first album, *Wonderwall Music*.

29 (113a) TEARDROPS *(4.01)* (116a) SAVE THE WORLD *(4.54)*

Dark Horse K 17837 – July 31, 1981

The second single from *Somewhere In England* failed to enter the *NME* or BMRB charts, even though it was released in a picture sleeve.

30 THE BEST OF GEORGE HARRISON

Music For Pleasure MFP 50523 – November 25, 1981

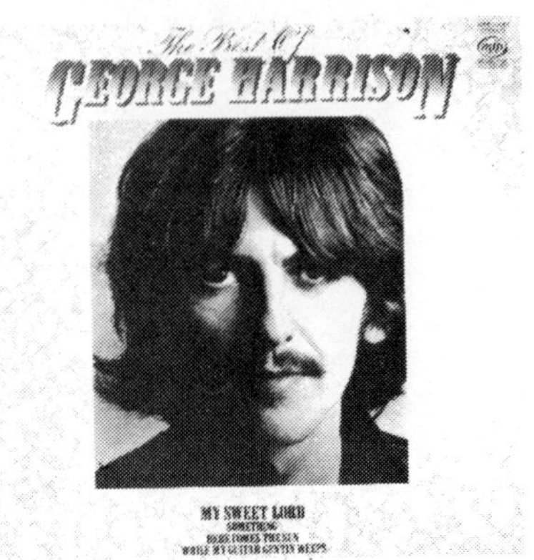

The second selection of Beatle reissues on EMI's budget label, Music For Pleasure, included *The Best Of George Harrison* album, along with John's *Rock 'n' Roll* and Ringo's *Blast From Your Past*. George's album was reissued in a new sleeve, using the picture of George which originally appeared in *The Beatles* white album of 1968.

A SIDE (THE BEATLES)

(See the Beatles British section in *The Long and Winding Road,* page 113.)

B SIDE (GEORGE HARRISON)

23f **MY SWEET LORD** *(4.38)*

55c **GIVE ME LOVE (GIVE ME PEACE ON EARTH** *(3.32)*

77c **YOU** *(3.40)*

45b **BANGLA DESH** *(3.56)*

74d **DARK HORSE** *(3.51)*

26d **WHAT IS LIFE** *(5.20)*

31 (117) WAKE UP MY LOVE *(3.30)* (118) GREECE *(3.57)*

Dark Horse 929864-7 – November 8, 1982

George's only singles release of 1982, which was a trailer for his album released the same day, *Gone Troppo*. The single did not enter the charts, not being helped by the fact that George refused to promote the single in any way.

32 GONE TROPPO

Dark Horse 923734-1 – November 8, 1982

1943 WAS A GREAT YEAR FOR MUSIC

·GEORGE·
HARRISON

THIRTY
·THREE & 1/3°·

K 56319

33⅓ YEARS ON....

DARK HORSE RECORDS
RELEASE HIS NEW ALBUM

MARKETED BY WEA RECORDS

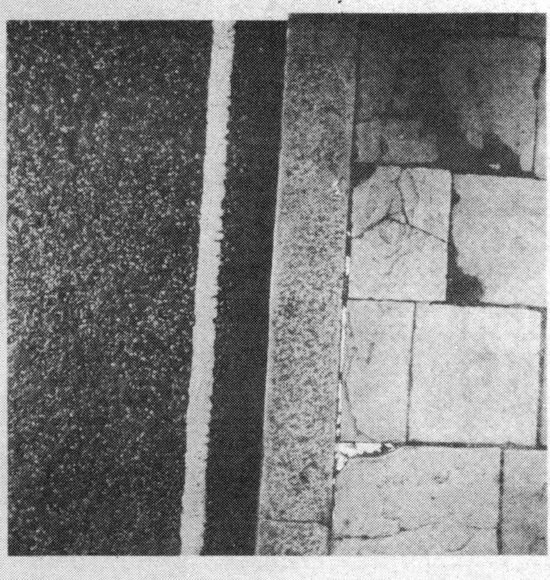

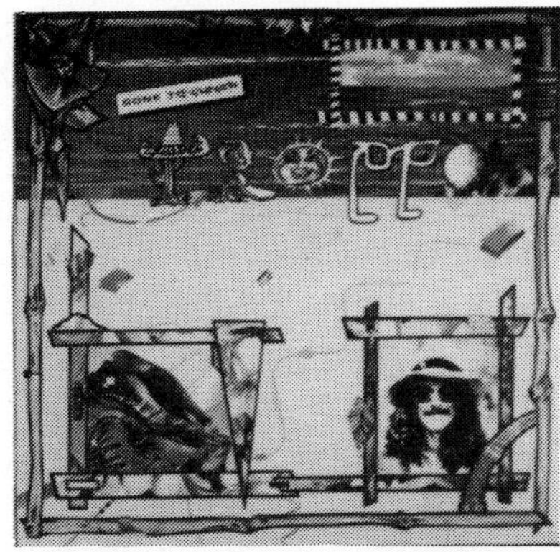

As with the single, George failed to promote *Gone Troppo*, and therefore it did not enter the *NME* or BMRB charts. The recordings were produced by George, Ray Cooper and Phil McDonald with a basic instrumental line-up of: George/guitars, bass, synthesizers, marimba, Jal-Tarang and mandolin; Ray Cooper/percussion, Fender Rhodes, glockenspeil, marimba and synthesizer; Herbie Flowers/bass; Mike Moran/keyboards, synthesizer, bass synthesizer and piano; and Henry Spinetti/drums.

The following musicians contributed to only certain tracks: Gary Brooker/synthesizer (*Unknown Delight*); Joe Brown/mandolin (*Mystical One*); Alan Jones/bass (*Dream Away*); Jim Keltner/percussion (*Gone Troppo*) and drums (*Baby Don't Run Away*); Neil Larson/piano (*Unknown Delight*); Jon Lord/synthesizer (*Circles*); Dave Mattacks/drums (*Dream Away*); Billy Preston/keyboards and synthesizer (*Greece*) and organ and piano (*Circles*) and Willie Weeks/bass (*Unknown Delight*).

The striking and decorative album sleeve was designed by "Legs" Larry Smith, ex of the Bonzo Dog Band, featuring a cover picture of George by Terry O'Neill. The inner sleeve, as well as containing the song lyrics, also includes an instruction on how to make cement!

A SIDE

117a **WAKE UP MY LOVE** *(3.32)*

119 **THAT'S THE WAY IT GOES** *(3.32)*

120 **I REALLY LOVE YOU** *(2.54)*

118a **GREECE** *(3.57)*

121 **GONE TROPPO** *(4.24)*

B SIDE

122 **MYSTICAL ONE** *(3.40)*

123 **UNKNOWN DELIGHT** *(4.15)*

124 **BABY DON'T RUN AWAY** *(3.59)*

125 **DREAM AWAY** *(4.28)*

126 **CIRCLES** *(3.44)*

George composed all the songs on the album, except the 1961 doo wop song, *I Really Love You*, written by one L. Swearingen, and originally recorded by The Stereos, whose version was a Top 30 US hit in 1961. More recently, it was also recorded by Rocky Sharpe and the Replays, but was not a hit.

Wake Up My Love features George playing bass, while the bass voice on *That's The Way It Goes* is supplied by Willie Greene. Although George sings lead vocals on most tracks, on *I Really Love You* he is joined by Willie Greene, Bobby King and Pico Payne (who have appeared on several LPs by Ry Cooder) on both lead and backing vocals. On *Gone Troppo*, George's lead vocal is backed by the voices of Joe and Vicki Brown. Joe Brown also supplies mandolin, duetting with George, on *Mystical One*.

Unknown Delight again features vocal backing by Willie Greene, Bobby King and Pico Payne, while Billy Preston and Rodina Sloan supply the same service on *Baby Don't Run Away*. *Dream Away* is the song George wrote for the *Time Bandits* film, made by his company Hand Made Films, and is heard playing over the closing credits. For the film – starring John Cleese, Michael Palin, Sean Connery, Shelley Duvall and Sir Ralph Richardson – George composed a complete incidental score, although the proposed soundtrack never materialised. The song features Billy Preston, Syreeta and Sarah Ricor on backing vocals. The last track, *Circles*, features the synthesizer of ex-Deep Purple member, Jon Lord.

GEORGE – US SECTION

1 WONDERWALL MUSIC

Apple ST 3350 – December 2, 1968

Wonderwall Music was the second Beatle solo album in America (*Two Virgins* was released there in November 1968). The album performed decidedly better in the charts than *Two Virgins*, rising to No. 49 for two weeks on March 1, 1969. The album entered the Top 100 on February 1, 1969, at No. 72, after being in the lower regions of the Top 200 for three weeks. The album stayed in the Top 100 for eleven weeks and in the Top 200 for sixteen weeks. (Tracks and sleeve same as British release.)

2 ELECTRONIC SOUND

Zapple ST 3358 – May 26, 1969

George's second album, which failed to enter the Top 100 album charts, only breaking into the Top 200 for two weeks, and peaking at No. 191 in July 1969. (Tracks and sleeve same as British release.)

3 (23) MY SWEET LORD (25) ISN'T IT A PITY

Apple 2995 – November 23, 1970

In America, *My Sweet Lord* was released prior to the *All Things Must Pass* album. It entered the charts within a week of release on November 28, at No. 72, jumping to No. 13 the following week (December 5), by which time it had sold 500,000. By December 14 it had passed the million mark, being awarded a Gold Award from RIAA, and on December 26 it finally reached the No. 1 spot, where it stayed for four weeks. For three weeks, between January 2 and January 16, George held the Top US singles and album positions with *My Sweet Lord* and *All Things Must Pass*. By the end of 1970, after six weeks on release, the single had sold over two million and – as it stayed in the charts for fourteen weeks – American sales must be little short of three million.

4 ALL THINGS MUST PASS

Apple STCH 639 – November 27, 1970

All Things Must Pass entered the Top 100 charts at No. 5 on December 19, having sold 750,000 by December 5, and passed one million sales by December 17, 1970, receiving a Gold Award from RIAA. On January 2, 1971, it rose to No. 1 in the Billboard charts, where it stayed for seven weeks, by which time it had sold two and a half million copies. The album stayed in the Billboard Top 30 for nineteen weeks, the Top 100 for twenty-seven weeks and the Top 200 for thirty-eight weeks. (Cover as British release.)

RECORD ONE A SIDE

22 **I'D HAVE YOU ANYTIME**

23a **MY SWEET LORD**

24 **WAH-WAH**

25a **ISN'T IT A PITY (version one)**

(Remainder of album same as British release.)

5 (26a) WHAT IS LIFE (32a) APPLE SCRUFFS

Apple 1828 – February 15, 1971

Not released in Britain as a single, the second release from *All Things Must Pass* entered the Billboard chart on February 27 at No. 66, rising to No. 10 on March 27 and staying in the Top 100 for nine weeks.

6 (45) BANGLA DESH (46) DEEP BLUE

Apple 1836 – July 28, 1971

Bangla Desh entered the Billboard charts on August 14 at No. 67, rising to No. 23 for two weeks on September 11 and featuring in the chart for seven weeks.

7 THE CONCERT FOR BANGLA DESH

Apple STCX 3385 – December 20, 1971

Although the Bangla Desh album appeared in America about three weeks before its British release, George had numerous problems with the album in the United States. Capitol Records initially refused to release the album unless it was financially rewarding to them, but George argued that with Phil Spector mixing the tapes free of charge, Apple supplying the booklet and album design at no charge, and all the other record companies involved giving their permission for their artists to appear, Capitol also had to forfeit something. George threatened to take the album to CBS if Capitol didn't give way, but it was eventually released by Capitol, who presented Apple with a cheque for $3,750,000 as advance payment on sales.

The album entered the Billboard Top 100 charts on January 8, 1972, at No. 14, rising to No. 2 on January 22 where it remained for five weeks, and staying in the Top 100 for thirty weeks, and in the Top 30 for twenty-two of them. The album was listed in the Billboard Top 200 album charts for forty-one weeks, and received an RIAA Gold Award on January 4, 1974. (Tracks and sleeve same as British release.)

8 (55) GIVE ME LOVE (GIVE ME PEACE ON EARTH) (56) MISS O'DELL

Apple 1862 – May 7, 1973

George's second No. 1 single in America entered the Billboard charts on May 19 at No. 59. It rose for one week to No. 1 on June 30, and stayed in the Top 100 for fourteen weeks, nine of which were spent in the Top 30. As in Britain, the "B" side, *Miss O'Dell*, has never appeared on another George Harrison record released in America. *Give Me Love* was the first track released as a 45 from the *Living In The Material World* album.

9 LIVING IN THE MATERIAL WORLD

Apple SMAS 3410 – May 30, 1973

Living In The Material World entered the Billboard Top 100 LP chart on June 16 at No. 11, rising to No. 1 on June 23 for the first of five weeks at the top of the chart. It gave George his second double top in the US charts on June 30, when *Give Me Love* was at No. 1 in the single charts, and *Living* at No. 1 in the album charts. The album received a Gold Award on June 1, 1973, and eventually sold over two million copies in America. It was in the Billboard Top 100 for twenty-one weeks, and in the Top 200 for twenty-six weeks. A second single was nearly released from the album, *Don't Let Me Wait Too Long* (Apple 1866), but was withdrawn before release. (Tracks and sleeve as British release.)

10 (74) DARK HORSE (68) I DON'T CARE ANYMORE

Apple 1877 – November 18, 1974

The American trailer for the *Dark Horse* album was the title track, which entered the Billboard Top 100 at No. 69 on November 23, peaked at No. 15 on January 11, 1975, and was in the Top 30 for four weeks, and in the Top 100 for ten weeks. As with the British release, *I Don't Care Anymore* did not appear on any other Harrison release in the United States.

11 DARK HORSE

Apple SMAS 3418 – December 9, 1974

Dark Horse entered the Billboard Top 100 album charts on December 28 at No. 58, rising to No. 4 on January 25, 1975, staying in the chart for thirteen weeks, and receiving an RIAA Gold Award on December 16, 1974. (Sleeve same as British release.)

A SIDE

69 **HARI'S ON TOUR (EXPRESS)**

70 **SIMPLY SHADY**

71 **SO SAD**

72 **BYE BYE LOVE**

73 **MAYA LOVE**

B SIDE

67 **DING DONG DING DONG**

74a **DARK HORSE**

75 **FAR EAST MAN**

76 **IT IS "HE"**

12 (67a) DING DONG DING DONG (69a) HARI'S ON TOUR (EXPRESS)

Apple 1879 – December 23, 1974

Possibly released too close to Christmas to be a festive hit, *Ding Dong* only reached No. 36 in the Billboard Hot Hundred, on February 8, 1975, after entering on January 11, 1975, at No. 81, and being in the chart for six weeks. It was George's first single which failed to enter the Billboard Top 30.

13 (77) YOU (78) WORLD OF STONE

Apple 1884 – September 15, 1975

You entered the Billboard Hot 100 on September 20 at No. 75, rising to No. 20 for two weeks from November 1, and staying in the chart for ten weeks, five of them in the Top 30. (Picture sleeve same as British release.)

14 EXTRA TEXTURE (Read All About It)

Apple SW 3420 – September 22, 1975

Extra Texture entered the Top 100 album charts on October 11 at No. 34, rising to No. 8 for three weeks on October 25, passing the million dollar sales mark by November 11, 1975, and receiving a Gold Award from RIAA. The album stayed in the Top 100 for eight weeks and in the Top 200 for eleven weeks. (Tracks and sleeve same as British release.)

15 (80a) THIS GUITAR (CAN'T KEEP FROM CRYING) (73a) MAYA LOVE

Apple 1885 – December 8, 1975

George's last Apple single in America, and his first not to enter the American charts.

16 THE BEST OF GEORGE HARRISON

Capitol ST 11578 – November 8, 1976

This compilation album, featuring seven of George's Beatle songs and six solo hits, entered the Billboard Top 200 on November 27, rising to No. 31 and staying in the chart for fifteen weeks. It received an RIAA Gold Award (million dollar sale) on February 15, 1977.

A SIDE (THE BEATLES)

(See the Beatles British section in *The Long and Winding Road,* page 113.)

B SIDE (GEORGE HARRISON)

23b **MY SWEET LORD**

55b **GIVE ME LOVE (GIVE ME PEACE ON EARTH)**

77b **YOU**

45a **BANGLA DESH**

74b **DARK HORSE**

26b **WHAT IS LIFE**

17 (87) THIS SONG (88) LEARNING HOW TO LOVE YOU

Dark Horse DRC 8294 – November 15, 1976

George's first American Dark Horse single, *This Song* entered the Billboard Top 100 on November 20, rising to No. 25 and staying in the chart for eleven weeks.

18 THIRTY THREE & ⅓

Dark Horse DH 3005 – November 24, 1976

George's first album release on his own Dark Horse label entered the Billboard Top 200 chart on December 11, 1976, and rose to No. 11. It stayed in the chart for twenty-one weeks, and received an RIAA Gold Award (million dollars sale) on January 19, 1977. (Tracks and sleeve same as British release.)

19 (96a) CRACKERBOX PALACE (88b) LEARNING HOW TO LOVE YOU

Dark Horse DRC 8313 – January 24, 1977

Crackerbox Palace was not released as a single in Britain, but in America it proved to be another Top 20 hit for George, entering the Billboard charts on January 29, rising to No. 19, and staying in the chart for eleven weeks. George's liking for *Learning How To Love You* prompted him to include it for a second time as the "B" side coupling (the track had appeared previously with *This Song*).

20 (74c) DARK HORSE (77c) YOU

Capitol Star Line 6245 – April 4, 1977

With some of George's early singles deleted, Capitol's policy of reissuing hit songs on their Star Line label extended to their first Harrison reissue of *Dark Horse* and *You* – taken from the *Dark Horse* and *Extra Texture* albums respectively.

21 (101) BLOW AWAY (100) SOFT-HEARTED HANA

Dark Horse DRC 8763 – February 14, 1979

George's "come-back" single after his 1977 rest, became his tenth hit single in the United States, entering the Billboard Hot Hundred on March 3, rising to No. 16, and staying in the chart for fourteen weeks.

22 GEORGE HARRISON

Dark Horse DHK 3255 – February 14, 1979

George's eighth Top 100 Billboard album, *George Harrison* entered the chart on March 17, and rose to No. 14, staying in the chart for eighteen weeks. (Sleeve as British release.)

A SIDE

97 LOVE COMES TO EVERYONE

98 NOT GUILTY

99 HERE COMES THE MOON

100a SOFT-HEARTED HANA

101a BLOW AWAY

B SIDE

102 FASTER

103 DARK SWEET LADY

104 YOUR LOVE IS FOREVER

105 SOFT TOUCH

106 IF YOU BELIEVE

23 (97a) LOVE COMES TO EVERYONE (105a) SOFT TOUCH

Dark Horse DRC 8844 – May 9, 1979

George's second single (and first for Dark Horse) not to enter the Billboard charts (excepting reissues), and the second single release from the *George Harrison* album.

24 DARK HORSE

Capitol SN-16055 – October, 1980

As with EMI in Britain, Capitol deleted several original Beatles solo albums, and reissued them in their budget series. *Dark Horse* appeared with John's *Mind Games* and *Rock 'n' Roll* albums and Ringo's *Ringo* album. The reissue, like the British release, had a new front and back cover.

A SIDE

69b HARI'S ON TOUR (EXPRESS)

70a SIMPLY SHADY

71a SO SAD

72a BYE BYE LOVE

73b MAYA LOVE

B SIDE

67b DING DONG DING DONG

74d DARK HORSE

75a FAR EAST MAN

76a IT IS "HE"

25 LIVING IN THE MATERIAL WORLD

Capitol SN-16216 – February, 1981

The second reissue of a deleted Harrison

album, *Living In The Material World* reappeared in a single sleeve, and not the gatefold sleeve of the original release.

A SIDE

55c GIVE ME LOVE (GIVE ME PEACE ON EARTH)

57a SUE ME SUE YOU BLUES

58a THE LIGHT THAT HAS LIGHTED THE WORLD

59a DON'T LET ME WAIT TOO LONG

60a WHO CAN SEE IT

61a LIVING IN THE MATERIAL WORLD

B SIDE

62a THE LORD LOVES THE ONE (THAT LOVES THE LORD)

63a BE HERE NOW

64a TRY SOME BUY SOME

65a THE DAY THE WORLD GETS 'ROUND'

66a THAT IS ALL

26 EXTRA TEXTURE (Read All About It)

Capitol SN-16217 – February, 1981

Reissued simultaneously with *Living In The Material World, Extra Texture* appeared on the Capitol budget label, in a single sleeve, and not the textured and die-cut cover of the original release.

A SIDE

77d YOU

79a THE ANSWER'S AT THE END

80b THIS GUITAR (CAN'T KEEP FROM CRYING)

81a OOH BABY (YOU KNOW THAT I LOVE YOU)

78b WORLD OF STONE

B SIDE

82a A BIT MORE OF YOU

83a CAN'T STOP THINKING ABOUT YOU

84a TIRED OF MIDNIGHT BLUE

85a GREY CLOUDY LIES

86a HIS NAME IS LEGS (LADIES AND GENTLEMEN)

29 (107) ALL THOSE YEARS AGO (108) WRITING'S ON THE WALL

Dark Horse DRC 49725 – May 11, 1981

George's biggest America hit since *Give Me Love* in 1973, *All Those Years Ago* reached No. 2 in the Billboard charts, after entering on May 23, and staying in the chart for thirteen weeks. (Picture sleeve same as British release.)

28 SOMEWHERE IN ENGLAND

Dark Horse DHK 3492 – June 1, 1981

Boosted by the hit single *All Those Years Ago, Somewhere In England* rose to No. 11 in the Billboard Top 200, after entering on June 20, 1981, and it stayed in the chart for twelve weeks. (Tracks and sleeve same as British release.)

29 (113a) TEARDROPS (116a) SAVE THE WORLD

Dark Horse DRC 79825 – July 24, 1981

George's second single of 1982 failed to enter the Billboard Hot Hundred, bubbling under the charts for a few weeks.

30 (107b) ALL THOSE YEARS AGO (113b) TEARDROPS

Dark Horse GDRC 0410 – November 4, 1981

As Warner Brothers distributed Dark Horse Records in the United States, they had the right to re-release George's singles. This release was their first oldies release, coupling both singles from the *Somewhere In England* album.

31 (117) WAKE UP MY LOVE (118) GREECE

Dark Horse 7-29864 – November ?, 1982

George's first new single for over a year entered the Billboard chart on November 20, peaked at No. 53 on December 4, and remained in the chart for six weeks.

32 GONE TROPPO

Dark Horse 1-23734 – November ?, 1982

George's only album release of 1982 failed to achieve the chart success of his previous LP, entering on November 27 at No. 119, and rising to No. 108 on December 11. It continued to feature in the chart until the end of 1982. (Sleeve and tracks same as British release.)

RINGO STARR

1 SENTIMENTAL JOURNEY

Apple PCS 7101 – March 27, 1970

Ringo's first solo album, featuring a selection of standards, entered the *NME* charts on April 22 at No. 16. It rose to No. 15 the following week, and stayed in the chart for four weeks.

For his first solo album, Ringo decided to record the old "standards" that he could remember from his childhood, and he consulted his parents and family before choosing the titles. He started recording the album in September 1969 (when *Night And Day*, *Star Dust* and *Blue Turning Grey Over You* were recorded) followed by further sessions during November and December 1969. A final session in February 1970 produced *Whispering Grass*, *Bye Bye Blackbird* and *Love Is A Many Splendoured Thing*, along with two unused numbers, *Autumn Leaves* and *I'll Be Looking At The Moon*. The album was produced by George Martin, using the George Martin Orchestra, with arrangements for each song being carried out by various well-known musicians or composers.

The album sleeve features photographs by Richard Polak; the front cover shows the Empress Pub, in High Park Street, Liverpool (Ringo's local), which was a short distance from his childhood homes in Madryn Street and Admiral Grove. Ringo is superimposed standing in front of the pub, while his relatives appear likewise in the pub windows.

A SIDE

1 **SENTIMENTAL JOURNEY** *(3.25)*

2 **NIGHT AND DAY** *(2.24)*

3 **WHISPERING GRASS (DON'T TELL THE TREES)** *(2.35)*

4 **BYE BYE BLACKBIRD** *(2.10)*

5 **I'M A FOOL TO CARE** *(2.39)*

6 **STAR DUST** *(3.16)*

B SIDE

7 **BLUE TURNING GREY OVER YOU** *(3.18)*

8 **LOVE IS A MANY SPLENDOURED THING** *(3.04)*

9 **DREAM** *(2.41)*

10 **YOU ALWAYS HURT THE ONE YOU LOVE** *(2.18)*

11 **HAVE I TOLD YOU LATELY THAT I LOVE YOU** *(2.43)*

12 **LET THE REST OF THE WORLD GO BY** *(2.55)*

Sentimental Journey, arranged by Richard Perry (who was later to produce two albums for Ringo), was written by Bud Green, Les Brown and Ben Homer, and was originally recorded by Les Brown and his Orchestra, with vocals by Doris Day. The record reached No. 1 for nine weeks in America, becoming a million seller, and also Doris Day's first big hit.

Night And Day, written by Cole Porter, was arranged for Ringo by Chico O'Farrell, and originally appeared in the 1932 musical *Gay Divorcee*, sung by Fred Astaire and Claire Luce. *Whispering Grass* was arranged by well-known orchestra leader, Ron Goodwin, and was written by Fred and Doris Fisher, and originally recorded by the Ink Spots, in 1940.

Bye Bye Blackbird, arranged for Ringo by Bee Gee Maurice Gibb, was written by Mort Dixon and Ray Henderson in 1927 for vaudeville star George Price. The Beatles' old Hamburg friend and ex-Manfred Mann bass player, Klaus Voorman, arranged *I'm A Fool To Care*, which was written in 1948 by Country and Western songwriter Ted Daffan. It became a hit for Les Paul and Mary Ford in 1954 and a million seller for Joe Barry in 1961.

Star Dust, one of the world's most popular songs, with over 1,100 different recorded versions, was written in 1927 by Hoagy Carmichael, with words added by Mitchell Parish in 1929. It was first recorded in 1927, but first sold a million for Artie Shaw and his Orchestra in 1940. A second version by Billy Ward and the Dominoes also sold a million in 1957. Ringo's version was arranged by Paul McCartney.

Blue Turning Grey Over You was arranged by Oliver Nelson, written by Andy Razaf and Thomas "Fats" Waller, and recorded by Louis Armstrong and his Orchestra in 1930. *Love Is A Many Splendoured Thing*, arranged by Quincy Jones

Week ending April 4, 1970

WORLD'S **LARGEST** CIRCULATION OF **ANY** MUSIC PAPER

NMExclusive Part one of . . .

LED ZEPPELIN ASK-IN by RITCHIE YORKE

KENNY ROGERS | CLIFF | *RUFFIN, WALKER*

BLACK SABBATH | *ANDY* | TOP POP NEWS

ELVIS: WILL HE COME?

Ringo Starr
Beacoups of Blues.
Apple Records PAS 10002

– ace American producer – was written by Paul Francis Webster (words) and Sammy Fain (music) for the film of the same name, winning an Academy Award for Best Film Song of 1955. The song was made a chart hit by the Four Aces who scored a No. 1 America million seller.

George Martin arranged *Dream*, originally written by Johnny Mercer for his 1945 American CBS Radio Show, but recorded by The Pied Pipers, with the Paul Weston Orchestra, giving them a hit million seller. *You Always Hurt The One You Love*, arranged by John Dankworth, well-known jazz musician and orchestra leader, was written by Allan Roberts (words) and Doris Fisher (music). It was recorded by the Mills Brothers, giving them a four week No. 1 and America million seller in 1944.

Elmer Bernstein arranged *Have I Told You Lately That I Love You*, a song written by Scott Wiseman, and originally recorded by Foy Willing and the Riders of The Purple Sage. *Let The Rest Of The World Go By*, arranged by Les Reed, is the oldest song on the album; dating from 1919, when it was written by J. Keirn Brennan and Ernest K. Ball, being performed by George J. Trinkaus and his band.

2 BEAUCOUPS OF BLUES

Apple PAS 10002 – September 25, 1970

Although regarded by many reviewers at the time as a better album than *Sentimental Journey*, *Beaucoups Of Blues* – Ringo's second solo album – did not enter the *NME* album charts.

Whilst Ringo was assisting George to record his *All Things Must Pass* album, Pete Drake, an American pedal steel guitarist also helping with George's album, suggested that Ringo should record a Country and Western album, and offered to assist him. Originally Ringo wanted to record the album in London, using imported Country and Western musicians, allowing himself several weeks to complete the album. Pete Drake persuaded Ringo that it would take too long to record the album in London, and that he could complete the whole album in a few days in Nashville, USA. The album was recorded between June 30 and July 1, 1970, at the Music City Recorders Studio in Nashville, Tennessee, using over twenty of Nashville's top country musicians under the production guidance of Pete Drake. The album was engineered by Scotty Moore, legendary guitarist of Elvis Presley's first group, who was also Presley's manager for a short time and supplied guitar on all his early recordings. Drake commissioned a host of Country and Western writers to compose songs especially for Ringo, who was given almost a hundred to choose from, and he eventually recorded many more than were needed for the album. At one time, a second album of country songs was being considered but this never materialised.

The recordings featured the following musicians: Buddy Harman (bass); Charlie Daniels (guitar), Dave Kirby (guitar), Chuck Howard (guitar), The Jordanaires (backing vocals – who backed Elvis Presley on his first recording sessions for RCA in Nashville in January 1956 and on many later recordings), Charlie McCoy (harmonica), Sorrels Pickard (guitar), Jerry Kennedy (guitar), Jerry Shook (guitar), George Richey, Grover Lavender, Jim Buchanan (fiddle), Roy Huskey Jnr (bass), Pete Drake (pedal steel guitar), Ringo (acoustic guitar and drums), D.J. Fontana (drums), Ben Keith (steel guitar), Jerry Reed (guitar – he has written many hit songs, including *Guitar Man* recorded by Elvis Presley) and Jeannie Kendall.

The gatefold sleeve, designed by John Kosh, features photographs taken in Nashville by Marshall Fallwell Jnr, including a back cover shot showing most of the musicians on the album.

A SIDE

13 **BEAUCOUPS OF BLUES** *(2.30)*

14 **LOVE DON'T LAST LONG** *(2.43)*

15 **FASTEST GROWING HEARTACHE IN THE WEST** *(2.33)*

16 **WITHOUT HER** *(2.33)*

17 **WOMAN OF THE NIGHT** *(2.20)*

18 **I'D BE TALKING ALL THE TIME** *(2.08)*

B SIDE

19 **$15 DRAW** *(3.27)*

20 **WINE, WOMEN AND LOUD HAPPY SONGS** *(2.17)*

21 **I WOULDN'T HAVE YOU ANY OTHER WAY** *(2.56)*

22 **LOSER'S LOUNGE** *(2.22)*

23 **WAITING** *(2.54)*

24 **SILENT HOMECOMING** *(3.53)*

All but one of the songs on the album were written in 1970 and given to Ringo, eight of them composed by two musicians playing on the album. *Beaucoups Of Blues* was written by Buzz Rabin and was nearly released in Britain as a single (it was announced in the music press for release in either November or December 1970). Chuck Howard, who also contributed guitar to the album, composed *Love Don't Last Long, I Wouldn't Have You Any Other Way* and *Waiting*; he also co-composed *I'd Be Talking All The Time* with Larry Kingston. Sorrels Pickard, another guitarist heard on the album, composed *Without Her, Woman Of The Night, $15 Draw* and *Silent Homecoming.* Larry Kingston also composed *Wine, Women And Loud Happy Songs* in 1968, and co-composed *Fastest Growing Heartache In The West* with Fred Dycus. *Loser's Lounge* was written by Bobby Pierce.

3 (26) IT DON'T COME EASY *(2.59)* (27) EARLY 1970 *(2.18)*

Apple R 5898 – April 9, 1971

Ringo's first solo single entered the *NME* charts on April 21 at No. 12, rising to No. 5 for two weeks, on May 5, and staying in the charts for nine weeks. Having sold a million in the United States, the global sales of *It Don't Come Easy* must be close to two million.

Ringo composed *It Don't Come Easy* in 1970. There were supposedly three recorded versions of the song, including one with Klaus Voorman/bass and George Harrison/guitar, and another with Eric Clapton on guitar. The released version, recorded on March 8, 1970, at EMI and Trident Studios, features Klaus Voorman/bass, Steven Stills and George Harrison/guitars, Ringo/drums and Ron Cattermole/saxophone and trumpet.

Early 1970, Ringo's song to his three fellow Beatles, features George playing guitar and supplying backing vocals, and Ringo on acoustic guitar, drums and piano. Both numbers were produced by George Harrison. The single was mastered by George Peckham ("PECKO" AND "PORKY" appearing on the run-out grooves) and was packaged in a picture sleeve.

THE CONCERT FOR BANGLA DESH

By George Harrison and Friends

Apple STCX 3385 – January 7, 1972

Ringo's only live recording to feature his vocal talents is included on George's *Concert For Bangla Desh*, in which Ringo performs a live version of *It Don't Come Easy*, managing to forget the words in places. He plays drums throughout the second, third, fourth and sixth sides, and tambourine during the fifth side, which features Bob Dylan. (For further information, track listing and sleeve see George Harrison British section, page **120**.)

RECORD TWO A SIDE TRACK ONE

28 **IT DON'T COME EASY** *(2.38)*

4 (29) BACK OFF BOOGALOO *(3.18)* (30) BLINDMAN *(2.40)*

Apple R 5944 – March 17, 1972

Another big hit for Ringo, *Back Off Boogaloo* entered the *NME* charts on March 29 at No. 26, rising to No. 2 for one week on April 26 (*Amazing Grace* by the Royal Scots Dragoon Guards, Pipes, Drums and Band, was at No. 1) and staying in the chart for nine weeks.

Back Off Boogaloo was written by Ringo, and produced by George Harrison. It features George/guitar, Gary Wright/keyboards, Klaus Voorman/bass, Ringo/drums and vocals, and backing vocalists

Ringo Starr

OUT SOON

It don't come easy

Apple Records R 5898

ANOTHER MONSTER FROM APPLE

Listen now ring 247 6693

R 5944

Madeline Bell, Lesley Duncan and Jean Gilbert. *Boogaloo* was supposedly one of Paul's nicknames. *Blindman*, written by Ringo for his 1971 film of the same name, was produced by Ringo and Klaus Voorman. The single appeared in a picture sleeve, and also featured blue "Apple" labels.

TOMMY

By The London Symphony Orchestra and Chamber Choir with Guest Soloists

Ode 99001 – November 24, 1972

Ringo's first guest appearance on a concept album was playing the part of Uncle Ernie in the Lou Reizner production of Pete Townshend's classic rock opera *Tommy*. The album entered the *NME* charts on January 9, 1973, at No. 23, its highest position, staying in the chart for three weeks. Album sales exceeded a global million by March 1973.

It was Lou Reizner's idea to re-record *Tommy* using an orchestra with an all-star cast of guest vocalists, and he started to produce the album in September 1971. Recording sessions began in March 1972 at Olympic Studios, London, through to September 1972, when Ringo recorded his vocals. As well as Ringo the all-star cast included: Pete Townshend/Narrator; Sandy Denny/Nurse; Graham Bell/Lover; Steve Winwood/Father; Maggie Bell/Mother; Richie Havens/Hawker; Merry Clayton/Acid Queen; Roger Daltrey/Tommy; John Entwistle/Cousin Kevin; Rod Stewart/Local Lad and Richard Harris/The Doctor. The London Symphony Orchestra and Chamber Choir was conducted by David Measham.

The two LP set came in an elaborate package of a gatefold double album enclosed inside a thick cardboard sleeve, plus a thirty-two page four colour booklet featuring illustrations and lyrics. The package was designed by Wilkes and Braun Inc., with photographs by Phil Marco, Ethan Russell and Tom Wilkes. (The double album features sides one and four on the first LP, and sides two and three on the second LP.)

A SIDE

OVERTURE
Pete Townshend

IT'S A BOY
Sandy Denny

1921
Graham Bell, Steve Winwood & Maggie Bell

AMAZING JOURNEY
Pete Townshend

SPARKS
London Symphony Orchestra

EYESIGHT TO THE BLIND
Richie Havens

CHRISTMAS
Steve Winwood & Roger Daltrey

B SIDE

COUSIN KEVIN
John Entwistle

THE ACID QUEEN
Merry Clayton

UNDERTURE
London Symphony Orchestra

DO YOU THINK IT'S ALRIGHT
Maggie Bell

31 **FIDDLE ABOUT** *(1.26)*
Ringo Starr

PINBALL WIZARD
Rod Stewart

C SIDE

THERE'S A DOCTOR I'VE FOUND
Steve Winwood

GO TO THE MIRROR BOY
Richard Harris, Roger Daltrey & Steve Winwood

TOMMY CAN YOU HEAR ME?
Maggie Bell

SMASH THE MIRROR
Maggie Bell

I'M FREE
Roger Daltrey

MIRACLE CURE
Chambre Choir

SENSATION
Roger Daltrey

D SIDE

SALLY SIMPSON
Pete Townshend

WELCOME
Roger Daltrey

32 TOMMY'S HOLIDAY CAMP *(1.27)*
Ringo Starr

WE'RE NOT GONNA TAKE IT/
SEE ME FEEL ME
Roger Daltrey

5 (33) PHOTOGRAPH *(3.55)*
(34) DOWN AND OUT *(2.59)*

Apple R 5992 – October 19, 1973

Ringo's third solo single, and third hit, entered the *NME* charts on October 23 at No. 28. It dropped out of the chart for one week, re-entered at No. 20 on November 6, after which it climbed to No. 4 for one week on November 20, and remained in the chart for eight weeks. The single sold over one and a half million globally.

The single was recorded between March and July 1973, during the *Ringo* album sessions – the "A" side being produced by Richard Perry, and the "B" side by George Harrison and Richard Perry. *Photograph* was written by Ringo and George, and features Ringo and Jim Keltner/drums; George Harrison/twelve string guitar and harmony vocal; Nicky Hopkins/piano; Klaus Voorman/bass; Vini Poncia/acoustic guitar; Jimmy Calvert/acoustic guitar; Lon and Derrek Van Eaton/percussion; and Bobby Keyes/tenor saxophone solo, with the orchestra and chorus arranged by Jack Nitzsche.

Down And Out was written by Ringo, and is not included on any other of his record releases. The single appeared in a picture sleeve, with a matching label design.

6 RINGO

Apple PCTC 252 – November 9, 1973

Ringo entered the *NME* album charts on November 27 at No. 21, climbing to No. 6 on January 1, 1974. It then dropped down the charts, until the release of *You're*

Sixteen as a single caused the album to rise to No. 13 on March 5, 1974. The album stayed in the charts for eighteen weeks, and has probably sold around two million globally.

Most of the album was recorded between March and July, 1973, at Sunset Sound, Los Angeles, and Apple Studios, London, with some additional recordings at The Burbank Studios, Sound Labs and Producers Workshop, Los Angeles, and EMI Studios, London. The album was produced by Richard Perry, and features a galaxy of star musicians including: John Lennon/piano; George Harrison/guitar; Klaus Voorman/bass & upright bass; Billy Preston/organ and piano; Jim Keltner/drums; Marc Bolan/ guitar; James Booker/piano; Milt Holland/percussion; Tom Scott/horns and saxophones; Nicky Hopkins/piano; Vini Poncia/acoustic guitar and percussion; Jimmy Calvert/guitar and acoustic guitar; Robbie Robertson/guitar; Levon Helm/mandolin; Rick Danko/fiddle; David Bromberg/fiddle and banjo; Garth Hudson/accordian; Paul McCartney/mouth sax solo, piano and synthesizer; Steve Cropper/electric guitar; Chuck Findley/horns and Tom Hensley/piano.

The album appeared in a very elaborate gatefold sleeve, including a twenty-four page lyric book illustrated with ten lithographs by Klaus Voorman. The cover paintings were by Tim Bruckner, the front showing a stage containing a crowd of people, including all the musicians heard on the album. The album photography and design was by Barry Feinstein for Camouflage Productions.

A SIDE

35 I'M THE GREATEST *(3.22)*

36 HAVE YOU SEEN MY BABY *(3.42)*

33a PHOTOGRAPH *(3.56)*

37 SUNSHINE LIFE FOR ME (SAIL AWAY RAYMOND) *(2.43)*

photograph

RINGO STARR

Produced by Richard Perry

apple single R 5992

EMI

"You come on like a dream, peaches and cream,
Lips like strawberry wine,
You're sixteen, you're beautiful and you're mine." *

RINGO'S NEW SINGLE, "YOU'RE SIXTEEN."

R5995

Produced by Richard Perry

* REPRODUCED BY KIND PERMISSION OF JEWEL MUSIC PUBLISHING CO. LTD.

EMI

EMI Records Limited, 20 Manchester Square, London W1A 1ES
Sales and Distribution Centre, 1-3 Uxbridge Road, Hayes, Middlesex.

38 **YOU'RE SIXTEEN** *(2.45)*

B SIDE

39 **OH MY MY** *(4.16)*

40 **STEP LIGHTLY** *(3.14)*

41 **SIX O'CLOCK** *(4.04)*

42 **DEVIL WOMAN** *(3.58)*

43 **YOU AND ME (BABE)** *(4.31)*

As well as singing lead vocals on all tracks, Ringo also played drums throughout the album. *I'm The Greatest* was written for Ringo by John Lennon, who plays piano and supplies vocal harmonies, and is joined by George/guitar and Billy Preston/organ. *Have You Seen My Baby*, written by Randy Newman, features Marc Bolan on guitar. *Photograph* was previously released as a single, while *Sunshine Life For Me* was written for Ringo by George, while he was in Ireland with Donovan. George plays guitar, along with Robbie Robertson of the Band, the other members of that group being featured on mandolin, fiddles, banjo and accordian. George and Vini Poncia supply backing vocals.

The only "oldie" on the album, *You're Sixteen*, was written by Robert and Richard Sherman; it was originally recorded by Johnny Burnette, giving him a million seller in 1960. Ringo's version features backing vocals by Harry Nilsson, the piano of Nicky Hopkins, and Paul McCartney imitating a saxophone. *Oh My My*, written by Vini Poncia and Ringo, features the piano and organ of Billy Preston and backing vocals by Martha Reeves and Merry Clayton.

The only solo composition by Ringo on the album is *Step Lightly*, featuring Steve Cropper on electric guitar, and Ringo tap dancing. *Six O'Clock* was written by Paul and Linda McCartney for Ringo; they recorded the song in London and sent the tapes to Ringo in Los Angeles, where he recorded his version (dubbing Paul and Linda's vocals from their original version). The song features Paul on piano and synthesizer, with strings and flutes arranged by Paul. *Devil Woman*, co-written by Ringo and Vini Poncia, features Richard Perry, the producer, and Klaus Voorman on backing vocals. *You and Me (Babe)* was written by George Harrison and Mal Evans, and features George on electric guitar.

7 (38a) YOU'RE SIXTEEN *(2.45)* (42a) DEVIL WOMAN *(3.53)*

Apple R 5995 – February 8, 1974

Ringo's third global million-selling single, which entered the *NME* charts on February 12 at No. 26, rising to No. 4 on March 12, and staying in the chart for nine weeks. Having passed the million sale in the US alone, the single must have sold nearly two million globally. The release of the single, in a picture sleeve, boosted the *Ringo* album (from which both tracks were extracted) back up the album charts. The single appeared on the "Starr" label.

8 (44) ONLY YOU (AND YOU ALONE) *(3.22)* (45) CALL ME *(4.02)*

Apple R 6000 – November 15, 1974

Ringo's last chart single (so far), *Only You* entered the *NME* charts for one week at No. 25 on December 3, although it stayed in the BMRB Top 75 for eleven weeks, rising to No. 28. John Lennon suggested to Ringo that he should record *Only You*, and eventually assisted him in recording the song. Lennon played acoustic guitar, while Ringo and Jim Keltner played drums, Billy Preston/electric piano, Jesse Ed Davis and Steve Cropper/electric guitars with Harry Nilsson providing backing vocals. *Only You (And You Alone)* was written by Buck Ram and Ande Rand for The Platters, a vocal group managed by Ram, who scored a million seller with the song in 1955.

Call Me, an original Ringo composition, features Ringo/drums, Steve Cropper/guitar, Klaus Voorman/bass and David Foster/piano, with backing vocals by Lon and Derrek Van Eaton, Vini Poncia, Richard Perry, Klaus Voorman and Cynthia Webb. The single, taken from the *Goodnight Vienna* album which was released the same day, appeared in a picture sleeve, and featured a new label, showing "celestial bodies".

9 GOODNIGHT VIENNA

Apple PCS 7168 – November 15, 1974

Ringo's last chart album to date, *Goodnight Vienna* entered the *NME* Top 30 album charts on December 10 at No. 24, for one week only.

The album was recorded during the summer of 1974, at Sunset Sound and Producers' Workshop, Los Angeles, with Richard Perry producing Ringo for the last time (up to 1982). The album was recorded using over twenty-five musicians, with a basic unit of Ringo and Jim Keltner/drums and Klaus Voorman/bass, with a variety of guitarists, keyboard players and horn players on each number: John Lennon/piano (*Goodnight Vienna*), guitar (*All By Myself*) and acoustic guitar (*Only You*); Billy Preston/clavinet (*Goodnight Vienna*) and electric piano (*Only You*); Lon Van Eaton/guitar (*Goodnight Vienna* and *Occapella*), acoustic guitar (*Husbands And Wives*) and horns (*Goodnight Vienna*); Jesse Ed Davis/guitar (*Goodnight Vienna, Occapella, No No Song* and *Only You*); Carl Fortina/accordian (*Goodnight Vienna* and *Husbands And Wives*); Dr. John/electric piano (*Occapella*), piano (*Oo-Wee* and *All By Myself*); Dennis Coffey/guitar (*Oo-Wee*); Vini Poncia/acoustic guitar (*Husbands And Wives*); Richard Bennett/ electric guitar (*Husbands And Wives*); Tom Hensley/electric piano (*Husbands And Wives*); Elton John/piano (*Snookeroo*); Robbie Robertson/guitar (*Snookeroo*); James Newton Howard/synthesizer (*Snookeroo*); Alvin Robinson/guitar (*All By Myself*); Steve Cropper/guitar (*Call Me* and *Only You*); David Foster/piano (*Call Me*); Nicky Hopkins/electric piano (*No No Song*); Lincoln Mayorga/piano (*Easy For Me*); and horn players Trevor Lawrence, Steve Madaio, Bobby Keyes, Lou McCreery and Chuck Findley.

The album sleeve was designed by Roy Kohara, with a front cover illustration taken from the 1951 classic science fiction film *The Day The Earth Stood Still*, directed by Robert Wise and starring Michael Rennie as Klaatu. Klaatu is seen on the cover emerging from his "flying saucer" (Ringo's head being superimposed onto the original picture) with his nine foot tall robot Gort. The inner sleeve featured song lyrics and pictures taken by Larry Emerine at the recording sessions for the album.

A SIDE

46 **GOOD NIGHT VIENNA** *(2.33)*

47 **OCCAPELLA** *(2.50)*

48 **OO-WEE** *(3.40)*

49 **HUSBANDS AND WIVES** *(3.29)*

50 **SNOOKEROO** *(3.23)*

B SIDE

51 **ALL BY MYSELF** *(3.18)*

45a **CALL ME** *(4.05)*

52 **NO NO SONG** *(2.30)*

44a **ONLY YOU** *(3.23)*

53 **EASY FOR ME** *(2.17)*

54 **GOODNIGHT VIENNA (REPRISE)** *(1.16)*

Goodnight Vienna was written by John Lennon for Ringo, and features John playing piano, with backing vocals by Clydie King, The Blackberries and The "Masst Abbots". *Occapella*, written by Allen Toussaint and originally recorded by Lee Dorsey, features Dr. John on piano, with backing vocals by Jimmy Gilstrap, Joe Greene, Clydie King and Ira Hawkins. Ringo wrote *Oo-Wee* with Vini Poncia, who supplies harmony vocal, with backing vocals by Clydie King and The Blackberries.

Husbands And Wives, written and recorded by Roger Miller in 1966, features an electric guitar solo by Richard Bennett with Vini Poncia supplying harmony vocals. *Snookeroo* was especially written by Elton John and Bernie Taupin for Ringo, and features Elton on piano, along with Robbie Robertson (of The Band) on guitar, with vocal backing by Linda Lawrence, Clydie King and Joe Greene.

All By Myself, another Vini Poncia/Ringo composition, features John Lennon and Alvin Robinson on guitars, with vocal backing by Richard Perry, Vini Poncia,

"ONLY YOU"
THE FIRST SINGLE FROM

RINGO STARR'S
NEW ALBUM
GOODNIGHT VIENNA

PCS 7168 (Available on Cassette and Cartridge)
Produced by RICHARD PERRY

on apple records
R 6000
Marketed by EMI Records

RINGO STARR

GOODNIGHT VIENNA

Produced by RICHARD PERRY

Don't Forget:

"KLAATU BARADA NIKTO"

on apple records and tapes
PCS 7168
Marketed by EMI Records

Clydie King, Linda Lawrence and Joe Greene. *Call Me* was written by Ringo and was featured on the "B" side of the *Only You* single. *No No Song* was written by Hoyt Axton and given to Ringo, and features backing vocals by Harry Nilsson. Nilsson composed *Easy For Me*, with Lincoln Mayorga on piano, strings arranged by Trevor Lawrence and Vini Poncia, and Richard Perry conducting. The album finishes with a reprise of *Goodnight Vienna* – a different recording from the first – featuring an introduction by John Lennon, who instructs "OK with gusto, boys, with gusto."

10 (50a) SNOOKEROO *(3.24)* (48a) OO-WEE *(3.40)*

Apple R 6004 – February 21, 1975

Ringo's sixth single, his second single release from *Goodnight Vienna*, and his first not to make the charts. With this single and all subsequent releases, (singles and albums to date) Ringo has enjoyed no chart success whatsoever. Both tracks were taken from the *Goodnight Vienna* album and the single did not appear in a picture sleeve.

11 BLAST FROM YOUR PAST

Apple PCS 7170 – December 12, 1975

A fairly predictable *Greatest Hits* package of Ringo's Apple recordings, which features all eight American chart singles, five of which were British hits, along with one "B" side and an album track. The album was obviously compiled with the American market in mind, as *Beaucoups Of Blues*, *No No Song* and *Oh My My* had not been released as singles in Britain, though the latter two were to become Ringo's last Apple single. The album track, *I'm The Greatest*, was lifted from *Ringo*, while *Early 1970* was originally the "B" side to *It Don't Come Easy*. For British fans, the obvious omission was the American only "B" side to *Beaucoups Of Blues*, *Coochy Coo*, which never appeared on a British release.

Blast From Your Past was the last album to appear on the Apple label in Britain, and featured a red Apple on both "A" and "B" sides of the record. The sleeve, designed by Roy Kohara, features photographs by Emerson/Loew, with special photographic effects by Daniel Catherine. The inner sleeve included the song lyrics, plus a series of black and white photographs of Ringo. The outer sleeve contains a quote by "a local Gynecologist" (sic): "You don't have to be first But make sure you're not last!"

A SIDE

38b **YOU'RE SIXTEEN** *(2.43)*

52a **NO NO SONG** *(2.28)*

26a **IT DON'T COME EASY** *(2.59)*

33b **PHOTOGRAPH** *(3.55)*

29a **BACK OFF BOOGALOO** *(3.16)*

B SIDE

44b **ONLY YOU (AND YOU ALONE)** *(3.23)*

13a **BEAUCOUPS OF BLUES** *(2.31)*

39a **OH MY MY** *(4.15)*

27a **EARLY 1970** *(2.18)*

35a **I'M THE GREATEST** *(3.21)*

12 (39b) OH MY MY *(2.20)* (52b) NO NO SONG *(2.26)*

Apple R 6011 – January 9, 1976

Ringo's last Apple single – which coupled two songs that had previously been Top 5 hits in America, *Oh My My* (No. 5) and *No No Song* (No. 3) – originally appeared on *Ringo* and *Goodnight Vienna* respectively. The single was released to promote the *Blast From Your Past* album, on which they both appeared (*Oh My My* being a shortened version of the single), but neither the single nor the album enjoyed any chart success. The single was released in a plain sleeve.

13 RINGO'S ROTOGRAVURE

Polydor 2302 040 – September 17, 1976

Ringo's first Polydor album was recorded during April and May 1976, with Arif Mardin producing. It features well over thirty musicians, including many star names. Ringo and Jim Keltner play drums

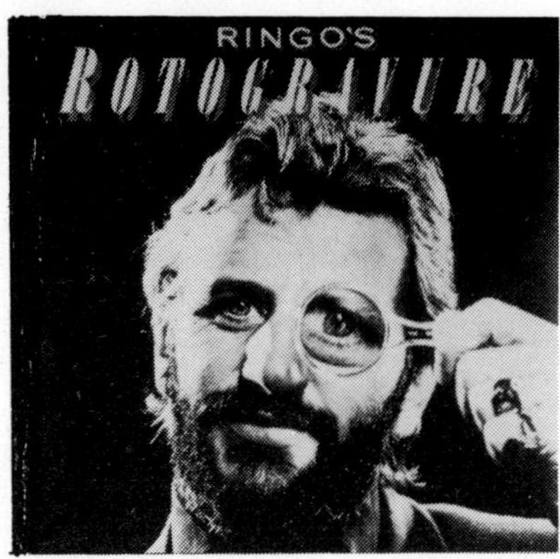

on all tracks except *Las Brisas*, with the following additional instrumentation: guitars/Peter Frampton (*A Dose Of Rock 'n' Roll*), Danny Kortchmar (*A Dose Of Rock 'n' Roll, Cookin'* and *Lady Gaye*), Jesse Ed Davis (*A Dose Of Rock 'n' Roll* and *Lady Gaye*), Mac Rebennack (*Cookin'*), Lon Van Eaton (*Hey Baby, Pure Gold, Cryin', You Don't Know Me At All, I'll Still Love You* and *This Be Called A Song*) and Eric Clapton (*This Be Called A Song*); bass guitar/Klaus Voorman (*A Dose Of Rock 'n' Roll, Pure Gold, I'll Still Love You* and *Lady Gaye*), Cooker Lo Presti (*Hey Baby, Cryin'* and *You Don't Know Me At All*) and Will Lee (*Cookin'*); pedal steel/Sneaky Pete (*Cryin'*); keyboards/Mac Rebennack (alias Dr. John) (*A Dose Of Rock 'n' Roll* and *Lady*, organ/*Cookin'*), John Jarvis (*Hey Baby, Pure Gold* and *You Don't Know Me At All* & piano/*Cryin'*), Jane Getz (*Pure Gold* & piano/*I'll Still Love You* and *This Be Called A Song*), Arif Mardin (electric piano/*Cryin'* & Arp String Ensemble/*I'll Still Love You*), John Lennon (piano/*Cookin'*); percussion/King Errisson (*Cookin'*), George Devens (congas/*Pure Gold* & marimba/*Lady Gaye*) and Robert Greenidge (steel drum/*This Be Called A Song*) and horns: trumpets/Randy Brecker (*A Dose Of Rock 'n' Roll* and *Hey Baby*), Alan Rubin (*A Dose Of Rock 'n' Roll*) and Alan Young (*Hey Baby*); tenor saxophone/Michael Brecker (*A Dose Of Rock 'n' Roll, Hey Baby* and *Lady Gaye*), George Young (*A Dose Of Rock 'n' Roll* and *Hey Baby*) and Lou Marini (*Lady Gaye*) and baritone saxophone/Lewis Delgatto (*A Dose Of Rock 'n' Roll, Hey Baby* and *Lady Gaye*).

Backing vocals were supplied by the following: Melissa Manchester (*A Dose Of Rock 'n' Roll, Cookin'* and *This Be Called A Song*), Duitch Helmer (*A Dose Of Rock 'n' Roll, You Don't Know Me At All* & *Cookin'*), Joe Bean (*A Dose Of Rock 'n' Roll* & *This Be Called A Song*), Vini Poncia (*A Dose Of Rock 'n' Roll, You Don't Know Me At All, This Be Called A Song* & *Las Brisas*), The Mad Mauries (*Hey Baby*) – these people also supply claps on *Hey Baby* – Paul and Linda McCartney (*Pure Gold*), David Lasley (*I'll Still Love You* and *Lady Gaye*) and The "Fab" Harry (Nilsson) (*Lady Gaye*). All strings and horn arrangements were by Arif Mardin.

Several people were involved in the production of the sleeve design. The original idea for the sleeve came from Ringo, with design by John Kosh. The front cover photograph was taken by David Alexander who – with Mark Hanauer – took the thirty-six photographs on the inner spread of the gatefold sleeve. The back cover picture, taken by Tommy Hanley, shows the graffiti covered front door to the Apple offices in Savile Row. Original copies of the album included a magnifying glass to examine the graffiti, which obviously refers to the Beatles, and includes such gems as: "Give John A Green Card", "We Love The Beatles", "Get Lost Rollers The Beatles Are The Best THAT'S WHAT SHE THINKS That's What I Know", "Keep On Rocking All Of You" and "Long Live The Beatles".

A SIDE

55 **A DOSE OF ROCK 'N' ROLL** *(3.24)*

56 **HEY BABY** *(3.10)*

57 **PURE GOLD** *(3.13)*

58 **CRYIN'** *(3.17)*

59 **YOU DON'T KNOW ME AT ALL** *(3.14)*

B SIDE

60 **COOKIN' (IN THE KITCHEN OF LOVE)** *(3.40)*

61 **I'LL STILL LOVE YOU** *(2.56)*

62 **THIS BE CALLED A SONG** *(3.13)*

63 **LAS BRISAS** *(3.33)*

64 **LADY GAYE** *(2.56)*

65 **SPOOKY WEIRDNESS** *(1.24)*

A Dose Of Rock 'n' Roll was given to Ringo by Carl Grossman, the composer, and features three guitars played by Frampton, Kortchmar and Davis. *Hey Baby* was written by Margaret Cobb and Bruce Channel in 1961. Channel had a million-selling hit with the song in 1962, which reached No. 1 in the US and No. 2 in Britain.

Pure Gold was written by Paul McCartney for Ringo (who sings with Vini Poncia) and features Paul and Linda on backing vocals. *Cryin'* was co-written by Vini Poncia and Ringo; Sneaky Pete plays

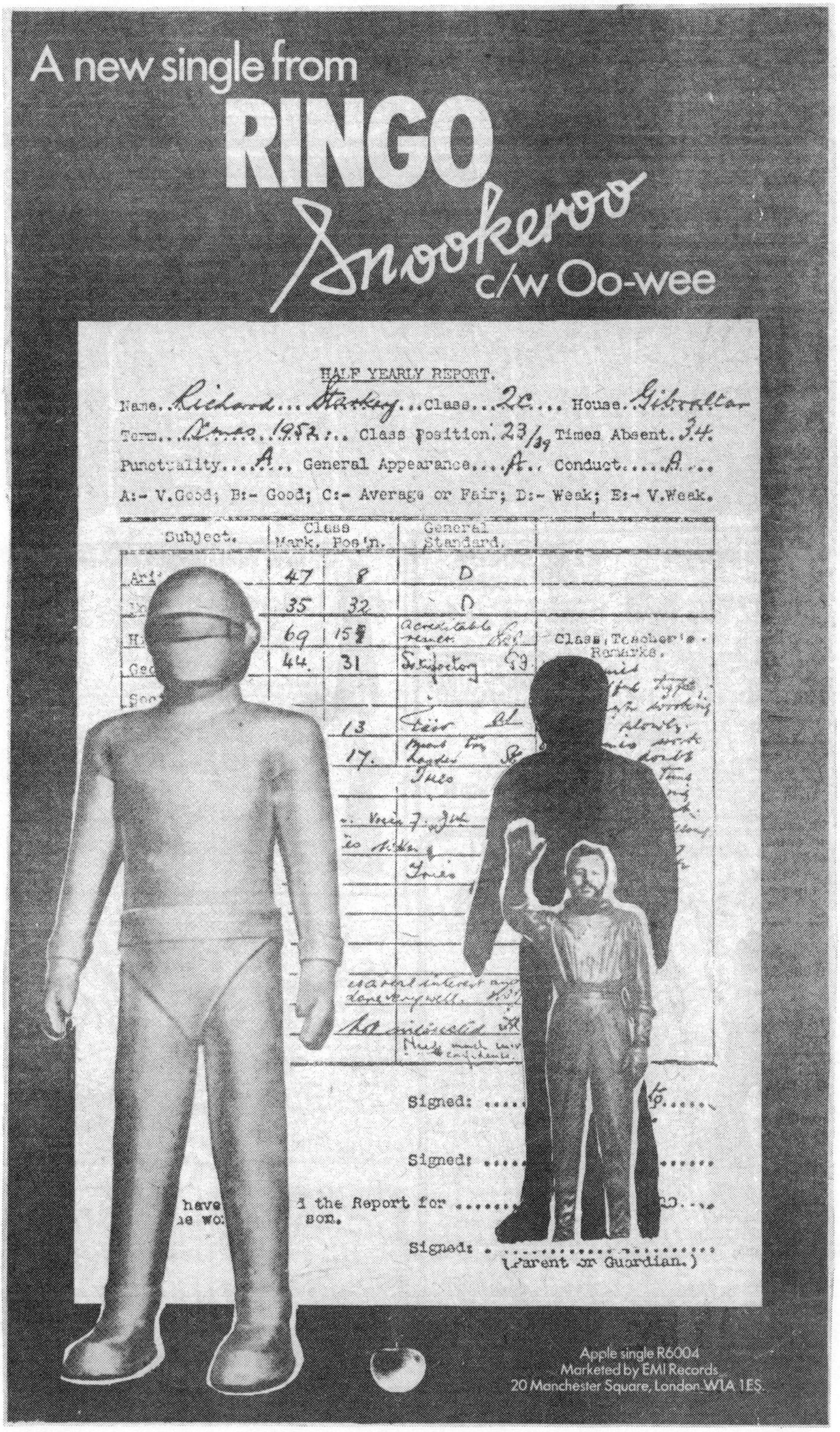

A new single from

RINGO

Snookeroo

c/w Oo-wee

HALF YEARLY REPORT.

Name. Richard ... Starkey ... Class ... 2C ... House. Gibraltar

Term ... Xmas 1952 ... Class Position. 23/39 Times Absent. 34.

Punctuality ... A .. General Appearance ... A .. Conduct ... A ...

A:- V.Good; B:- Good; C:- Average or Fair; D:- Weak; E:- V.Weak.

Subject.	Class Mark.	Class Pos'n.	General Standard.	
Ari	47	8	D	
	35	32	D	
H	69	15	Acceptable	Class Teacher's Remarks.
Geo	44.	31	Satisfactory	
Soc				
		13	Fair	
		17.		

Signed: ....

Signed: ....

have ... the Report for ....
... son.

Signed: .... (Parent or Guardian.)

Apple single R6004
Marketed by EMI Records
20 Manchester Square, London W1A 1ES.

RINGO STAR★R

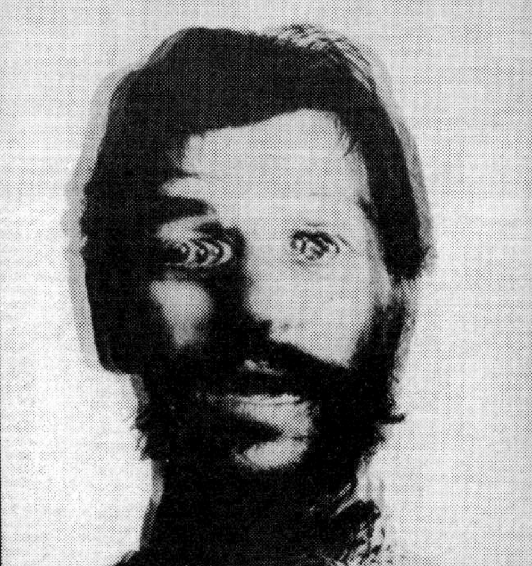

BLAST *from your* PAST

PCS 7170*

HIS NEW ALBUM

YOU'RE SIXTEEN, NO NO SONG, IT DON'T COME EASY, PHOTOGRAPH, BACK OFF BOOGALOO, ONLY YOU (AND YOU ALONE), BEAUCOUPS OF BLUES, OH MY MY, EARLY 1970, I'M THE GREATEST.

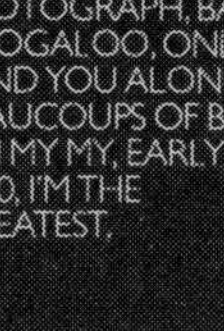

OUT NOW FOR CHRISTMAS

* Also available on tape

Marketed by EMI Records Limited, 20, Manchester Square, London W1A 1ES pedal steel guitar. *You Don't Know Me At All,* written by Dave Jordan, was given to Ringo, as was *This Be Called A Song,* written by and featuring Eric Clapton.

Cookin' (In The Kitchen Of Love) was written for Ringo by John Lennon who, with Yoko, assisted with the recording in Los Angeles by playing piano. *I'll Still Love You* was originally called "When Every Song Is Sung", and was written by George Harrison, who recorded the song several times – with Ronnie Spector, Cilla Black and Leon and Mary Russell – but never completed it. George eventually gave it to Ringo, but could not attend the recording session; so Lon Van Eaton deputised for him, producing a very "Harrisonesque" guitar sound.

Las Brisas was co-written by Ringo and Nancy Andrews, an American model whom Ringo was dating at the time, and features a Mariachi Band from a Mexican restaurant. *Lady Gaye* was co-written by Vini Poncia, Ringo and Clifford T. Ward, who composed the hit single, *Gaye,* on which the song was based *Spooky Weirdness* is a piece of musical madness adlibbed in the studio.

14 (55a) A DOSE OF ROCK 'N' ROLL *(3.17)* (58a) CRYIN' *(3.16)*

Polydor 2001 694 – October 15, 1976

Ringo's first Polydor single, featuring two tracks from the Polydor album, *Ringo's Rotogravure,* had no chart success, and was not released in a picture sleeve.

15 (56a) HEY BABY *(3.08)* (64a) LADY GAYE *(2.55)*

Polydor 2001 699 – November 26, 1976

Although a big hit for Bruce Channel in 1962, Ringo's version of *Hey Baby* did not break his chart absence. Once again, it was released in a plain sleeve.

16 (66) DROWNING IN THE SEA OF LOVE *(3.41)* (67) JUST A DREAM *(4.17)*

Polydor 2001 734 – September 16, 1977

As a trailer to his next album, Ringo released his third Polydor single, but without chart success. *Drowning In The Sea Of Love* was written by Philadelphia based Kenny Gamble and Leon Huff, and was originally recorded by Joe Simon in 1971, becoming a million seller in the US. The number features Ringo and Steve Gadd on drums, with Dave Spinozza/lead guitar, Don Grolnick/keyboards, Tony Levin/bass and either Jeff Mironov or John Tropea/guitar. *Just A Dream* was written by Ringo and Vini Poncia, and is not featured on the *Ringo The 4th* album, from which the "A" side is taken. Both tracks were produced by Arif Mardin.

17 RINGO THE 4TH

Polydor 2310 556 – September 30, 1977

Although actually his sixth album, Ringo decided to call his second Polydor LP *Ringo The 4th,* choosing to disregard *Sentimental Journey* and *Beaucoups Of Blues.* He considered *Ringo* to be his first "true" solo album.

The album was produced by Arif Mardin, and engineered by Lew Hahn, using a main instrumental line-up of: Ringo and Steve Gadd/drums, David Spinozza/lead guitar, Jeff Mironov or John Tropea/guitars, Don Grolnick/keyboards and Tony Levin/bass on all tracks except *Sneaking Sally Through The Alley, Simple Love Song* and *Gypsies In Flight* (see below), with Ken Bischel/synthesizer, Don Brooks/harmonica, Randy Brecker/trumpet and Michael Brecker/tenor saxophone.

Backing vocals were supplied by Vini Poncia, Jimmy Gilstrap, Luther Vandross, Melissa Manchester, Debra Gray, Robin Clark, David Lasley, Maxine Anderson, Marietta Waters, Brie Howard, Joe Bean, Dutch Helmer, Lynn Pitney, Arnold McCuller and Rebecca Louis.

The album sleeve was designed by John Kosh, using photographs by Nancy Andrews and Lew Hahn.

A SIDE

66a **DROWNING IN THE SEA OF LOVE** *(5.07)*

68 **TANGO ALL NIGHT** *(4.54)*

69 **WINGS** *(3.24)*

70 **GAVE IT ALL UP** *(4.40)*

71 **OUT ON THE STREETS** *(4.21)*

B SIDE

72 **CAN SHE DO IT LIKE SHE DANCES** *(3.11)*

73 **SNEAKING SALLY THROUGH THE ALLEY** *(4.15)*

74 **IT'S NO SECRET** *(3.39)*

75 **GYPSIES IN FLIGHT** *(3.01)*

76 **SIMPLE LOVE SONG** *(2.56)*

Unlike his previous three albums, on this occasion Ringo did not receive any "give away" songs from his three fellow ex-Beatles, or from any other songwriters. All but four of the songs were jointly composed by Ringo and Vini Poncia. *Drowning In The Sea Of Love*, written by Kenny Gamble and Leon Huff, had been released as a single, while *Tango All Night* was written by Tom Seufert and Steve Hague, and was originally recorded by La Seine in 1976. Ringo's version eatures Bette Midler, Melissa Manchester and Vini Poncia on backing vocals.

Can She Do It Like She Dances was written by Steve Duboff and Gerry Robinson, and originally recorded by Gold Rush in 1975. *Sneaking Sally Through The Alley*, originally recorded by Lee Dorsey in 1970, was written by Allen Toussaint. This track features Cornell Dupree and Lon Van Eaton/guitars, Richard Tee/electric piano and clavinet, David Foster/clarinet, Chuck Rainey/bass, Ringo and Steve Gadd/drums and Nick Marrero/percussion.

Gypsies In Flight, written by Ringo and Vini Poncia, features David Bromberg/electric guitar, Dick Fegy/acoustic guitar, Hugh McDonald/bass, Jeff Gutcheon/electric piano and Ringo/snare drum and brush.

Wings, Gave It All Up, Out On The Streets, It's No Secret and *Simple Love Song* were all co-written by Ringo and Vini Poncia, with the last track featuring Danny Kortchmar and Lon Van Eaton/guitars, David Foster/piano and keyboards, Chuck Rainey/bass and Ringo/drums.

SCOUSE THE MOUSE

By Various Artists

Polydor 2480 429 – December 9, 1977

Ringo's second guest appearance on a concept album features him in the title role of a children's story written by

Donald Pleasence, the veteran British actor.

Donald Pleasence narrates the story of Scouse the Mouse, played by Ringo, with two other well-known British singers, Adam Faith and Barbara Dickson, playing Bonce and Molly Jolly respectively. The album was recorded at Berwick Street Studios, London, with Hugh Murphy producing and engineering. Ringo was only featured vocally on the album as the instrumental backing was supplied by: Henry Spinetti/drums, Gary Taylor/bass, Peter Solley and Tommy Eyre/piano, Peter Solley/organ, Phil Palmer, Ray Russell and Nigel Jenkins/electric guitars, Roger Brown and Gary Taylor/ acoustic guitars, Rod King/steel guitar and dobro, Keith Nelson/banjo, Graham Preskett/fiddle and mandolin, Simon Morton/percussion and Raphael Ravenscroft/flute, with backing vocals by Gary Taylor, Joanna Carlin, Pete Zorn, Paul Da Vinci and Roger Brown.

The album was released in conjunction with an illustrated book published by the New English Library, written by Donald Pleasence, with drawings by Gerry Potterton. The album included a free "Scouse The Mouse" colouring and drawing competition entry sheet for children aged five to ten, with two hundred copies of the book as prizes.

A SIDE

77 **LIVING IN A PET SHOP** *(2.33)*
Ringo as Scouse

SING A SONG FOR THE TRAGOPAN
Barbara Dickson as Molly Jolly

78 **SCOUSE'S DREAM** *(1.50)*
Ringo

SNOW UP YOUR NOSE FOR CHRISTMAS
Ben Chatterley as Olly Jolly

RINGO'S

ROTOGRAVURE

HIS NEW ALBUM OUT NOW

INCLUDING THE SINGLE

DOSE OF ROCK 'N' ROLL

PLUS FREE MAGNIFYING GLASS WITH EVERY L.P.

polydor

RECORDS AND TAPES

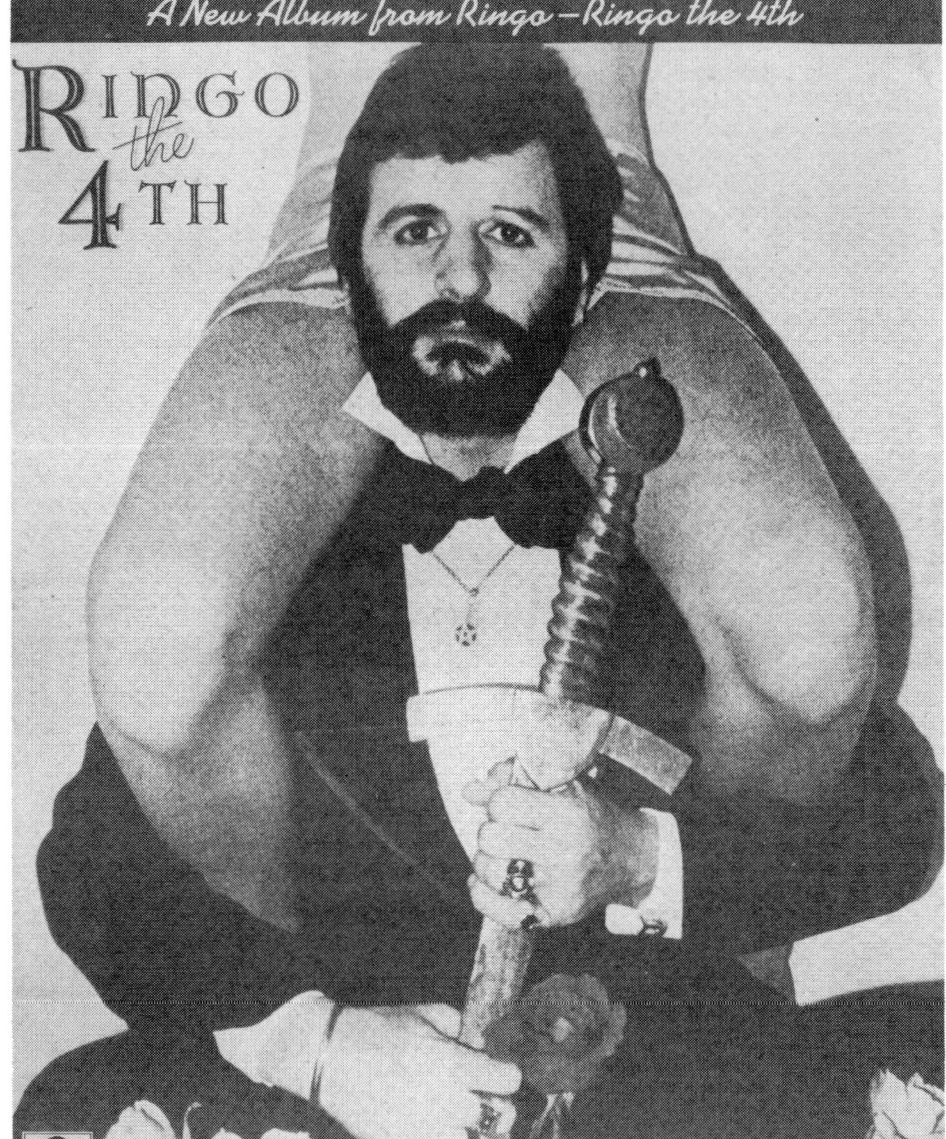

A New Album from Ringo – Ringo the 4th
RINGO the 4TH
Polydor
A New Single from Ringo – 'Drowning In the Sea Of Love

79 **RUNNING FREE** *(2.40)*
Ringo

AMERICA (A MOUSE'S DREAM)
Adam Faith as Bonce

SCOUSEY
Lucy Pleasence as Holly Jolly

B SIDE

80 **BOAT RIDE** *(1.53)*
Ringo

81 **SCOUSE THE MOUSE** *(2.40)*
Ringo

PASSENGER PIGEON
Barbara Dickson

82 **I KNOW A PLACE** *(1.32)*
Polly Pleasence as Polly Jolly
and Ringo as Scouse

CATERWAUL
(Instrumental)

83 **S. O. S.**
Ringo

ASK LOUEY
Rick Jones as Louey The Gull

84 **A MOUSE LIKE ME** *(4.16)*
Ringo

The story concerns a Liverpool mouse named Scouse, who gets bored with his ordinary life in a pet shop and then with a Liverpool family. After learning to speak English from the television, on which he sees a group called The Jollies, he decides to run away to become famous. Boarding the QE2, he meets The Jollies and sings with them, but Jeffrey (the ship's cat) accuses Scouse of imitating a human, and sentences him to be drowned. Scouse is thrown into the sea, where he drifts in his toy BEA bag, but is rescued by Louey the Gull, who sets him back onto the QE2 – bound for New York – where Scouse hopes for fame.

Although Ringo only sings eight of the fifteen songs on the album, he is also featured talking between numbers, most of which were written by Roger Brown, the musical director for the project. Brown composed *Living In A Pet Shop, Scouse's Dream, Running Free, America, Scousey, Boat Ride, Scouse The Mouse* and *S.O.S.*, and with Donald Pleasence *Sing A Song For The Tragopan* and *Passenger Pigeon.* Brown and Pleasence also co-composed *I Know A Place* with Ruan O'Lochlain, who composed the final song, *A Mouse Like Me* (which Ringo later re-recorded for his *Bad Boy* album as *A Man Like Me*). *Snow Up Your Nose For Christmas* was written by Meira and Donald Pleasence, while *Caterwaul* was composed by Jim Parker, musical arranger for the album.

18 BAD BOY

Polydor 2310 599 – June, 1978

Ringo's final Polydor album, and his last for three years, was produced by his long time friend and songwriting partner, Vini Poncia, who had assisted on all his albums since *Ringo* in 1973. The majority of Ringo's previous four albums had been recorded in Los Angeles, but for *Bad Boy* Ringo ventured outside America – to the Elite Recording Studio in the Bahamas and Can-Base Studio and Nimbus 9 in Canada. As well as Ringo on drums, the album features four anonymous musicians who are credited on the sleeve as: Push-a-lone/lead guitar, Git-tar/rhythm guitar, Hamisch Bissonette/synthesizers and Diesel/bass, with Vini Poncia's "Peaking Duck Orchestra and Chorus" (sic).

The album sleeve was designed by John Kosh (who else?) using front cover and inner sleeve photography by Nancy Andrews and back cover photography by Ringo.

A SIDE

85 **WHO NEEDS A HEART** *(3.47)*

86 **BAD BOY** *(3.13)*

87 **LIPSTICK TRACES (ON A CIGARETTE)** *(2.59)*

88 **HEART ON MY SLEEVE** *(3.19)*

89 **WHERE DID OUR LOVE GO** *(3.14)*

B SIDE

90 **HARD TIMES** *(3.31)*

91 **TONIGHT** *(2.55)*

92 **MONKEY SEE – MONKEY DO** *(3.35)*

93 **OLD TIME RELOVIN'** *(4.16)*

94 **A MAN LIKE ME** *(2.59)*

Only *Who Needs A Heart* and *Old Time Relovin'* were written by Ringo with Vini Poncia, the remaining eight songs being "oldies". *Bad Boy* was written by Lil Armstrong and Avon Long and was recorded by The Jive Bombers, featuring Clarence Palmer, whose version reached the US Top 40 during 1957. The song has also been released by Sha Na Na and Mink De Ville. *Lipstick Traces (On A Cigarette)* was written in 1962 by Naomi Neville, and originally recorded by Benny Spellman, whose version was a minor US hit in that year. *Heart On My Sleeve*, written by Benny Gallagher and Graham Lyle, gave that duo a Top Ten hit in May 1976 in the UK. *Where Did Our Love Go*, written by Ace Motown songwriters, Eddie Holland, Lamont Dozier and Brian Holland, gave The Supremes their first million seller in 1964, taking them to No. 1 in America.

Hard Times was originally recorded by its composer Peter Skellern, while *Tonight* was written by Ian McLagan (ex of the Faces) and John Pidgeon in 1977. *Monkey See – Monkey Do* was written by Michael Franks in 1975, and recorded by Melissa Manchester in 1977. *A Man Like Me* was adopted from the song *A Mouse Like Me,* written by Ruan O'Lochlain, and originally sung by Ringo in the *Scouse The Mouse* story album. The album finishes with a four second cymbal crash.

19 (87a) LIPSTICK TRACES (ON A CIGARETTE) *(2.59)*
(93a) OLD TIME RELOVIN' *(4.16)*

Polydor 2001 782 – June, 1978

Although *Lipstick Traces* was announced in the music press as the first single from the *Bad Boy* album, there appear to have been very few, if any, copies pressed; the release very shortly afterwards of *Tonight* seems to indicate that the idea of the *Lipstick Traces* single was abandoned.

20 (91a) TONIGHT *(2.50)*
(88a) HEART ON MY SLEEVE *(3.18)*

Polydor 2001 795 – July 21, 1978

With the poor sales of the first single release from *Bad Boy*, Polydor rushed out a second release – Ringo's final single for Polydor, and his last for over three years.

THE SONGS LENNON AND McCARTNEY GAVE AWAY

By Various Artists

EMI NUT 18 – April, 1979

During the Beatle years of 1963 to 1970, John and Paul composed several songs for other artists, never intending to release them officially by the Beatles. Many of these songs originally appeared only on singles, which later became very scarce and hard to find.

The twenty tracks cover every song John and Paul gave away between 1963 and 1969, although the one song sung by Ringo, written by John, is a little out of place. It dates from 1973, and would have fitted in better with a possible "Volume 2" of such songs from 1968 to the present. (This possible "Volume 2" could include such songs as: *Thingumybob*/The Black Dyke Mills Band, *Goodbye*/Mary Hopkin, *Come And Get It*/Badfinger, *God Save Us & Do The Oz*/The Elastic Oz Band, *The Ballad Of New York City*/David Peel and The Lower East Side, *Ten Years After On Strawberry Jam*/Scaffold, *4th Of July*/John Christie, *Mucho Mungo*/Harry Nilsson, *Leave It*/Mike McGear, *Mine For Me*/Rod Stewart, *Bridge Over The River Suite*/ Country Hams and *Let's Love*/Peggy Lee, along with the other songs John and Paul gave to Ringo.)

The album was compiled by Colin Miles, who also originated the sleeve concept, drawn and designed by Adam Yeldham. Colin Miles later left EMI and set up his own "See For Miles" "oldies" label, distributed by Charly Records. The album sleeve notes were written by the Beatles early PR man, Tony Barrow. The album was deleted by EMI on March 31, 1982.

A SIDE

35b **I'M THE GREATEST** *(3.20)*
Ringo Starr

ONE AND ONE IS TWO
The Strangers with Mike Shannon

FROM A WINDOW
Billy J. Kramer and The Dakotas

NOBODY I KNOW
Peter and Gordon

LIKE DREAMERS DO
The Applejacks

I'LL KEEP YOU SATISFIED
Billy J. Kramer and The Dakotas

LOVE OF THE LOVED
Cilla Black

WOMAN
Peter and Gordon

TIP OF MY TONGUE
Tommy Quickly

I'M IN LOVE
The Fourmost

B SIDE

HELLO LITTLE GIRL
The Fourmost

THAT MEANS A LOT
P.J. Proby

IT'S FOR YOU
Cilla Black

PENINA
Carlos Mendes

STEP INSIDE LOVE
Cilla Black

WORLD WITHOUT LOVE
Peter and Gordon

BAD TO ME
Billy J. Kramer and The Dakotas

I DON'T WANT TO SEE YOU AGAIN
Peter and Gordon

I'LL BE ON MY WAY
Billy J. Kramer and The Dakotas

CAT CALL
The Chris Barber Band

21 RINGO

Music For Pleasure MFP 50508 – November 27, 1980

Along with John's *Mind Games*, George's *Dark Horse* and the Beatles' *Rock And Roll Music Volumes 1 & 2*, *Ringo* was one of the first re-releases of Beatles material on a budget label. The album was reissued in a single sleeve, using a slightly amended front cover illustration from the original sleeve (the "Apple" and Latin quote is missing from the top), plus a completely revised back cover, featuring the song credits.

A SIDE

35c I'M THE GREATEST *(3.22)*

36a HAVE YOU SEEN MY BABY *(3.42)*

33c PHOTOGRAPH *(3.56)*

37a SUNSHINE LIFE FOR ME (SAIL AWAY RAYMOND) *(2.43)*

38c YOU'RE SIXTEEN, YOU'RE BEAUTIFUL (AND YOU'RE MINE) *(2.45)*

B SIDE

39c OH MY MY *(4.16)*

40a STEP LIGHTLY *(3.14)*

41a SIX O'CLOCK *(4.04)*

42a DEVIL WOMAN *(3.58)*

43a YOU AND ME (BABE) *(4.31)*

22 (95) WRACK MY BRAIN *(2.17)* (96) DRUMMING IS MY MADNESS *(3.26)*

RCA RCA 166 – November 13, 1981

Ringo's first official release for over three years featured two tracks from his first RCA album *Stop And Smell The Roses*, and appeared in a picture sleeve. *Wrack My Brain* was written for Ringo by George Harrison, who also produced the song, as well as playing both lead and acoustic guitars. Ringo plays drums, and is joined by Herbie Flowers/bass and tuba, Al Kooper/piano and electric guitar and Ray Cooper/piano, percussion, synthesizer and lead guitar. Background vocals were supplied by George and Ray Cooper using a vocoder.

Drumming Is My Madness was written for Ringo by Harry Nilsson, who also produced the song, using Ringo and Jim Keltner/drums, Dennis Budimir, Ritchie Zito and Fred Tackett/guitars, Dennis Belfield/bass, Jane Getz/piano, Jerry Jumonville/tenor saxophone, Bruce Paulson/trombone, Jim Gordon/baritone saxophone, Lee Thornburg/trumpet and Rick Riccio/flute.

The single was promoted with a specially prepared video of *Wrack My Brain*, which was aired several times on television, although it did not help sales and the single did not enter the charts.

23 STOP AND SMELL THE ROSES

RCA RCALP 6022 – November 20, 1981

Ringo's ninth album (excluding reissues) was originally titled *Can't Fight Lightning*, and was scheduled for American release in April 1981, but Ringo had a disagreement with CBS Records – who distributed Portrait Records in America – and he left the label. The proposed album was shelved, while Ringo looked around for another label, eventually signing with Boardwalk in the United States and RCA in Britain.

The album was recorded during July 1980, in Paris, with five different producers and seven engineers, using over twenty-five musicians and a dozen backing vocalists. The musicians can be broken down into five different units that worked with each producer. *Private Property*, *Attention* and *Sure To Fall* were recorded with Paul McCartney/bass, piano and percussion; Ringo/drums; Howie Casey/saxophones (not on *Sure To Fall*); Lawrence Juber/acoustic and electric guitars; and Lloyd Green/pedal steel guitar (*Sure To Fall* only).

Wrack My Brain and *You Belong To Me* feature George Harrison/lead guitar and acoustic guitar (*Wrack My Brain*); Ringo/drums; Herbie Flowers (*Wrack My Brain* only)/bass and tuba; Al Kooper/piano, guitar (*Wrack My Brain*) and synthesizer (*You Belong To Me*) and Ray Cooper/piano, synthesizer, lead guitar (*Wrack My Brain*) and tambourine (*You Belong To Me*).

The biggest unit was for *Drumming Is My Madness*, *Stop And Take The Time To Smell The Roses* and *Back Off Boogaloo* featuring Ringo/drums, Jerry Jumonville/tenor saxophone, Bruce Paulson/trombone, Jim Gordon/baritone saxophone, Lee Thornburg/trumpet, Dennis Budimir/guitar, Ritchie Zito/guitar, Jim Keltner/drums, Jane Getz/piano, Fred Tackett/guitar, Dennis Belfield/bass and Rick Riccio (*Drumming* only)/flute.

Dead Giveaway features Ron Wood/guitar, acoustic bass and saxophones, Ringo/drums, Wilton Felder/electric bass Joe Sample/piano and Greg Mathieson/piano.

You've Got A Nice Way features Steven Stills/lead guitar, Ringo/drums, Mike Finnigan/piano and organ, Mike Stergis/rhythm guitar, Joe Lala/percussion and Harley Thompson/bass.

The album sleeve, designed by John Kosh, features photography by Aaron Rapoport, and includes a dedication from Ringo to the other Beatles: "Thanks to my Three Brothers".

A SIDE

97 **PRIVATE PROPERTY** *(2.42)*

95a **WRACK MY BRAIN** *(2.19)*

96a **DRUMMING IS MY MADNESS** *(3.28)*

98 **ATTENTION** *(3.19)*

99 **STOP AND TAKE THE TIME TO SMELL THE ROSES** *(3.07)*

B SIDE

100 **DEAD GIVEAWAY** *(4.26)*

101 **YOU BELONG TO ME** *(2.07)*

102 **SURE TO FALL (IN LOVE WITH YOU)** *(3.40)*

103 **NICE WAY** *(3.29)*

104 **BACK OFF BOOGALOO** *(3.14)*

Private Property and *Attention* were written and produced by Paul McCartney, who also produced *Sure To Fall*. All three songs feature Linda McCartney, Sheila Casey, Lezlee Livrano Pariser and Paul on backing vocals. The album lyric sheet credits Lawrence Tuber as playing guitar on these tracks ("Tuber" should read

Juber, the Wings ex-guitarist). *Sure To Fall (In Love With You)* was written by Carl Perkins, Quinton Claunch and William Cantrell and was originally recorded by Carl Perkins and released in 1956. The song was also a favourite of the Beatles during their Liverpool and Hamburg club days.

Wrack My Brain, written by George, and *You Belong To Me* were produced by George, the latter being written by Pee Wee King, Redd Stewart and Chilton Price, and recorded by Jo Stafford, who scored a million-selling US No. 1 in 1952.

Drumming Is My Madness, written by Harry Nilsson, *Stop And Take The Time To Smell The Roses*, written by Harry and Ringo, and *Back Off Boogaloo* written by Ringo, were all produced by Harry Nilsson. *Back Off Boogaloo* is a new version of Ringo's 1972 hit, with a new arrangement by Van Dyke Parks, and features Harry Nilsson and Rick Riccio on backing vocals. The new arrangement includes parts of several other Beatles and Ringo songs: *With A Little Help From My Friends, Help!, Lady Madonna, Good Day Sunshine, It Don't Come Easy, Baby You're A Rich Man* and *With A Little Help From My Friends* repeated. (On the album lyric sheet the song is incorrectly titled *Back Off Bugaloo.*)

Dead Giveaway was co-written by Ringo and Ron Wood of The Rolling Stones. This duo also produced the song together, as well as supplying backing vocals. *You've Got A Nice Way* was written by Stephen Stills and Michael Stergis, it was produced by Stephen Stills, and features Stills, Mike Finnigan and Mike Stergis on backing vocals.

24 BLAST FROM YOUR PAST

Music For Pleasure MFP 50524 – November 25, 1981

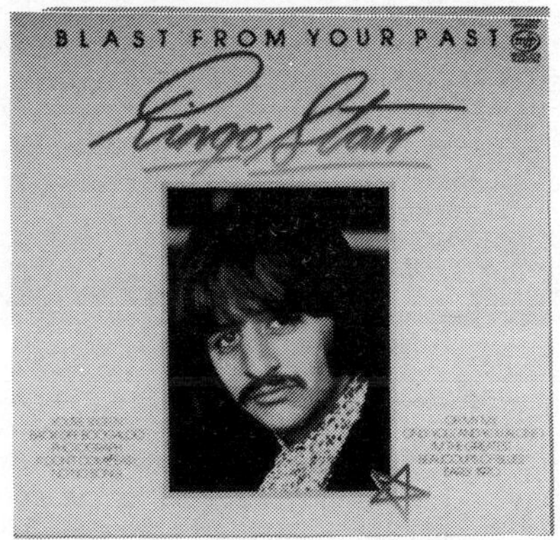

The second selection of Beatle releases on EMI's budget label, Music For Pleasure, included John's *Rock 'n' Roll*, George's *The Best Of George Harrison* and Ringo's *Blast From Your Past.* The album featured a completely new sleeve design using the picture of Ringo originally included in *The Beatles*, the white double album of 1968.

A SIDE

38d **YOU'RE SIXTEEN** *(2.43)*

52c **NO NO SONG** *(2.28)*

26b **IT DON'T COME EASY** *(2.59)*

33d **PHOTOGRAPH** *(3.55)*

29b **BACK OFF BOOGALOO** *(3.16)*

B SIDE

44c **ONLY YOU (AND YOU ALONE)** *(3.23)*

13b **BEAUCOUPS OF BLUES** *(2.31)*

39d **OH MY MY** *(4.15)*

27b **EARLY 1970** *(2.18)*

35d **I'M THE GREATEST** *(3.21)*

RINGO – US SECTION

1 SENTIMENTAL JOURNEY

Apple SW 3365 – April 24, 1970

Sentimental Journey sold 500,000 copies in the US before entering the Billboard charts on May 16, at No. 51. The album rose to No. 22 for one week on June 20, staying in the Top 30 for five weeks, the Top 100 for nine weeks and the Top 200 for fourteen weeks. (Tracks and sleeve same as British release.)

2 BEAUCOUPS OF BLUES

Apple SMAS 3368 – September 28, 1970

Although Country and Western music originated in the United States and remains very popular, Ringo's Country and Western album did poorly chartwise compared to his first album. *Beaucoups Of Blues* entered the Top 200 on October 17 at No. 141, rising to No. 65 – its highest position – on November 21, and staying in the Top 100 for nine weeks and in the Top 200 for fifteen weeks. (Tracks and sleeve same as British release.)

3 (13a) BEAUCOUPS OF BLUES (25) COOCHY COOCHY

Apple 2969 – October 5, 1970

Not released as a single in Britain, *Beaucoups Of Blues* only rose to No. 87 for two weeks from November 28 in the Billboard charts, after propping up the Top 100 on November 7 at No. 100.

The "B" side of the single featured a song, not released in Britain, called *Coochy Coo*, which was recorded during the Nashville sessions. Written by Ringo, it was originally twenty-eight minutes long!

4 (26) IT DON'T COME EASY (27) EARLY 1970

Apple 1831 – April 16, 1971

Ringo's second American single outsold his three fellow Beatles' respective singles of the same period, *Power To The People, Another Day* and *Bangla Desh*. The single entered the Billboard charts on May 1 at No. 49, rising to No. 4 for two weeks on June 5; it stayed in the Top 30 for eleven weeks, and in the Top 100 for twelve weeks. The single sold a million by August 3, 1971, receiving an RIAA Gold Award. (Sleeve same as British release.)

THE CONCERT FOR BANGLA DESH

By George Harrison and Friends

Apple STCX 3385 – December 20, 1971

Ringo guested at George's *Concert For Bangla Desh*, playing drums and singing *It Don't Come Easy*. (See original British release under Ringo and George, and American release under George.)

5 (28) BACK OFF BOOGALOO (29) BLINDMAN

Apple 1849 – March 20, 1972

Back Off Boogaloo entered the Billboard Hot Hundred on April 1, at No. 88, rising to No. 9 for two weeks on May 13, and staying in the Top 30 for six weeks and the Top 100 for ten weeks. (Sleeve same as British release.)

TOMMY

By The London Symphony Orchestra, Chamber Choir and Guest Vocalists.

Ode SP 99001 – November 27, 1972

Although not a big seller in Britain, the L.S.O.'s interpretation of *Tommy* (Pete Townshend's celebrated rock opera) was a huge success in America, where it entered the Billboard album Top 200 on December 9 at No. 136, receiving an RIAA Gold Award on December 13, and rising to No. 5 for three weeks on January 27, 1973. The album stayed in the Top 30 for eleven weeks, the Top 100 for nineteen weeks and the Top 200 for twenty-four weeks. The album received a Grammy Award for Best Album Package in 1973. (Tracks and sleeve same as British release.)

6 (33) PHOTOGRAPH (34) DOWN AND OUT

Apple 1865 – September 24, 1973

Ringo's first American No. 1, and his second US million seller. *Photograph* entered the Billboard charts on October 6 at No. 74, rising to No. 1 for one week on November 24, and staying in the Top 30 for eleven weeks. The single stayed in the Top 200 for sixteen weeks, receiving an RIAA Gold Award on December 28, 1973. (Picture sleeve same as British release.)

7 RINGO

Apple SWAL 3413 – November 2, 1973

Starr's best-selling American album, *Ringo* entered the Billboard charts at No. 15 on November 17, having received an RIAA Gold Award on November 8, 1973. The album rose to No. 2 for two weeks on December 1, staying in the Top 30 for eighteen weeks, the Top 100 for thirty-two weeks and the Top 200 for thirty-seven weeks, and selling a million copies by August 1974. (Tracks and sleeve same as British release.)

8 (38a) YOU'RE SIXTEEN (42a) DEVIL WOMAN

Apple 1870 – December 3, 1973

Ringo's second America No. 1 and his third US million-selling single entered the Billboard Hot Hundred on December 22 at No. 50 (while *Photograph* was still in the charts at No. 8) and rose five weeks later to No. 1 on January 26, 1974, for one week. It sold more than one million copies by January 31, 1974, and qualified for an RIAA Gold Award. The single stayed in the Top 30 for eleven weeks and in the Top 100 for fourteen weeks. (Picture sleeve as British release.)

9 (39a) OH MY MY (40a) STEP LIGHTLY

Apple 1872 – February 18, 1974

The third singles release from *Ringo, Oh My My* was not released in Britain at this time. However, in America it became Ringo's fifth consecutive Top Ten hit. It entered the Billboard charts on March 9 at No. 65, rising to No. 5 for one week on April 27, and staying in the Top 30 for nine weeks and in the Top 100 for thirteen weeks. (Not released in a picture sleeve.)

10 (44) ONLY YOU (AND YOU ALONE) (45) CALL ME

Apple 1876 – November 11, 1974

Ringo's seventh American single, a trailer for the *Goodnight Vienna* album, entered the Billboard Hot Hundred on November 16 at No. 63, rising to No. 6 for one week on January 11, 1975, and becoming his sixth consecutive Top Ten single. It was in the Top 30 for eight weeks and in the Top 100 for fifteen weeks. (Picture sleeve same as British release.)

11 GOODNIGHT VIENNA

Apple SW 3417 – November 18, 1974

Ringo's second Gold Award album, *Goodnight Vienna* entered the Billboard album charts on November 30 at No. 70, achieving one million dollars worth of sales by December 9, 1974. It rose to No. 8 for two weeks on January 11, 1975, and stayed in the Top 30 for nine weeks, the Top 100 for twenty weeks and the Top 200 for twenty-five weeks. (Tracks and sleeve same as British release.)

12 (52a) NO NO SONG (50a) SNOOKEROO

Apple 1880 – January 27, 1975

In Britain, *Snookeroo* was released as the "A" side coupled with *Oo-Wee*; in America it was coupled with *No No Song* as a double "A" side, and charted as such. The single entered the Billboard chart on February 8 at No. 78, rising to No. 3 for two weeks on April 5, becoming Ringo's seventh consecutive Top Ten single. It stayed in the Top 30 for eight weeks and in the Top 100 for fourteen weeks.

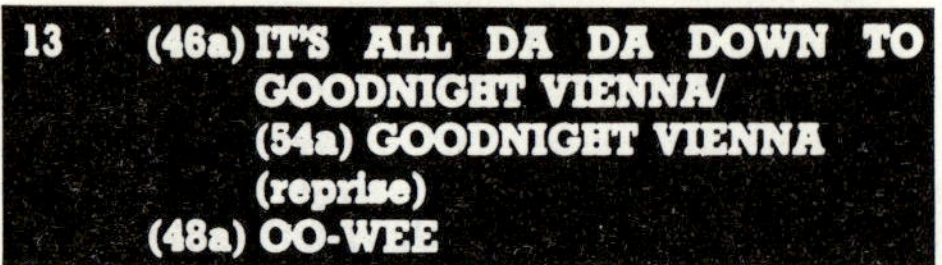

13 (46a) IT'S ALL DA DA DOWN TO GOODNIGHT VIENNA/ (54a) GOODNIGHT VIENNA (reprise) (48a) OO-WEE

Apple 1882 – June 2, 1975

The third release from *Goodnight Vienna* coupled the two versions of *Goodnight Vienna* together as a medley (Capitol's idea), giving Ringo his ninth consecutive Top 100 hit. The single did not reach the Top 30, his first comparative failure since *Beaucoups Of Blues* (his first single release). The single entered the Billboard Hot Hundred on June 14 at No. 82, rising to No. 31 for two weeks on July 31, and staying in the Top 100 for seven weeks.

14 BLAST FROM YOUR PAST

Apple SW 3422 – November 20, 1975

Ringo's greatest hits package was obviously based on his American singles, as eight of the ten tracks were US Top 100 hits, including seven Top Ten entries and two chart toppers. Up to November 1975, Ringo had released nine singles in America, all of which had entered the Billboard Top 100; and with seven being Top Tenners, he had a better hit average than John, Paul or George. John had released twelve singles with only four Top Tenners, Paul fourteen, with ten Top Tenners (although four were No. 1's), and George had seven releases, with only three Top Ten entries (two being No. 1's). The album entered the Billboard Top 200 on December 6 at No. 176, rising to No. 30 and staying in the chart for eleven weeks. (Sleeve same as British release.)

A SIDE

38b YOU'RE SIXTEEN

52b NO NO SONG

26a IT DON'T COME EASY

33b PHOTOGRAPH

29a BACK OFF BOOGALOO

B SIDE

44b ONLY YOU (AND YOU ALONE)

13b BEAUCOUPS OF BLUES

39b OH MY MY

27a EARLY 1970

35a I'M THE GREATEST

15 (55) A DOSE OF ROCK 'N' ROLL (58) CRYIN'

Atlantic 45-3361 – September 20, 1976

Ringo's first Atlantic single entered the Billboard chart on September 25, reaching No. 26 and staying in the chart for nine weeks. This was Ringo's last US Top 30 entry to date.

16 RINGO'S ROTOGRAVURE

Atlantic SD 18193 – September 27, 1976

Ringo's last appearance in the album Top 30 was with his first Atlantic album, *Ringo's Rotogravure*, which entered the Billboard Top 200 chart on October 9, reaching No. 28, and staying in the chart for nine weeks. (Sleeve same as British release.)

A SIDE

55a A DOSE OF ROCK 'N' ROLL

56 HEY BABY

57 PURE GOLD

58a CRYIN'

59 YOU DON'T KNOW ME AT ALL

B SIDE

60 COOKIN' (IN THE KITCHEN OF LOVE)

61 I'LL STILL LOVE YOU

62 THIS BE CALLED A SONG

63 LAS BRISAS

64 LADY GAYE

65 SPOOKY WEIRDNESS

17 (56a) HEY BABY (64a) LADY GAYE

Atlantic 45-3371 – November 22, 1976

With *Hey Baby*, taken from *Ringo's Rotogravure* album, Ringo made his last chart appearance of the seventies. The single entered the charts on January 29, 1977, but reached only No. 74, staying in the chart for a mere three weeks.

18 (69) WINGS (67) JUST A DREAM

Atlantic 3429 – July 25, 1977

The first single release from Ringo's second Atlantic album, *Ringo The 4th*, sank without trace, even though the "B" side was not to appear on the album.

19 RINGO THE 4TH

Atlantic SO 19108 – September 26, 1977

After the non-appearance of the previous singles in the single charts, it was hardly surprising that the album would only rise to No. 162 in the Billboard Top 200 LP charts. It remained in the chart for six weeks, after entering on October 15. (Sleeve same as British release.)

A SIDE

66 DROWNING IN THE SEA OF LOVE

68 TANGO ALL NIGHT

69a WINGS

70 GAVE IT ALL UP

71 OUT ON THE STREETS

B SIDE

72 CAN SHE DO IT LIKE SHE DANCES

73 SNEAKING SALLY THROUGH THE ALLEY

74 IT'S NO SECRET

75 GYPSIES IN FLIGHT

76 SIMPLE LOVE SONG

20 (66a) DROWNING IN THE SEA OF LOVE (67a) JUST A DREAM

Atlantic 3412 – October 18, 1977

Ringo's last record release for Atlantic also failed to make the charts. *Drowning* should have been the first release from the *Ringo The 4th* album as a single, but was substituted with *Wings*. When this single flopped, *Drowning* was hurriedly released, using the same "B" side as the earlier record.

21 (87) LIPSTICK TRACES (ON A CIGARETTE) (93) OLD TIME RELOVIN'

Portrait 6-70015 – April 18, 1978

A change of label to Portrait did not help Ringo's chart performance, his first single for his new company making no impression on the charts.

22 BAD BOY

Portrait JR-35378 – April 21, 1978

Ringo's first and only album for Portrait made a brief appearance in the Top 200 charts; it reached No. 129 and stayed in the chart for six weeks, after entering on May 20. (Sleeve same as British release.)

A SIDE

85 WHO NEEDS A HEART

86 BAD BOY

87a LIPSTICK TRACES (ON A CIGARETTE)

88 HEART ON MY SLEEVE

89 WHERE DID OUR LOVE GO

B SIDE

90 HARD TIMES

91 TONIGHT

92 MONKEY SEE – MONKEY DO

93a OLD TIME RELOVIN'

94 A MAN LIKE ME

23 (88a) HEART ON MY SLEEVE (85a) WHO NEEDS A HEART

Portrait 6-70018 – July 6, 1978

In America, Portrait played safe, releasing a song that had already proved to be hit material for its composers, Gallagher and Lyle, but Ringo's version of *Heart On My Sleeve* still failed to enter the charts.

24 RINGO

Capitol SN-16114 – October, 1980

As in Britain, Capitol re-released several old "Beatle" albums on its budget label. *Ringo* was reissued in a new single sleeve.

A SIDE

35b I'M THE GREATEST

36a HAVE YOU SEEN MY BABY

33c PHOTOGRAPH

37a SUNSHINE LIFE FOR ME (SAIL AWAY RAYMOND)

38c YOU'RE SIXTEEN

B SIDE

39c OH MY MY

40b STEP LIGHTLY

41a SIX O'CLOCK

42b DEVIL WOMAN

43a YOU AND ME (BABE)

25 SENTIMENTAL JOURNEY

Capitol SN-16218 – February, 1981

The second budget reissue of Ringo's old Capitol/Apple catalogue featured his first album and *Goodnight Vienna*. (Tracks and sleeve same as original release.)

26 GOODNIGHT VIENNA

Capitol SN-16219 – February, 1981

A SIDE

46b GOODNIGHT VIENNA

47a OCCAPELLA

48b OO-WEE

49a HUSBANDS AND WIVES

50b SNOOKEROO

B SIDE

51a ALL BY MYSELF

45b CALL ME

52c NO NO SONG

44c ONLY YOU (AND YOU ALONE)

53a EASY FOR ME

54b GOODNIGHT VIENNA (reprise)

27 BEAUCOUPS OF BLUES

Capitol SN-16235 – September, 1981

A SIDE

13c BEAUCOUPS OF BLUES

14a LOVE DON'T LAST LONG

15a FASTEST GROWING HEARTACHE IN THE WEST

16a WITHOUT HER

17a WOMAN OF THE NIGHT

18a I'D BE TALKING ALL THE TIME

B SIDE

19a $15 DRAW

20a WINE, WOMEN AND LOUD HAPPY SONGS

21a I WOULDN'T HAVE YOU ANY OTHER WAY

22a LOSER'S LOUNGE

23a WAITING

24a SILENT HOMECOMING

28 BLAST FROM YOUR PAST

Capitol SN-16236 – September, 1981

A SIDE

38d YOU'RE SIXTEEN

52d NO NO SONG

26b IT DON'T COME EASY

33d PHOTOGRAPH

29b BACK OFF BOOGALOO

B SIDE

44d ONLY YOU (AND YOU ALONE)

13d BEAUCOUPS OF BLUES

39d OH MY MY

27b EARLY 1970

35c I'M THE GREATEST

With these two last releases, all of Ringo's Apple albums were reissued on the Capitol budget series, *Beaucoups Of Blues* appearing in a single sleeve, and not in the original gatefold cover.

29 (95) WRACK MY BRAIN (96) DRUMMING IS MY MADNESS

Boardwalk NB7-11-130 – October 27, 1981

Ringo's first Top 100 singles entry since 1976 and *Hey Baby, Wrack My Brain* peaked at No. 38, after entering on November 7, and stayed in the Billboard charts for eleven weeks. (Picture sleeve same as British release.)

30 STOP AND SMELL THE ROSES

Boardwalk NB1-33246 – October 27, 1981

Although voted the "Worst Record Of 1981" in the United States, Ringo's first new album in three years entered the Billboard Top 100 on December 5, and reached No. 98, staying in the Top 200 for five weeks. (Tracks and sleeve same as British release.)

31 (97a) PRIVATE PROPERTY (99a) STOP AND TAKE THE TIME TO SMELL THE ROSES

Boardwalk NB7-11-134 – January 13, 1982

Ringo's second single release from his Boardwalk album, and another flop.

"DAYTIME NIGHTIME SUFFERING"
Wings
45 R.P.M
RECORD

HAIR PEACE
BED PEACE

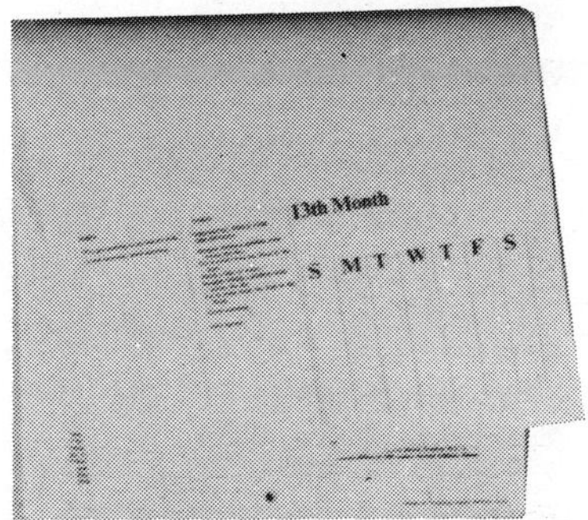
13th Month
S M T W T F S

JOHN & YOKO CALENDAR

APPENDIX 1

CHRONOLOGICAL RECORD RELEASES IN GREAT BRITAIN

This appendix lists all solo releases in chronological order, giving the appropriate record number for each solo section, i.e. "J" = John Lennon, "P" = Paul McCartney, "G" = George Harrison and "R" = Ringo Starr, in the left-hand column. Where a "C" appears, this indicates a compilation album, which does not receive a record number. Singles are listed in upper and lower case, while album titles appear in UPPER CASE only.

RECORD NUMBER	RECORD TITLE	ARTIST	LABEL	CATALOGUE NUMBER	RELEASE DATE
1968					
G1	WONDERWALL MUSIC	George Harrison	Apple	SAPCOR 1	1/11
J1	UNFINISHED MUSIC No. 1 – TWO VIRGINS	John Lennon & Yoko Ono	Track/ Apple	613012 (SAPCOR 2)	29/11
1969					
J2	UNFINISHED MUSIC No. 2 – LIFE WITH THE LIONS	John Lennon & Yoko Ono	Zapple	ZAPPLE 01	9/5
G2	ELECTRONIC SOUND	George Harrison	Zapple	ZAPPLE 02	9/5
J3	Give Peace A Chance/ Remember Love	Plastic Ono Band	Apple	APPLE 13	4/7
J4	Cold Turkey/ Don't Worry Kyoko	Plastic Ono Band	Apple	APPLES 1001	24/10
J5	THE WEDDING ALBUM	John Lennon & Yoko Ono	Apple	SAPCOR 11	7/11
J6	THE PLASTIC ONO BAND – LIVE PEACE IN TORONTO 1969	Plastic Ono Band	Apple	CORE 2001	12/12
1970					
J7	Instant Karma/ Who Has Seen The Wind	Lennon/Ono with The Plastic Ono Band	Apple	APPLES 1003	6/2
R1	SENTIMENTAL JOURNEY	Ringo Starr	Apple	PCS 7101	27/3
P1	McCARTNEY	Paul McCartney	Apple	PCS 7102	17/4
R2	BEAUCOUPS OF BLUES	Ringo Starr	Apple	PAS 10002	25/9
G3	ALL THINGS MUST PASS	George Harrison	Apple	STCH 639	27/11
J8	JOHN LENNON/PLASTIC ONO BAND	John Lennon & The Plastic Ono Band	Apple	PCS 7124	11/12
1971					
G4	My Sweet Lord/ What Is Life	George Harrison	Apple	R 5884	15/1
P2	Another Day/ Oh Woman Oh Why	Paul McCartney	Apple	R 5889	19/2
J9	Power To The People/ Open Your Box	John Lennon/Yoko Ono & The Plastic Ono Band	Apple	R 5892	12/3
R3	It Don't Come Easy/ Early 1970	Ringo Starr	Apple	R 5898	9/4
P3	RAM	Paul & Linda McCartney	Apple	PAS 10003	21/5
J	God Save Us/ Do The Oz	Bill Elliot & The Elastic Oz Band	Apple	APPLE 36	16/7

G5	Bangla Desh/ Deep Blue	George Harrison	Apple	R 5912	30/7
P4	The Back Seat Of My Car/ Heart Of The Country	Paul & Linda McCartney	Apple	R 5914	13/8
J10	IMAGINE	John Lennon & The Plastic Ono Band with The Flux Fiddlers	Apple	PAS 10004	8/10
P5	WILD LIFE	Wings	Apple	PCS 7142	3/12
1972					
G6	THE CONCERT FOR BANGLA DESH	George Harrison & Friends	Apple	STCX 3385	7/1
P6	Give Ireland Back To The Irish/Version	Wings	Apple	R 5936	25/2
R4	Back Off Boogaloo/ Blindman	Ringo Starr	Apple	R 5944	17/3
P7	Mary Had A Little Lamb/ Little Woman Love	Wings	Apple	R 5949	12/5
J11	SOMETIME IN NEW YORK CITY	John & Yoko/Plastic Ono Band with Elephant's Memory & Invisible Strings	Apple	PCSP 716	15/9
J12	Happy Xmas (War Is Over)/ Listen The Snow Is Falling	John & Yoko/Plastic Ono Band & Harlem Community Choir	Apple	R 5970	24/11
RC	TOMMY	London Symphony Orchestra/Guests	Ode	99001	24/11
P8	Hi, Hi, Hi/ C Moon	Wings	Apple	R 5973	1/12
1973					
P9	My Love/ The Mess	Paul McCartney & Wings	Apple	R 5985	23/3
P10	RED ROSE SPEEDWAY	Paul McCartney & Wings	Apple	PCTC 251	3/5
G7	Give Me Love (Give Me Peace On Earth)/Miss O'Dell	George Harrison	Apple	R 5988	25/5
P11	Live And Let Die/I Lie Around	Wings	Apple	R 5987	1/6
G8	LIVING IN THE MATERIAL WORLD	George Harrison	Apple	PAS 10006	21/6
PC	LIVE AND LET DIE	Soundtrack	United Artists	UAS 29475	6/7
R5	Photograph/ Down And Out	Ringo Starr	Apple	R 5992	19/10
P12	Helen Wheels/ Country Dreamer	Paul McCartney & Wings	Apple	R 5993	26/10
J13	Mind Games/ Meat City	John Lennon	Apple	R 5994	16/11
R6	RINGO	Ringo Starr	Apple	PCTC 252	9/11
J14	MIND GAMES	John Lennon	Apple	PCS 7165	16/11
P13	BAND ON THE RUN	Paul McCartney & Wings	Apple	PAS 10007	30/11
1974					
R7	You're Sixteen/ Devil Woman	Ringo Starr	Apple	R 5995	8/2
P14	Jet/Let Me Roll It	Paul McCartney & Wings	Apple	R 5996	18/2
P15	Band On The Run/Zoo Gang	Paul McCartney & Wings	Apple	R 5997	28/6

J15	Whatever Gets You Thru The Night/Beef Jerky	John Lennon	Apple	R 5998	4/10
J16	WALLS AND BRIDGES	John Lennon	Apple	PCTC 253	4/10
P	Walking In The Park With Eloise/Bridge Over The River Suite	The Country Hams	EMI	EMI 2220	18/10 (re-issued 1/3/82)
P16	Junior's Farm/Sally G	Paul McCartney & Wings	Apple	R 5999	25/10
R8	Only You/Call Me	Ringo Starr	Apple	R 6000	15/11
R9	GOODNIGHT VIENNA	Ringo Starr	Apple	PCS 7168	15/11
G9	Ding Dong/ I Don't Care Anymore	George Harrison	Apple	R 6002	6/12
G10	DARK HORSE	George Harrison	Apple	PAS 10008	20/12

1975

J17	No. 9 Dream/What You Got	John Lennon	Apple	R 6003	31/1
P17	Sally G/Junior's Farm	Paul McCartney & Wings	Apple	R 5999	7/2
J18	ROCK 'N' ROLL	John Lennon	Apple	PCS 7169	21/2
R10	Snookeroo/Oo-Wee	Ringo Starr	Apple	R 6004	21/2
G11	Dark Horse/ Hari's On Tour (Express)	George Harrison	Apple	R 6001	28/2
J	Philadelphia Freedom/ I Saw Her Standing There	The Elton John Band	DJM	DJS 354	28/2
J19	Stand By Me/ Move Over Ms. L	John Lennon	Apple	R 6005	18/4
P18	Listen To What The Man Said/Love In Song	Wings	Apple	R 6006	16/5
P19	VENUS AND MARS	Wings	Capitol	PCTC 254	30/5
P20	Letting Go/ You Gave Me The Answer	Wings	Capitol	R 6008	5/9
G12	You/World Of Stone	George Harrison	Apple	R 6007	12/9
G13	EXTRA TEXTURE (READ ALL ABOUT IT)	George Harrison	Apple	PAS 10009	30/9
J20	Imagine/Working Class Hero	John Lennon	Apple	R 6009	24/10
J21	SHAVED FISH (COLLECTABLE LENNON)	John Lennon	Apple	PCS 7173	24/10
P21	Venus And Mars/Rock Show/ Magneto And Titanium Man	Wings	Capitol	R 6010	28/11
R11	BLAST FROM YOUR PAST	Ringo Starr	Apple	PCS 7170	12/12

1976

R12	Oh My My/No No Song	Ringo Starr	Apple	R 6011	9/1
G14	This Guitar (Can't Keep From Crying)/Maya Love	George Harrison	Apple	R 6012	6/2
P22	WINGS AT THE SPEED OF SOUND	Wings	Parlophone	PAS 10010	26/3
P23	Silly Love Songs/ Cook Of The House	Wings	Parlophone	R 6014	30/4
P24	Let 'em In/ Beware My Love	Wings	Parlophone	R 6015	23/7
R13	RINGO'S ROTOGRAVURE	Ringo Starr	Polydor	2302 040	17/9
R14	A Dose Of Rock 'n' Roll/ Cryin'	Ringo Starr	Polydor	2001 694	15/10
G15	This Song/ Learning How To Love You	George Harrison	Dark Horse	K 16856	19/11
G16	THIRTY THREE & ⅓	GEORGE HARRISON	Dark Horse	K 56319	19/11

G17	THE BEST OF GEORGE HARRISON	George Harrison	Parlophone	PAS 10011	20/11
R15	Hey Baby/Lady Gaye	Ringo Starr	Polydor	2001 699	26/11
P25	WINGS OVER AMERICA	Wings	Parlophone	PCSP 720	10/12
G18	My Sweet Lord/ What Is Life	George Harrison	Apple	R5884	?/12
1977					
P26	Maybe I'm Amazed/Soily	Wings	Parlophone	R 6017	4/2
G19	True Love/Pure Smokey	George Harrison	Dark Horse	K 16896	18/2
P	Uncle Albert/Admiral Halsey/Eat At Home	Percy Thrillington	Regal Zonophone	EMI 2594	?/4
P	THRILLINGTON	Percy Thrillington	Regal Zonophone	EMC 3175	29/4
G20	It's What You Value/ Woman Don't You Cry For Me	George Harrison	Dark Horse	K 16967	10/6
R16	Drowning In The Sea Of Love/Just A Dream	Ringo Starr	Polydor	2001 734	16/9
R17	RINGO THE 4TH	Ringo Starr	Polydor	2310 556	30/9
P27	Mull Of Kintyre/ Girls School	Wings	Capitol	R 6018	11/11
RC	SCOUSE THE MOUSE	Various	Polydor	2480429	9/12
1978					
P28	With A Little Luck/ Backwards Traveller/ Cuff Link	Wings	Parlophone	R 6019	23/3
P29	LONDON TOWN	Wings	Parlophone	PAS 10012	31/3
R18	BAD BOY	Ringo Starr	Polydor	2310 599	?/4
R19	Lipstick Traces/ Old Time Relovin'	Ringo Starr	Polydor	2001 782	?/6
P30	I've Had Enough/ Deliver Your Children	Wings	Parlophone	R 6020	16/6
R20	Tonight/ Heart On My Sleeve	Ringo Starr	Polydor	2001 795	21/7
P31	London Town/I'm Carrying	Wings	Parlophone	R 6021	15/9
P32	WINGS GREATEST	Wings	Parlophone	PCTC 256	1/12
1979					
G21	GEORGE HARRISON	George Harrison	Dark Horse	K 56562	23/2
G22	Blow Away/Soft Touch	George Harrison	Dark Horse	K 17327	2/3
P33	Goodnight Tonight/ Daytime Nightime Suffering	Wings	Parlophone	R 6023	23/3
P34	Goodnight Tonight/ Daytime Nightime Suffering	Wings	Parlophone	12Y R 6023	?/3
RC	THE SONGS LENNON AND McCARTNEY GAVE AWAY	Various	EMI	NUT 18	?/4
G23	Love Comes To Everyone/ Soft-Hearted Hana	George Harrison	Dark Horse	K 17284	?/5
G/JC	A MONUMENT TO BRITISH ROCK	Various	Harvest	EMTV 17	4/5
P35	Old Siam Sir/Spin It On	Wings	Parlophone	R 6026	1/6
P36	BACK TO THE EGG	Wings	Parlophone	PCTC 257	8/6
G24	Faster/ Your Love Is Forever	George Harrison	Dark Horse	K 17423	20/7

G25	Faster/Your Love is Forever (picture disc)	George Harrison	Dark Horse	K 17423P	?/7
P37	Getting Closer/ Baby's Request	Wings	Parlophone	R 6027	10/8
P	Seaside Woman/ B Side To Seaside	Suzy And The Red Stripes	A&M	AMS 7461	?/8
P	Seaside Woman/ B Side To Seaside (box set)	Suzy And The Red Stripes	A&M	AMSP 7461	?/8
P38	Wonderful Christmastime/ Rudolph The Red Nosed Reggae	Paul McCartney	Parlophone	R 6029	16/11

1980

PC	THE SUMMIT	Various	K-tel	NE 1067	19/1
P39	Coming Up/Coming Up (Live At Glasgow)/Lunchbox/Odd Sox	Paul McCartney	Parlophone	R 6035	11/4
P40	McCARTNEY II	Paul McCartney	Parlophone	PCTC 258	16/5
P41	Waterfalls/ Check My Machine	Paul McCartney	Parlophone	R 6037	14/6
P	Seaside Woman/ B Side To Seaside	Linda McCartney	A&M	AMS 7548	18/7
P	Seaside Woman/ B Side To Seaside (twelve-inch)	Linda McCartney	A&M	AMSP 7548	18/7
P42	Temporary Secretary/ Secret Friend	Paul McCartney	Parlophone	12 R 6039	15/9
J22	(Just Like) Starting Over/ Kiss Kiss Kiss	John Lennon & Yoko Ono	Geffen	K 79186	24/10
J23	DOUBLE FANTASY	John Lennon & Yoko Ono	Geffen	K 99131	17/11
R21	RINGO	Ringo Starr	Music For Pleasure	MFP 50508	27/11
J24	MIND GAMES	John Lennon	Music For Pleasure	MFP 50509	27/11
G26	DARK HORSE	George Harrison	Music For Pleasure	MFP 50510	27/11
GC	THE GUINNESS ALBUM – HITS OF THE 70'S	Various	CBS	S CBS 10020	5/12

1981

J25	Woman/Beautiful Boys	John Lennon & Yoko Ono	Geffen	K 79195	16/1
P43	THE McCARTNEY INTERVIEW	Paul McCartney	Parlophone	CHAT 1	23/2
J	I Saw Her Standing There/ Whatever Gets You Thru The Night/Lucy In The Sky With Diamonds	Elton John & John Lennon	DJM	DJS 10965	13/2
J26	Watching The Wheels/ Yes, I'm Your Angel	John Lennon & Yoko Ono	Geffen	K 79207	27/3
PC	THE CONCERTS FOR KAMPUCHEA	Various	Atlantic	K 60153	3/4
G27	All Those Years Ago/ Writings On The Wall	George Harrison	Dark Horse	K 17807	15/5
G28	SOMEWHERE IN ENGLAND	George Harrison	Dark Horse	K 56870	5/6
J27	JOHN LENNON (box set)	John Lennon	Apple	JLB 8	15/6
G29	Teardrops/Save The World	George Harrison	Dark Horse	K 17837	31/7
R22	Wrack My Brain/ Drumming Is My Madness	Ringo Starr	RCA	RCA 166	13/11
R23	STOP AND SMELL THE ROSES	Ringo Starr	RCA	RCALP 6022	20/11
J28	ROCK 'N' ROLL	John Lennon	Music For Pleasure	MFP 50522	25/11

G30	**THE BEST OF GEORGE HARRISON**	**George Harrison**	Music For Pleasure	MFP 50523	25/11
R24	**BLAST FROM YOUR PAST**	**Ringo Starr**	Music For Pleasure	MFP 50524	25/11
1982					
PC	**JAMES BOND GREATEST HITS**	**Various**	Liberty	EMTV 007	8/3
P44	**Ebony And Ivory/ Rainclouds**	**Paul McCartney with Stevie Wonder**	Parlophone	R 6054	29/3
P45	**Ebony And Ivory/Rainclouds/ Ebony And Ivory (twelve-inch)**	**Paul McCartney with Stevie Wonder**	Parlophone	12 R 6054	?/3
P46	**TUG OF WAR**	**Paul McCartney**	Parlophone	PCTC 259	26/4
P47	**Take It Away/ I'll Give You A Ring**	**Paul McCartney**	Parlophone	R 6056	21/6
P48	**Take It Away/I'll Give You A Ring/Dress Me Up As A Robber (twelve-inch)**	**Paul McCartney**	Parlophone	12 R 6056	5/7
P49	**Tug Of War/Get It**	**Paul McCartney**	Parlophone	R 6057	20/9
G31	**Wake Up My Love/Greece**	**George Harrison**	Dark Horse	929864-7	8/11
G32	**GONE TROPPO**	**George Harrison**	Dark Horse	923734-1	8/11
J29	**THE JOHN LENNON COLLECTION**	**John Lennon**	Parlophone	EMTV 37	8/11
J30	**Love/Gimme Some Truth**	**John Lennon**	Parlophone	R 6059	15/11
P	**The Girl Is Mine/ Can't Get Outta The Rain**	**Michael Jackson and Paul McCartney**	Epic	EPC A2729	29/11
P	**The Girl Is Mine/ Can't Get Outta The Rain (picture disc)**	**Michael Jackson and Paul McCartney**	Epic	EPC A 11-2729	?/11

CHRONOLOGICAL RECORD RELEASES IN THE UNITED STATES OF AMERICA

RECORD NUMBER	RECORD TITLE	ARTIST	LABEL	CATALOGUE NUMBER	RELEASE DATE
1968					
J1	UNFINISHED MUSIC No. 1 – TWO VIRGINS	John Lennon & Yoko Ono	Apple	T 5001	11/11
G1	WONDERWALL MUSIC	George Harrison	Apple	ST 3350	2/12
1969					
J2	UNFINISHED MUSIC No. 2 – LIFE WITH THE LIONS	John Lennon & Yoko Ono	Zapple	ST 3357	26/5
G2	ELECTRONIC SOUND	George Harrison	Zapple	ST 3358	26/5
J3	Give Peace A Chance/ Remember Love	Plastic Ono Band	Apple	1809	7/7
J4	Cold Turkey/ Don't Worry Kyoko	Plastic Ono Band	Apple	1813	20/10
J5	THE WEDDING ALBUM	John Lennon & Yoko Ono	Apple	SMAX 3361	20/10
J6	THE PLASTIC ONO BAND – LIVE PEACE IN TORONTO 1969	Plastic Ono Band	Apple	SW 3362	12/12
1970					
J7	Instant Karma/ Who Has Seen The Wind	Lennon/Ono with The Plastic Ono Band	Apple	1818	20/2
P1	McCARTNEY	Paul McCartney	Apple	STAO 3363	20/4
R1	SENTIMENTAL JOURNEY	Ringo Starr	Apple	SW 3365	24/4
R2	BEAUCOUPS OF BLUES	Ringo Starr	Apple	SMAS 3368	28/9
R3	Beaucoups of Blues/Coochy Coo	Ringo Starr	Apple	2969	5/10
G3	My Sweet Lord/ Isn't It A Pity (version 1)	George Harrison	Apple	2995	23/11
G4	ALL THINGS MUST PASS	George Harrison	Apple	STCH 639	27/11
J8	JOHN LENNON/ PLASTIC ONO BAND	John Lennon and The Plastic Ono Band	Apple	SW 3372	11/12
J9	Mother/Why	John Lennon/Yoko Ono & Plastic Ono Band	Apple	1827	28/12
1971					
G5	What Is Life/ Apple Scruffs	George Harrison	Apple	1828	15/2
P2	Another Day/ Oh Woman Oh Why	Paul McCartney	Apple	1829	22/2
J10	Power To The People/ Touch Me	John Lennon/Yoko Ono & Plastic Ono Band	Apple	1830	22/3
R4	It Don't Come Easy/ Early 1970	Ringo Starr	Apple	1831	16/4
P3	RAM	Paul & Linda McCartney	Apple	SMAS 3375	17/5
J	God Save Us/Do The Oz	Bill Elliot & The Elastic Oz Band	Apple	1835	7/7
G6	Bangla Desh/Deep Blue	George Harrison	Apple	1836	28/7
P4	Uncle Albert/Admiral Halsey/Too Many People	Paul & Linda McCartney	Apple	1837	2/8

J11	**IMAGINE**	**John Lennon**	Apple	SW 3379	9/9
J12	**Imagine/It's So Hard**	**John Lennon**	Apple	1840	11/10
J13	**Happy Xmas (War Is Over)/ Listen The Snow Is Falling**	**John & Yoko/Plastic Ono Band & The Harlem Community Choir**	Apple	1842	1/12
P5	**WILD LIFE**	**Wings**	Apple	SW 3386	7/12
G7	**THE CONCERT FOR BANGLA DESH**	**George Harrison & Friends**	Apple	STCX 3385	20/12
1972					
P6	**Give Ireland Back To The Irish/version**	**Wings**	Apple	1847	28/2
R5	**Back off Boogaloo/ Blindman**	**Ringo Starr**	Apple	1849	20/3
J14	**Woman Is The Nigger Of The World/Sisters O Sisters**	**John Lennon/Yoko Ono & Plastic Ono Band**	Apple	1848	24/4
P7	**Mary Had A Little Lamb/ Little Woman Love**	**Wings**	Apple	1851	29/5
J15	**SOMETIME IN NEW YORK CITY**	**John & Yoko/Plastic Ono Band with Elephant's Memory & Invisible Strings**	Apple	SVBB 3392	12/6
RC	**TOMMY**	**London Symphony Orchestra & Guests**	Ode	SP 99001	27/11
P8	**Hi, Hi, Hi/C Moon**	**Wings**	Apple	1857	4/12
1973					
P9	**My Love/The Mess**	**Paul McCartney & Wings**	Apple	1861	9/4
P10	**RED ROSE SPEEDWAY**	**Paul McCartney & Wings**	Apple	SMAL 3409	30/4
G8	**Give Me Love (Give Me Peace On Earth)/Miss O'Dell**	**George Harrison**	Apple	1862	7/5
G9	**LIVING IN THE MATERIAL WORLD**	**George Harrison**	Apple	SMAS 3410	30/5
P11	**Live And Let Die/ I Lie Around**	**Wings**	Apple	1863	18/6
PC	**LIVE AND LET DIE**	**Soundtrack**	United Artists	LA 100-G	2/7
R6	**Photograph/Down And Out**	**Ringo Starr**	Apple	1865	24/9
J16	**Mind Games/Meat City**	**John Lennon**	Apple	1868	29/10
R7	**RINGO**	**Ringo Starr**	Apple	SWAL 3413	2/11
J17	**MIND GAMES**	**John Lennon**	Apple	SW 3414	2/11
P12	**Helen Wheels/ Country Dreamer**	**Paul McCartney & Wings**	Apple	1869	12/11
R8	**You're Sixteen/ Devil Woman**	**Ringo Starr**	Apple	1870	3/12
P13	**BAND ON THE RUN**	**Paul McCartney & Wings**	Apple	SO 3415	5/12
1974					
P14	**Jet/Mamunia**	**Paul McCartney & Wings**	Apple	1871	28/1
P15	**Jet/Let Me Roll It**	**Paul McCartney & Wings**	Apple	1871	18/2
R9	**Oh My My/Step Lightly**	**Ringo Starr**	Apple	1872	18/2
P16	**Band On The Run/Nineteen Hundred And Eighty Five**	**Paul McCartney & Wings**	Apple	1873	8/4
J18	**Whatever Gets You Thru The Night/Beef Jerky**	**John Lennon**	Apple	1874	23/9

J19	WALLS AND BRIDGES	John Lennon	Apple	SW 3416	26/9
P17	Junior's Farm/Sally G	Paul McCartney & Wings	Apple	1875	4/11
R10	Only You (And You Alone)/ Call Me	Ringo Starr	Apple	1876	11/11
R11	GOODNIGHT VIENNA	Ringo Starr	Apple	SW 3417	18/11
G10	Dark Horse/ I Don't Care Anymore	George Harrison	Apple	1877	18/11
P	Walking In The Park With Eloise/Bridge Over The River Suite	The Country Hams	EMI	3977	2/12
G11	DARK HORSE	George Harrison	Apple	SMAS 3418	9/12
J20	No. 9 Dream/What You Got	John Lennon	Apple	1878	16/12
G12	Ding Dong Ding Dong/ Hari's On Tour (Express)	George Harrison	Apple	1879	23/12

1975 ....

P18	Sally G/Junior's Farm	Paul McCartney & Wings	Apple	1875	20/1
R12	No No Song/Snookeroo	Ringo Starr	Apple	1880	27/1
J21	ROCK 'N' ROLL	John Lennon	Apple	SK 3419	17/2
J	Philadelphia Freedom/ I Saw Her Standing There	The Elton John Band	MCA	40364	24/2
J22	Stand By Me/Move Over Ms. L	John Lennon	Apple	1881	10/3
P19	Listen To What The Man Said/Love In Song	Wings	Capitol	4091	23/5
P20	VENUS AND MARS	Wings	Capitol	SMAS 11419	27/5
R13	It's All Da Da Down To Goodnight Vienna/Oo-Wee	Ringo Starr	Apple	1882	2/6
G13	You/World Of Stone	George Harrison	Apple	1884	15/9
G14	EXTRA TEXTURE (READ ALL ABOUT IT)	George Harrison	Apple	SW 3420	22/9
P21	Letting Go/ You Gave Me The Answer	Wings	Capitol	4145	29/9
J23	SHAVED FISH (COLLECTABLE LENNON)	John Lennon	Apple	SW 3421	24/10
P22	Venus And Mars/Rock Show/ Magneto And Titanium Man	Wings	Capitol	4175	27/10
R14	BLAST FROM YOUR PAST	Ringo Starr	Apple	SW 3422	20/11
G15	This Guitar (Can't Keep From Crying)/Maya Love	George Harrison	Apple	1885	8/12

1976 ....

P23	WINGS AT THE SPEED OF SOUND	Wings	Capitol	SW 11525	25/3
P24	Silly Love Songs/ Cook Of The House	Wings	Capitol	4256	1/4
P25	Let 'em In/ Beware My Love	Wings	Capitol	4293	28/6
R15	A Dose Of Rock 'n' Roll/ Cryin'	Ringo Starr	Atlantic	45-3361	20/9
R16	RINGO'S ROTOGRAVURE	Ringo Starr	Atlantic	SD 18193	27/9
G16	THE BEST OF GEORGE HARRISON	George Harrison	Capitol	ST 11578	8/11
G17	This Song/ Learning How To Love You	George Harrison	Dark Horse	DRC 8294	15/11
R17	Hey Baby/Lady Gaye	Ringo Starr	Atlantic	45-3371	22/11

G18	**THIRTY THREE & ⅓**	**George Harrison**	Dark Horse	DH 3005	24/11
P26	**WINGS OVER AMERICA**	**Wings**	Capitol	SWCO 11593	10/12
1977					
G19	**Crackerbox Palace/ Learning How To Love You**	**George Harrison**	Dark Horse	DRC 8313	24/1
P27	**Maybe I'm Amazed/Soily**	**Wings**	Capitol	4385	7/2
J24	**Stand By Me/ Woman Is The Nigger Of The World**	**John Lennon**	Capitol Star Line	6244	4/4
G20	**Dark Horse/You**	**George Harrison**	Capitol Star Line	6245	4/4
P	**Seaside Woman/ B Side To Seaside**	**Suzy & The Red Stripes**	Epic	8-50403	31/5
R18	**Wings/Just A Dream**	**Ringo Starr**	Atlantic	3429	25/7
R19	**RINGO THE 4TH**	**Ringo Starr**	Atlantic	SD 19108	26/9
R20	**Drowning In The Sea Of Love/Just A Dream**	**Ringo Starr**	Atlantic	3412	18/10
P28	**Mull Of Kintyre/ Girls School**	**Wings**	Capitol	4504	14/11
1978					
P29	**With A Little Luck/ Backwards Traveller/ Cuff Link**	**Wings**	Capitol	4559	20/3
P30	**LONDON TOWN**	**Wings**	Capitol	SW 11777	31/3
R21	**Lipstick Traces/ Old Time Relovin'**	**Ringo Starr**	Portrait	6-70015	18/4
R22	**BAD BOY**	**Ringo Starr**	Portrait	JR-35378	21/4
P31	**I've Had Enough/ Deliver Your Children**	**Wings**	Capitol	4594	12/6
R23	**Heart On My Sleeve/ Who Needs A Heart**	**Ringo Starr**	Portrait	6-70018	6/7
P32	**London Town/I'm Carrying**	**Wings**	Capitol	4625	21/8
P33	**WINGS GREATEST**	**Wings**	Capitol	SOO 11905	22/11
P34	**BAND ON THE RUN (picture disc)**	**Paul McCartney & Wings**	Capitol	SEAX 11901	?/12
1979					
G21	**Blow Away/ Soft-Hearted Hana**	**George Harrison**	Dark Horse	DRC 8763	14/2
G22	**GEORGE HARRISON**	**George Harrison**	Dark Horse	DHK-3255	14/2
P35	**Goodnight Tonight/ Daytime Nightime Suffering**	**Wings**	Columbia	3-10939	15/3
P36	**Goodnight Tonight/ Daytime Nightime Suffering (twelve-inch)**	**Wings**	Columbia	23-10940	15/3
G23	**Love Comes To Everyone/ Soft Touch**	**George Harrison**	Dark Horse	DRC 8844	9/5
P37	**BACK TO THE EGG**	**Wings**	Columbia	FC-36057	24/5
P38	**Getting Closer/ Spin It On**	**Wings**	Columbia	3-11020	5/6
P39	**Arrow Through Me/ Old Siam Sir**	**Wings**	Columbia	1-11070	14/8
P40	**Wonderful Christmastime/ Rudolph The Red Nosed Reggae**	**Paul McCartney**	Columbia	1-11162	20/11

1980 ....

P41	Coming Up (Live At Glasgow)/Lunch Box/ Odd Sox	Paul McCartney	Columbia	1-11263	15/4
P42	McCARTNEY II	Paul McCartney	Columbia	FC-36511	21/5
P43	McCARTNEY	Paul McCartney	Columbia	FC-36478	22/5
P44	RAM	Paul & Linda McCartney	Columbia	FC-36479	22/5
P45	WILD LIFE	Wings	Columbia	FC-36480	22/5
P46	RED ROSE SPEEDWAY	Paul McCartney & Wings	Columbia	FC-36481	22/5
P47	BAND ON THE RUN	Paul McCartney & Wings	Columbia	FC-36482	22/5
P48	Waterfalls/ Check My Machine	Paul McCartney	Columbia	1-11335	22/7
P49	VENUS AND MARS	Wings	Columbia	FC-36801	25/9
J25	(Just Like) Starting Over/ Kiss Kiss Kiss	John Lennon & Yoko Ono	Geffen	GEF-49604	23/10
G24	DARK HORSE	George Harrison	Capitol	SN-16055	–/10
J26	MIND GAMES	John Lennon	Capitol	SN-16068	–/10
J27	ROCK 'N' ROLL	John Lennon	Capitol	SN-16069	–/10
R24	RINGO	Ringo Starr	Capitol	SN-16114	–/10
J28	DOUBLE FANTASY	John Lennon & Yoko Ono	Geffen	GHS-2001	17/11
P50	THE McCARTNEY INTERVIEW	Paul McCartney	Columbia	PC-36987	4/12
P51	Getting Closer/ Goodnight Tonight	Wings	Columbia Hall Of Fame	13-33405	4/12
P52	My Love/Maybe I'm Amazed	Paul McCartney & Wings/ Paul McCartney	Columbia Hall Of Fame	13-33407	4/12
P53	Uncle Albert/Admiral Halsey/Jet	Paul & Linda McCartney/ Paul McCartney & Wings	Columbia Hall Of Fame	13-33408	4/12
P54	Band On The Run/ Helen Wheels	Paul McCartney & Wings	Columbia Hall Of Fame	13-33409	4/12

1981 ....

J29	Woman/Beautiful Boys	John Lennon & Yoko Ono	Geffen	49644	12/1
G25	LIVING IN THE MATERIAL WORLD	George Harrison	Capitol	SN-16216	–/2
G26	EXTRA TEXTURE (READ ALL ABOUT IT)	George Harrison	Capitol	SN-16217	–/2
R25	SENTIMENTAL JOURNEY	Ringo Starr	Capitol	SN-16218	–/2
R26	GOODNIGHT VIENNA	Ringo Starr	Capitol	SN-16219	–/2
J30	Watching The Wheels/ Yes, I'm Your Angel	John Lennon & Yoko Ono	Geffen	49695	13/3
PC	THE CONCERTS FOR KAMPUCHEA	Various artists	Atlantic	SD 2 7005	30/3
P55	BAND ON THE RUN (half-speed master)	Paul McCartney & Wings	Columbia	HC 46482	24/4
G27	All Those Years Ago/ Writing On The Wall	George Harrison	Dark Horse	DRC 49725	11/5
G28	SOMEWHERE IN ENGLAND	George Harrison	Dark Horse	DHK 3492	1/6
J31	(Just Like) Starting Over/ Woman	John Lennon	Geffen	GGEF 0408	5/6
P56	Silly Love Songs/ Cook Of The House	Wings	Columbia	18-02171	12/6
P57	WINGS AT THE SPEED OF SOUND	Wings	Columbia	FC-37409	13/7

G29	Teardrops/ Save The World	George Harrison	Dark Horse	DRC 79825	24/7
R27	BEAUCOUPS OF BLUES	RINGO STARR	Capitol	SN-16235	–/9
R28	BLAST FROM YOUR PAST	Ringo Starr	Capitol	SN-16236	–/9
R29	Wrack My Brain/ Drumming Is My Madness	Ringo Starr	Boardwalk	NB7-11-130	27/10
R30	STOP AND SMELL THE ROSES	Ringo Starr	Boardwalk	NB1-33246	27/10
G30	All Those Years Ago/ Teardrops	George Harrison	Dark Horse	GDRC 0410	4/11
J32	Watching The Wheels/ Beautiful Boy	John Lennon	Geffen	GGEF 0415	4/11
1982					
R31	Private Property/ Stop And Take The Time To Smell The Roses	Ringo Starr	Boardwalk	NB7-11-134	13/1
P58	Ebony And Ivory/ Rainclouds	Paul McCartney with Stevie Wonder	Columbia	18-02860	2/4
P59	Ebony And Ivory/ Rainclouds/Ebony And Ivory (twelve-inch)	Paul McCartney with Stevie Wonder	Columbia	44-02878	16/4
P60	TUG OF WAR	Paul McCartney	Columbia	TC 37462	26/4
P61	Take It Away/ I'll Give You A Ring	Paul McCartney	Columbia	18-03018	29/6
P62	Take It Away/ I'll Give You A Ring/ Dress Me Up As A Robber (twelve-inch)	Paul McCartney	Columbia		?/6
P63	Tug of War/Get It	Paul McCartney	Columbia	38-03235	14/9
	The Girl Is Mine/ Can't Get Out Of The Rain	Michael Jackson/ Paul McCartney	Epic	34-03288	3/10
G31	Wake Up My Love/Greece	George Harrison	Dark Horse	7-29864	?/11
G32	GONE TROPPO	George Harrison	Dark Horse	1-23734	?/11
J33	THE JOHN LENNON COLLECTION	John Lennon	Geffen	GHSP 2023	10/11
J34	Happy Xmas (War Is Over)/ Beautiful Boy (Darling Boy)	John Lennon	Geffen	7-29855	17/11

APPENDIX 2

WITH A LITTLE HELP TO THEIR FRIENDS

In *The Long And Winding Road*, this appendix only dealt with songs that John, Paul and George had written for other artists between 1963 and 1969. This expanded "With A Little Help To Their Friends" appendix now includes these compositions up to the end of 1982 (as well as some omitted from the original period) and also contains two new sections dealing with the Beatles' extra-curricular activities outside their own recording commitments, i.e. their production and session work for other artists.

The three lists are restricted (where possible) to the original appearance of each recording, as most artists and labels tend to reissue and re-package their recorded output fairly frequently. It is therefore beyond the scope of this book to include a complete discography of such releases. The three sections, (A) "Songs", (B) "Production" and (C) "Sessions", are divided into four lists covering each Beatle in chronological order according to release dates of the British issues.

The "Songs" lists give label, catalogue numbers and release dates for both British and American releases, while the "Production" and "Sessions" lists are based solely on British releases, except where recordings did not receive a British release, and therefore American issues are included. The "Production" and "Sessions" lists give individual song titles and singles, with album titles in CAPITALS. Where songs were co-written or recordings co-produced, the second party is named in brackets. The "Production" listing has been simplified by not including singles taken from albums (unless they include a non-album "B" side), even where a single appeared before the album.

WITH A LITTLE HELP TO THEIR FRIENDS JOHN SONGS

SONG TITLE	ARTIST – ALBUM TITLE	UK LABEL/NUMBER US LABEL/NUMBER	UK RELEASE US RELEASE
Bad To Me	Billy J. Kramer & The Dakotas	Parlophone R 5049 Liberty 55626	26/7/63 23/9/63
Hello Little Girl	The Fourmost	Parlophone R 5056 Atco 6280	30/8/63 15/11/63
I'm In Love	The Fourmost	Parlophone R 5078 Atco 6285	15/11/63 10/2/64
God Save Us (with Yoko Ono) Do The Oz (with Yoko Ono)	The Elastic Oz Band	Apple APPLE 36 Apple 1835	16/7/71 7/7/71
I'm The Greatest	Ringo Starr – LP *Ringo*	Apple PCTC 252 Apple SWAL 3413	9/11/73 2/11/73
Mucho Mungo/ Mt. Elga (with Nilsson)	Harry Nilsson – LP *Pussy Cats*	RCA APL 1-0570 RCA CPL 1-0570	30/8/74 19/8/74
(It's All Da-Da-Down To) Goodnight Vienna	Ringo Starr – LP *Goodnight Vienna*	Apple PCS 7168 Apple SW 3417	15/11/74 18/11/74
Rock And Roll People	Johnny Winter LP *John Dawson Winter*	Blue Sky 80586 Blue Sky PZ 33292	7/2/75 25/11/74
Fame (with David Bowie & Luther Vandross)	David Bowie – LP *Young Americans*	RCA RS 1006 RCA APL 1-0998	28/3/75 10/3/75
Move Over Ms. L	Keith Moon – LP *Two Sides Of The Moon*	Polydor 2442-134 Track 2136	23/5/75 17/3/75
Cookin' (In The Kitchen Of Love)	Ringo Starr – LP *Ringo's Rotogravure*	Polydor 2302 040 Atlantic SD 18193	17/9/76 27/9/76

WITH A LITTLE HELP TO THEIR FRIENDS PAUL SONGS

I'll Be On My Way	Billy J. Kramer & The Dakotas	Parlophone R 5023 Liberty 55586	26/4/63 10/6/63
Tip Of My Tongue	Tommy Quickly	Piccadilly 7N 35137	30/7/63
Love Of The Loved	Cilla Black	Parlophone R 5065	27/9/63

I'll Keep You Satisfied	Billy J. Kramer & The Dakotas	Parlophone R 5073 Liberty 55643	1/11/63 11/11/63
A World Without Love	Peter And Gordon	Columbia DB 7225 Capitol 5175	28/2/64 27/4/64
One And One Is Two	The Strangers with Mike Shannon	Philips BF 1335	8/5/64
Nobody I Know	Peter And Gordon	Columbia DB 7292 Capitol 5211	29/5/64 15/6/64
Like Dreamers Do	The Applejacks	Decca F 11916 London 9681	5/6/64 6/7/64
From A Window	Billy J. Kramer & The Dakotas	Parlophone R 5156 Imperial 66051	17/7/64 12/8/64
It's For You	Cilla Black	Parlophone R 5162 Capitol 5258	31/7/64 17/8/64
I Don't Want To See You Again	Peter And Gordon	Columbia DB 7356 Capitol 5272	11/9/64 21/9/64
That Means A Lot	P.J. Proby	Liberty 10215 Liberty 55806	17/9/65 5/7/65
Woman (as "Webb")	Peter And Gordon	Columbia DB 7834 Capitol 5579	11/2/66 10/1/66
Love In The Open Air (Family Way Theme)	The George Martin Orchestra LP – *The Family Way* soundtrack	Decca SKL 4847 London MS 82007	6/1/67 12/6/67
Catcall	The Chris Barber Band	Marmalade 598-005	20/10/67
Step Inside Love	Cilla Black	Parlophone R 5674 Bell 726	8/5/68 6/5/67
Thingumybob	John Foster and Sons Ltd. Black Dyke Mills Band	Apple APPLE 4 Apple 1800	6/9/68 26/8/68
Goodbye	Mary Hopkin	Apple APPLE 10 Apple 1806	28/3/69 7/4/69
Penina	Carlos Mendes (Portuguese release only)	Parlophone QMSP 16459	18/7/69
Come And Get It	Badfinger	Apple APPLE 20 Apple 1815	5/12/69 12/1/70
Six O'Clock	Ringo Starr – LP *Ringo*	Apple PCTC 252 Apple SWAL 3413	9/11/73 2/11/73
Ten Years After On Strawberry Jam (with Linda McCartney)	Scaffold	Warner Brothers K 16400 Warner Brothers 8001	24/5/74 29/7/74
4th Of July	John Christie	Polydor 2058-496 Capitol 3928	28/6/74 1/7/74
Leave It/ Sweet Baby (with Mike McGear)	Mike McGear	Warner Brothers K 16446 Warner Brothers 8037	6/9/74 28/10/74
Mine For Me	Rod Stewart – LP *Smiler*	Mercury 9104-001 Mercury SRM 1-1017	27/9/74 7/10/74
What Do We Really Know Norton (with Mike McGear) Have You Got Problems (with Mike McGear) The Casket (with Roger McGough) Rainbow Lady (with Mike McGear) Simply Love (with Mike McGear) Givin' Grease A Ride (with Mike McGear) The Man Who Found God On The Moon (with Mike McGear)	Mike McGear – LP *McGear*	Warner Brothers K 56051 Warner Brothers BS 2825	27/9/74 14/10/74

Bridge Over The River Suite (with Linda)	The Country Hams	EMI 2220 EMI 3977	18/10/74 2/12/74
Let's Love	Peggy Lee	Warner Brothers K 10527 Atlantic 3215	25/10/74 7/10/74
Dance The Do (with Mike McGear)	Mike McGear	Warner Brothers K 16573	4/7/75
Pure Gold	Ringo Starr – LP *Ringo's Rotogravure*	Polydor 2302 040 Atlantic SD 18193	17/9/76 27/9/76
Giddy	Roger Daltrey – LP *One Of The Boys*	Polydor 2442 146	13/5/77
Send Me Your Heart (with Denny Laine)	Denny Laine – LP *Japanese Tears*	Scratch SCRL 5001	?/12/80
Private Property & Attention	Ringo Starr – LP *Stop And Smell The Roses*	RCA RCALP 6022 Boardwalk NB1-33246	20/11/81 27/10/81

WITH A LITTLE HELP TO THEIR FRIENDS GEORGE SONGS

Sour Milk Sea	Jackie Lomax	Apple APPLE 3 Apple 1802	6/9/68 26/8/68
Badge (with Eric Clapton)	Cream – LP *Goodbye*	Polydor 583-053 Atco SD 7001	28/2/69 5/2/69
Ain't That Cute (with Doris Troy)	Doris Troy	Apple APPLE 24 Apple 1820	13/2/70 16/3/70
Give Me Back My Dynamite (with Doris Troy)	Doris Troy – LP *Doris Troy*	Apple SAPCOR 13 Apple ST 3371	11/9/70 9/11/70
Gonna Get My Baby Back (with Starkey, Troy & Stills)			
You Give Me Joy Joy (with Starkey, Troy & Stills)			
Sing One For The Lord (with Preston)	Billy Preston – LP *Encouraging Words*	Apple SAPCOR 14 Apple ST 3370	11/9/70 9/11/70
Try Some Buy Some/ Tandoori Chicken (with Phil Spector)	Ronnie Spector	Apple APPLE 33 Apple 1832	16/4/71 19/4/71
Sue Me Sue You Blues	Jesse Ed Davis	Atco 6873 (US only)	25/1/72
The Holdup (with David Bromberg)	David Bromberg – LP *David Bromberg*	CBS 64906 Columbia C31104	2/6/72 16/2/72
Photograph (with Ringo Starr)	Ringo Starr	Apple R 5992 Apple 1865	19/10/73 24/9/73
So Sad	Alvin Lee & Mylon Lefevre – LP *On The Road To Freedom*	Chrysalis CHR 1054 Columbia KC 32729	2/11/73 7/12/73
Sunshine Life For Me (Sail Away Raymond) You And Me, Babe (with Mal Evans)	Ringo Starr – LP *Ringo*	Apple PCTC 252 Apple SWAL 3413	9/11/73 2/11/73
Far East Man (with Ron Wood)	Ron Wood – LP *I've Got My Own Album To Do*	Warner Brothers K 56065 Warner Brothers BS 2819	27/9/74 23/9/74
The Pirate Song (with Eric Idle)	Rutland Weekend Television Christmas Show 1975	(Not available on record)	
I'll Still Love You	Ringo Starr – LP *Ringo's Rotogravure*	Polydor 2302 040 Atlantic SD 18193	17/9/76 27/9/76
Wrack My Brain	Ringo Starr	RCA RCA 166 Broadwalk NB7-11-130	13/11/81 27/10/81

WITH A LITTLE HELP TO THEIR FRIENDS RINGO SONGS

Rock And Roller (with Billy Lawrie)	Billy Lawrie	RCA 2439	9/11/73

How Long Can Disco On (with Harry Nilsson)	Harry Nilsson – LP *Flash Harry*	Mercury 6302 022	?/9/80

WITH A LITTLE HELP TO THEIR FRIENDS PRODUCTION JOHN

You've Got to Hide Your Love Away	The Silkie	Fontana	10/9/70
YOKO ONO/PLASTIC ONO BAND (with Yoko Ono)	Yoko Ono/Plastic Ono Band	Apple	17/12/70
God Save Us/Do The Oz ("A" side with Yoko, Mal Evans & Phil Spector. "B" side with Yoko & Phil Spector)	Bill Elliot & The Elastic Oz Band	Apple	16/7/71
FLY (with Yoko Ono)	Yoko Ono & Plastic Ono Band	Apple	3/12/71
THE POPE SMOKES DOPE (with Yoko Ono)	David Peel & The Lower East Side	Apple (US only)	28/4/72
ELEPHANT'S MEMORY (with Yoko Ono)	Elephant's Memory	Apple	10/11/72
APPROXIMATELY INFINITE UNIVERSE (with Yoko Ono)	Yoko Ono/Plastic Ono Band with Elephant's Memory	Apple	16/2/73
PUSSY CATS	Harry Nilsson	RCA	30/8/74

WITH A LITTLE HELP TO THEIR FRIENDS PRODUCTION PAUL

You've Got To Hide Your Love Away (with John)	The Silkie	Fontana	10/9/65
Got To Get You Into My Life	Cliff Bennett & The Rebel Rousers	Parlophone	5/8/66
From Head To Toe/Night Time	The Escorts	Columbia	18/11/66
Vegetables (SMILEY SMILE) (with The Beach Boys)	The Beach Boys	Brother	20/11/67
McGOUGH AND McGEAR	Roger McGough & Mike McGear	Parlophone	17/5/68
Those Were The Days/ Turn Turn Turn	Mary Hopkin	Apple	30/8/68
Thingumybob/Yellow Submarine	Black Dyke Mills Band	Apple	6/9/68
I'm The Urban Spaceman (as Apollo C. Vermouth)	The Bonzo Dog Band	Liberty	11/10/68
POSTCARD	Mary Hopkin	Apple	21/2/69
Rosetta	The Fourmost	CBS	21/2/69
Goodbye/Sparrow	Mary Hopkin	Apple	28/3/69
Come And Get It	Badfinger	Apple	5/12/69
Thumbin' A Ride ("B" side of *How The Web Was Woven* UK only)	Jackie Lomax	Apple	6/2/70
Que Sera Sera (Whatever Will Be Will Be/Fields Of St. Etienne	Mary Hopkin	Apple (US only)	5/6/70
Liverpool Lou/Ten Years After On Strawberry Jam	Scaffold	Warner Brothers	24/5/74
Leave It/Sweet Baby	Mike McGear	Warner Brothers	6/9/74
McGEAR	Mike McGear	Warner Brothers	27/9/74
Walking In The Park with Eloise/ Bridge Over The River Suite	The Country Hams	EMI	18/10/74

Dance The Do/Norton	Mike McGear	Warner Brothers	4/7/75
HOLLY DAYS	Denny Laine	EMI	6/5/77
Seaside Woman/ B Side to Seaside	Suzy And The Red Stripes	A&M	?/8/79
Private Property; Attention & Sure To Fall (In Love With You) (on STOP AND SMELL THE ROSES)	Ringo Starr	RCA	20/11/81

WITH A LITTLE HELP TO THEIR FRIENDS PRODUCTION GEORGE

IS THIS WHAT YOU WANT	Jackie Lomax	Apple	21/3/69
THAT'S THE WAY GOD PLANNED IT (three tracks by Wayne Schuler)	Billy Preston	Apple	22/8/69
Hare Krishna Mantra/Prayer To The Spiritual Masters	Radha Krishna Temple (London)	Apple	29/8/69
All That I've Got (I'm Gonna Give To You)	Billy Preston	Apple	30/1/70
How The Web Was Woven	Jackie Lomax	Apple	6/2/70
Ain't That Cute	Doris Troy	Apple	13/2/70
Govinda/Govinda Jai Jai	Radha Krishna Temple (London)	Apple	6/3/70
Long As I Got My Baby ("B" side of My Sweet Lord)	Billy Preston	Apple	(withdrawn)
ENCOURAGING WORDS (with Billy Preston)	Billy Preston	Apple	11/9/70
It Don't Come Easy/Early 1970	Ringo Starr	Apple	16/4/71
Try Some Buy Some/Tandoori Chicken (with Phil Spector)	Ronnie Spector	Apple	16/4/71
THE RADHA KRISHNA TEMPLE	Radha Krishna Temple	Apple	28/5/71
Joi Bangla/Oh Bhaugowan/ Raga Mishra	Ravi Shankar	Apple	27/8/71
RAGA (original soundtrack)	Ravi Shankar	Apple (US only)	7/12/71
I'd Die Babe; Name Of The Game; Suitcase & Day After Day (on STRAIGHT UP)	Badfinger	Apple	11/2/72
Back Off Boogaloo	Ringo Starr	Apple	17/3/72
Sweet Music (on BROTHER)	Lon & Derrek Van Eaton	Apple	9/2/73
IN CONCERT 1972 (with Zakir Hussein & Phil McDonald)	Ravi Shankar & Ali Akbar Khan	Apple	13/4/73
Down And Out ("B" side of Photograph)	Ringo Starr	Apple	19/10/73
THE PLACE I LOVE	Splinter	Dark Horse	20/9/74
SHANKAR FAMILY AND FRIENDS	Shankar Family & Friends	Dark Horse	20/9/74
Lonely Man (on HARDER TO LIVE)	Splinter	Dark Horse	24/10/75
Lumberjack Song	Monty Python's Flying Circus	Charisma	14/11/75
RAVI SHANKAR'S MUSIC FESTIVAL FROM INDIA	Ravi Shankar	Dark Horse	19/3/76
TWO MAN BAND (Executive producer with Dennis Morgan)	Splinter	Dark Horse	7/10/77

Wrack My Brain & You Belong To Me (on STOP AND SMELL THE ROSES)	Ringo Starr	RCA	20/11/81

WITH A LITTLE HELP TO THEIR FRIENDS – SESSIONS JOHN

	SONG/ALBUM TITLE	ARTIST	LABEL	RELEASE
	Song/album title	Artist	Label	Release
backing vocal (with Paul)	We Love You	Rolling Stones	Decca	18/8/67
voice	How I Won The War	Musketeer Gripweed & The Third Troop	United Artists	13/10/67
guitar	YOKO ONO/PLASTIC ONO BAND (all tracks except *AOS*)	Yoko Ono/Plastic Ono Band	Apple	17/12/70
	FLY	Yoko Ono & Plastic Ono Band	Apple	3/12/71
guitar	Midsummer New York; Mind Train; Mind Holes; Don't Worry Kyoko; Hirake; O 'Wind & Fly			
piano	Midsummer New York & Mrs Lennon			
organ	Mrs Lennon			
	APPROXIMATELY INFINITE UNIVERSE	Yoko Ono & Plastic Ono Band	Apple	16/2/73
Guitar (as Joel Nohnn)	Move On Fast & Is Winter Here To Stay			
	RINGO	Ringo Starr	Apple	9/11/73
piano & backing vocal	I'm The Greatest			
guitar, keyboards, percussion & backing vocal	ELEPHANT'S MEMORY	Elephant's Memory	Apple	10/11/73
	FEELING THE SPACE	Yoko Ono & Plastic Ono Band	Apple	23/11/73
guitar (as John O'Cean)	She Hits Back; Women Power & Men, Men, Men			
	GOODNIGHT VIENNA	Ringo Starr	Apple	15/11/74
piano	Goodnight Vienna			
guitar	All By Myself			
acoustic guitar	Only You (And You Alone)			
guitar & backing vocal	Lucy In The Sky With Diamonds/	Elton John	DJM	15/11/74
guitar (as Dr. Winston O'Boogie)	One Day At A Time			
guitar & vocal	I Saw Her Standing There ("B" side of Philadelphia Freedom)	Elton John Band	DJM	28/2/75
	YOUNG AMERICANS	David Bowie	RCA	28/3/75
guitar	Across The Universe			
	RINGO'S ROTOGRAVURE	Ringo Starr	Polydor	17/9/76
piano	Cookin' (In The Kitchen Of Love)			
guitar & keyboards	Walking On Thin Ice/	Yoko Ono	Geffen	20/2/81
voice	It Happened			

guitar & vocal	**I Saw Her Standing There/ Whatever Gets You Thru The Night/ Lucy In The Sky With Diamonds**	**Elton John Band with John Lennon**	DJM	13/3/81

WITH A LITTLE HELP TO THEIR FRIENDS – SESSIONS PAUL

tambourine	**I Knew Right Away**	**Alma Cogan**	Columbia	30/10/64
guitar	**You've Got To Hide Your Love Away**	**The Silkie**	Fontana	10/9/65
bass	**Mellow Yellow**	**Donovan**	Pye	?/2/67
backing vocal (with John)	**We Love You**	**The Rolling Stones**	Decca	18/8/67
drums	**And The Sun Will Shine**	**Paul Jones**	Columbia	8/3/68
tambourine & backing vocal	**Atlantis**	**Donovan**	Pye	22/11/68
	JAMES TAYLOR	**James Taylor**	Apple	6/12/68
bass	**Carolina In My Mind**			
bass, drums & backing vocal	**My Dark Hour**	**The Steve Miller Band**	Capitol	18/7/69
	NO SECRETS	**Carly Simon**	Elektra	15/12/72
backing vocal	**Night Owl**			
	RINGO	**Ringo Starr**	Apple	9/11/73
piano, synthesizer & backing vocal	**Six O'Clock**			
bass & backing vocal	**God Bless California**	**Thornton, Fradkin & Ungar & The Big Band**	ESP DISK (US only)	17/6/74
	WALKING MAN	**James Taylor**	Warner Brothers	28/6/74
backing vocal	**Rock 'n' Roll Music Now & Let It All Fall Down**			
	I SURVIVE	**Adam Faith**	Warner Brothers	20/9/74
synthesizer	**Change; Never Say Goodbye & Goodbye**			
backing vocal	**Star Song**			
	RINGO'S ROTOGRAVURE	**Ringo Starr**	Polydor	17/9/76
backing vocal	**Pure Gold**			
backing vocal	**One Of Those Days In England**	**Roy Harper**	Harvest	4/2/77
drums, guitar & harmony vocal	**HOLLY DAYS**	**Denny Laine**	EMI	6/5/77
?	**FREEZE FRAME**	**Godley and Creme**	Polydor	9/11/79
	JAPANESE TEARS	**Denny Laine**	Scratch	5/12/80
?	**I Would Only Smile; Weep For Love & Send Me Your Love**			
backing vocal	**All Those Years Ago**	**George Harrison**	Dark Horse	15/5/81
	STOP AND SMELL THE ROSES	**Ringo Starr**	RCA	20/11/81
bass & piano	**Private Property, Attention & Sure To Fall (In Love With You)**			
percussion	**Attention**			
backing vocal	**Private Property & Sure To Fall (In Love With You)**			

tambourine	You've Got To Hide Your Love Away	The Silkie	Fontana	10/9/65
	GOODBYE	Cream	Polydor	28/2/69
rhythm guitar (as L'Angelo Misterioso)	Badge			
	SONGS FOR A TAILOR	Jack Bruce	Polydor	29/8/69
rhythm guitar (as L'Angelo Misterioso)	Never Tell Your Mother She's Out Of Tune			
guitar	Instant Karma	Lennon/Ono & Plastic Ono Band	Apple	6/2/70
guitar	LEON RUSSELL	Leon Russell	A&M	24/4/70
guitar	DELANEY AND BONNIE ON TOUR	Delaney & Bonnie Bramlett	Atlantic	19/6/70
guitar	Jacob's Ladder/ Get Back	Doris Troy	Apple	28/8/70
guitar	DORIS TROY	Doris Troy	Apple	11/9/70
guitar	Tell The Truth	Derek & The Dominoes	ATCO (US only)	14/9/70
	THE WORST OF ASHTON, GARDNER & DYKE	Ashton, Gardner & Dyke	Capitol	5/2/71
guitar (as George O'Hara Smith)	I'm Your Spiritual Breadman			
guitar	It Don't Come Easy/ Early 1970	Ringo Starr	Apple	16/4/71
guitar	Stand For Our Right/ Can't See The Reason	Gary Wright	A&M	28/5/71
	IMAGINE	John Lennon	Apple	8/10/71
dobro	Crippled Inside			
slide guitar	I Don't Want To Be A Soldier Momma			
lead guitar	Gimme Some Truth			
guitar	Oh My Love			
guitar (as George H)	I WROTE A SIMPLE SONG	Billy Preston	A & M	14/1/72
guitar & slide guitar	FOOTPRINT	Gary Wright	A & M	21/1/72
guitar	Back Off Boogaloo	Ringo Starr	Apple	17/3/72
guitar	BOBBY KEYS	Bobby Keys	Warner Brothers	7/7/72
	SON OF SCHMILSSON	Harry Nilsson	RCA	28/7/72
slide guitar (as George Harrysong)	You're Breaking My Heart			
	SOMETIME IN NEW YORK CITY	John & Yoko & Plastic Ono Band with Elephant's Memory	Apple	15/9/72
guitar (as George Harrisong)	Cold Turkey & Don't Worry Kyoko			
	TO THE WORLD	Rudy Romero	Tumbleweed	1/12/72
guitar	Lovely Day; Nothin' Gonna Get You Down & Doing The Right Thing			
backing vocal	If I Had Time			
	THE TIN MAN WAS A DREAMER	Nicky Hopkins	CBS	27/7/73
guitar	Waiting For The Band; Edward; Spend On & Banana Anna			

	LOS COCHINOS	Cheech and Chong	Ode	28/9/73
guitar	Basketball Jones featuring Tyrone Shoelaces			
	IT'S LIKE YOU NEVER LEFT	Dave Mason	CBS	8/2/74
guitar	If You've Got Love			
acoustic guitar & backing vocal	Photograph	Ringo Starr	Apple	24/9/73
	RINGO	Ringo Starr	Apple	9/11/73
guitar	I'm The Greatest & Sunshine Life For Me			
acoustic guitar	Photograph			
electric guitar	You And Me (Babe)			
guitar				
backing vocal	Photograph & Sunshine Life For Me			
	SON OF DRACULA	Harry Nilsson	RCA	24/5/74
cow bell	Daybreak			
	THE PLACE I LOVE	Splinter	Dark Horse	20/9/74
guitar (as Hari Georgeson)	Gravy Train; Drink All Day; China Light; Somebody's City; The Place I Love; Situation Vacant & Haven't Got Time			
dobro (as Hari Georgeson)	Drink All Day			
harmonium (as P. Roducer)	Drink All Day & Costafine Town			
percussion (as Jai Raj Harisein)	Drink All Day; Somebody's City; Costafine Town; The Place I Love & Haven't Got Time			
mandolin (as Hari Georgeson)	China Light			
acoustic guitar (as Hari Georgeson)	China Light & Elly May			
bass & eight string bass (as Hari Georgeson)	Costafine Town			
Moog Synthesizer (as P. Roducer)	Elly May			
auto-harp electric & acoustic guitars (as Hari Georgeson)	SHANKAR FAMILY & FRIENDS	Shankar Family & Friends	Dark Horse	20/9/74
	IT'S MY PLEASURE	Billy Preston	A&M	19/7/75
guitar (as Hari Georgeson)	That's Life			
	HARD TIMES	Peter Skellern	Island	26/9/75
guitar	Make Love Not War			
	HARDER TO LIVE	Splinter	Dark Horse	24/10/75
guitar (as Hari Georgeson)	Lonely Man			
	NEW YORK CONNECTION	Tom Scott	Ode	2/4/76
slide guitar	Appolonia (Fostrata)			
	CROSSROADS	Larry Hosford	Shelter	6/7/76
harmony vocal	Wishing I Could			
slide guitar	Direct Me			
guitar	Round And Round/ I'll Bend For You	Splinter	Dark Horse (US only)	6/9/77
guitar	TWO MAN BAND	Splinter	Dark Horse	7/10/77
	THE VISITOR	Mick Fleetwood	RCA	30/6/81
12-string guitar & Slide guitar	Walk A Thin Line			

	STOP AND SMELL THE ROSES	Ringo Starr	RCA	20/11/81
lead & acoustic guitar & backing vocals	Wrack My Brain			
lead guitar	You Belong To Me			
guitar	THE CYCLE	Gary Brooker	Mercury	1/3/82
guitar	LEAD ME TO THE WATER	Gary Brooker	Mercury	?

WITH A LITTLE HELP TO THEIR FRIENDS – SESSIONS RINGO

backing vocal	America	Rory Storm & The Hurricanes	Parlophone	13/11/64
drums	WONDERWALL MUSIC	George Harrison	Apple	1/11/68
drums	New Day	Jackie Lomax	Apple	9/5/69
drums	Cold Turkey/Don't Worry Kyoko	Plastic Ono Band	Apple	24/10/69
voice	THE MAGIC CHRISTIAN MUSIC	Soundtrack album	Pye	10/4/70
voice	Hunting Scene			
drums	DORIS TROY	Doris Troy	Apple	11/9/70
	STEPHEN STILLS	Stephen Stills	Atlantic	27/11/70
drums (as Richie)	To A Flame & We Are Not Helpless			
drums	ALL THINGS MUST PASS	George Harrison	Apple	27/11/70
drums	JOHN LENNON/ PLASTIC ONO BAND	John Lennon & Plastic Ono Band	Apple	11/12/70
drums	YOKO ONO/ PLASTIC ONO BAND (not on Aos)	Yoko Ono & Plastic Ono Band	Apple	11/12/70
	THE LONDON HOWLIN' WOLF SESSIONS	Howlin' Wolf	Chess	20/8/71
drums (as Richie)	I Ain't Superstitious			
	B. B. KING IN LONDON	B.B. King	Probe	19/11/71
drums	Ghetto Woman; Wet Hayshake & Part-Time Love			
drums & tambourine	THE CONCERT FOR BANGLA DESH	George Harrison & Friends	Apple	7/1/72
drums	Oo Wee, Baby, I Love You	Bobby Hatfield	Elektra	10/3/72
	WIND OF CHANGE	Peter Frampton	A&M	26/5/72
drums	The Lodger & Alright			
drums	BOBBY KEYS	Bobby Keys	Warner Brothers	7/7/72
	SON OF SCHMILSSON	Harry Nilsson	RCA	28/7/72
drums (as Richie Snare)	Take 54; Spaceman; At My Front Door; Ambush & The Most Beautiful World In The World			
drums	BROTHER	Lon And Derrek Van Eaton	Apple	9/2/73
drums	LIVING IN THE MATERIAL WORLD	George Harrison	Apple	21/6/73
drums	LAND'S END	Jimmy Webb	Asylum	5/7/74
	PUSSY CATS	Harry Nilsson	RCA	30/8/74
drums	Save The Last Dance For Me; Loop De Loop; Rock Around The Clock; Subterranean Homesick Blues; Many Rivers To Cross & All My Life			

	SON OF DRACULA	Harry Nilsson	RCA	24/5/74
drums	Daybreak & At My Front Door			
drums	SHANKAR FAMILY AND FRIENDS	Shankar Family & Friends	Dark Horse	20/9/74
	DARK HORSE	George Harrison	Dark Horse	20/12/74
drums	So Sad & Ding Dong			
	STARTLING MUSIC	David Hentschel	Ring'O	18/4/75
finger clicks (as R.S.)	Step Lightly			
	DUIT ON MON DEI	Harry Nilsson	RCA	28/3/75
drums	Kojak Columbia			
backing vocal	Good For God			
	TWO SIDES OF THE MOON	Keith Moon	Polydor	23/5/75
announcements	Solid Gold			
drums & raps	Together			
	PLAYING POSSUM	Carly Simon	CBS	6/6/75
drums	More And More			
	STILLS	Stephen Stills	CBS	4/7/75
drums (as English Ritchie)	As I Come Of Age			
tambourine	Don't You Remember When	Vera Lynn	EMI	20/2/76
	LIES AND ALIBIES	Guthrie Thomas	Capitol	3/5/76
drums	Good Days Are Rollin' In; Band Of Steel & Ramblin' Cocaine Blues			
vocals	Band Of Steel			
	COMING OUT	Manhattan Transfer	Atlantic	27/8/76
drums	Ziny Lou & S.O.S.			
	LASSO FROM EL PASO	Kinky Friedman	Epic	25/2/77
voice of Jesus	Men's Room, LA			
	GOOD NEWS	Attitudes	Dark Horse	3/6/77
drums	Good News			
	SPARK IN THE DARK	The Alpha Band	Arista (US only)	26/9/77
drums	Born In Captivity & You Angel You			
	PUTTIN' ON THE STYLE	Lonnie Donegan	United Artists	/78
drums	Have a Drink On Me & Ham 'n' Eggs			
	THE LAST WALTZ	The Band	Warner Brothers	/78
drums	I Shall Be Released			
drums	TROUBLEMAKER	Ian McLagan	Mercury	/79
drums	FLASH HARRY	Harry Nilsson	Mercury	5/9/80
drums	All Those Years Ago	George Harrison	Dark Horse	15/5/81
drums	SOMEWHERE IN ENGLAND	George Harrison	Dark Horse	5/6/81
tom tom	Heart Of Mine	Bob Dylan	CBS	3/6/81

LENNON/ONO
with The Plastic Ono Band
INSTANT KARMA!
B/W Who has seen the wind?
Produced by Phil Spector
Ritten, Recorded, Remixed 27th Jan 1970
APPLE RECORDS APPLES 1003

Hi! Hi! Hi!

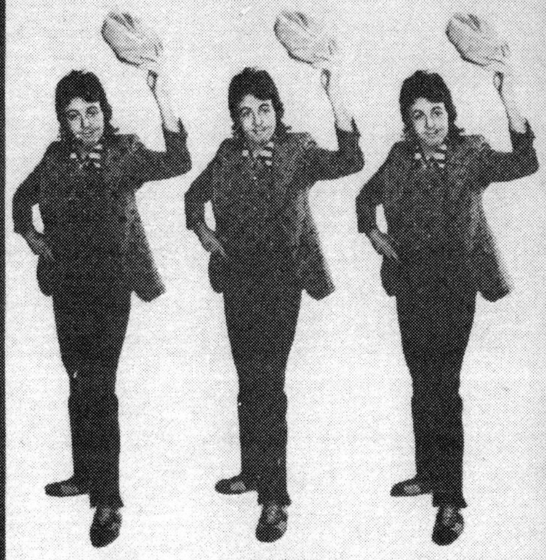

and

C. Moon

a new double 'A' side from

Paul McCartney and Wings

R5973

EMI

APPENDIX 3

THE BEATLES IN THE BMRB CHART 1962 – 1982

The British Market Research Bureau chart, compiled for the BBC and *Music Week*, became the "Chart Bible" after the publication of the excellent *Guinness Book Of British Hit Singles. Record Retailer*, which later became *Music Week*, first published a Top 50 singles chart on March 10, 1960, by basing their figures on the average from *NME, Melody Maker, Disc* and *Record Mirror*. In 1969 the British Phonographic Industry engaged the BMRB (British Market Research Bureau) to compile a weekly singles chart, which was broadcast by the BBC and published by *Music Week* and *Record Mirror*. On May 13, 1978, the Top 50 was extended to a Top 75, and at the end of 1982 – due to allegations of chart rigging – the BMRB lost the chart franchise, which was passed over to Gallup.

The Guinness Book of British Hit Singles first appeared in 1977, and instantly became one of the top-selling books in the country. It is updated every two years, and 1981 saw the appearance of the third edition, with the fourth due in 1983.

To fall into line with the companion volume to this book, this appendix includes all solo releases, as well as cover versions of songs written by the Beatles as solo artists, and individual Beatle production hits, (i.e. Badfinger's *Day After Day*, produced by George).

Up to the end of 1982, the individual Beatles' hits on the BMRB chart amounted to fifty-five, plus six re-entries. The individual Beatles' tallies are as follows: George – seven; John – fourteen (five re-entries); Paul – twenty-nine (one re-entry) and Ringo – five. The total number of hit cover versions amounts to five (one re-entry), with twelve "production" hits. These figures give a grand total of seventy-two (seven re-entries) Beatle-associated hits in the BMRB chart.

(The Beatles "production" hits are indicated by *, and where the hit was both written and produced by the Beatles, this is indicated by **.)

ARTIST	SONG TITLE	ENTRY DATE	HIGHEST POSITION/ WEEKS AT No. 1	WEEKS IN CHART
BADFINGER	Come And Get It**	10/1/70	4	11
	Day After Day*	29/1/72	10	11
BONZO DOG DOO-DAH BAND	I'm The Urban Spaceman*	6/11/68	5	14
DAVID BOWIE	Fame	2/8/75	17	8
RANDY CRAWFORD	Imagine	29/1/82	60	1
	Imagine (re-entry)	13/2/82	75	1
GEORGE HARRISON	My Sweet Lord	23/1/71	1/5	17
	Bangla Desh	14/8/71	10	9
	Give Me Love (Give Me Peace On Earth)	2/6/73	8	10
	Ding Dong	21/12/74	38	5
	You	11/10/75	38	5
	Blow Away	10/3/79	51	5
	All Those Years Ago	23/5/81	13	7
MARY HOPKIN	Those Were The Days*	4/9/68	1/6	21
	Goodbye**	2/4/69	2	14
MICHAEL JACKSON	Girlfriend	26/7/80	41	5
MICHAEL JACKSON & PAUL McCARTNEY	The Girl Is Mine	6/11/82	8	7
ELTON JOHN	Lucy In The Sky With Diamonds	23/11/74	10	10

ELTON JOHN & JOHN LENNON	I Saw Her Standing There	21/3/81	40	4
JOHN LENNON	Give Peace A Chance	9/7/69	2	13
	Cold Turkey	1/11/69	14	8
	Instant Karma	21/2/70	5	9
	Power To The People	20/3/71	7	9
	Happy Xmas (War Is Over)	9/12/72	4	8
	Mind Games	24/11/73	26	9
	Whatever Gets You Thru The Night	19/10/74	36	4
	Happy Xmas (War Is Over) (re-entry)	4/1/75	48	1
	Number 9 Dream	8/2/75	23	8
	Stand By Me	3/5/75	30	7
	Imagine	1/11/75	6	11
	(Just Like) Starting Over	8/11/80	1/1	14
	Happy Xmas (War Is Over) (re-entry)	20/12/80	2	8
	Imagine (re-entry)	27/12/80	1/4	12
	Woman	24/1/81	1/2	11
	Give Peace A Chance (re-entry)	24/1/81	33	5
	Watching The Wheels	4/4/81	30	6
	Happy Xmas (War Is Over) (re-entry)	19/12/81	28	4
	Love	20/11/82	41	5
PAUL McCARTNEY (& WINGS)	Another Day	27/2/71	2	12
	The Back Seat Of My Car	28/8/71	39	5
	Give Ireland Back To The Irish	26/2/72	16	8
	Mary Had A Little Lamb	27/5/72	9	11
	Hi Hi Hi/C Moon	9/12/72	5	13
	My Love	7/4/73	9	11
	Live And Let Die	9/6/73	9	13
	Live And Let Die (re-entry)	15/9/73	49	1
	Helen Wheels	3/11/73	12	12
	Jet	2/3/74	7	9
	Band On The Run	6/7/74	3	11
	Junior's Farm	9/11/74	16	10
	Listen To What The Man Said	31/5/75	6	8
	Letting Go	18/10/75	41	3
	Silly Love Songs	15/5/76	2	11
	Let 'Em In	7/8/76	2	10
	Maybe I'm Amazed	19/2/77	28	5
	Mull Of Kintyre	19/11/77	1/9	17
	With A Little Luck	1/4/78	5	9
	I've Had Enough	1/7/78	42	7
	London Town	9/9/78	60	4
	Goodnight Tonight	7/4/79	5	10
	Old Siam Sir	16/6/79	35	6
	Getting Closer/Baby's Request	1/9/79	60	3
	Wonderful Christmastime	1/12/79	6	8
	Coming Up	19/4/80	2	9
	Waterfalls	21/6/80	9	8
	Ebony And Ivory (with Stevie Wonder)	10/4/82	1/4	11
	Take It Away	3/7/82	15	10
	Tug Of War	9/10/82	53	3

MIKE McGEAR	Leave It**	5/10/74	36	4
OLIVIA NEWTON-JOHN	What Is Life	11/3/72	16	8
BILLY PAUL	Let 'em In	30/4/77	26	5
BILLY PRESTON	That's The Way God Planned It*	2/7/69	11	10
RADHA KRISHNA TEMPLE	Hare Krishna Mantra*	13/9/69	12	9
	Govinda*	28/3/70	23	8
ROXY MUSIC	Jealous Guy	21/2/81	1/2	11
SCAFFOLD	Liverpool Lou*	1/6/74	7	9
SILKIE	You've Got To Hide Your Love Away**	23/9/65	28	6
PHOEBE SNOW	Every Night	6/1/79	37	7
SPLINTER	Costafine Town*	2/11/74	17	10
RINGO STARR	It Don't Come Easy	17/4/71	4	11
	Back Off Boogaloo	1/4/72	2	10
	Photograph	27/10/73	8	13
	You're Sixteen	23/2/74	4	10
	Only You	30/11/76	28	11

'Amsterdam'
HAIR PEACE
BED PEACE
'John and Yoko'

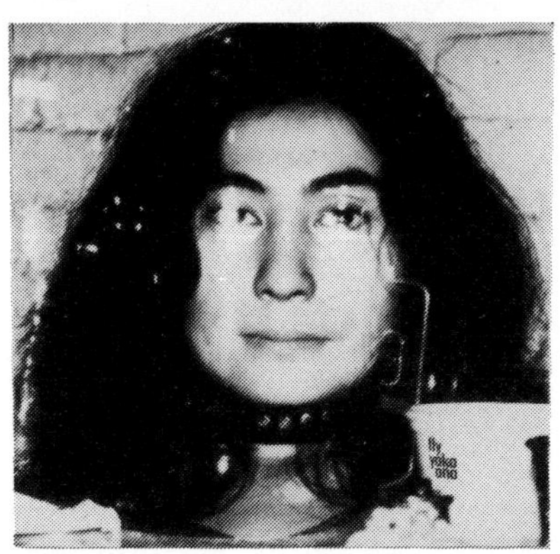

APPROXIMATELY
INFINITE
UNIVERSE
YOKO ONO

FEELING THE SPACE
YOKO ONO
134. Sphinx and Pyramids, Cairo, Egypt.

YOKO ONO MIND TRAIN
APPLE 41

YOKO ONO LISTEN THE SNOW IS FALLING
APPLE 41

WALKING ON THIN ICE
-FOR JOHN

APPENDIX 4

YOKO ONO

This appendix attempts to chronicle Yoko Ono's solo releases for Britain and America, as well as including her collaborations with John under their own names and the "Plastic Ono Band" tag (although these are only dealt with briefly, as they appear in full in the John Lennon section). The record and song numbering system is identical to that used for the Beatles sections, although only Yoko's own compositions are numbered.

1 **UNFINISHED MUSIC No. 1 – TWO VIRGINS**

By John Lennon and Yoko Ono

Apple SAPCOR 2 – November 29, 1968

Yoko's first collaboration with John, which produced this sound picture of avant-garde "music".

2 **UNFINISHED MUSIC No. 2 – LIFE WITH THE LIONS**

By John Lennon and Yoko Ono

Zapple ZAPPLE 01 – May 9, 1969

The second instalment of John and Yoko's avant-garde recordings.

3 **Give Pace A Chance**
(1) REMEMBER LOVE *(4.00)*

By The Plastic Ono Band

Apple APPLE 13 – July 4, 1969

Yoko wrote the "B" side of the first Plastic Ono Band single, and sings solo to John's acoustic guitar.

4 **Cold Turkey**
(2) DON'T WORRY KYOKO (MUMMY'S ONLY LOOKING FOR A HAND IN THE SNOW) *(4.52)*

By The Plastic Ono Band

Apple APPLES 1001 – October 24, 1969

It became a common occurrence for Yoko to write the "B" sides of the Plastic Ono Band singles, and again *Don't Worry Kyoko* is an Ono composition, sung by Yoko.

5 **THE WEDDING ALBUM**

By John Lennon and Yoko Ono

Apple SAPCOR 11 – November 7, 1969

Yoko's third LP collaboration with John produced this very elaborately packaged box set, containing another album of avant-garde recordings.

6 **THE PLASTIC ONO BAND – LIVE PEACE IN TORONTO 1969**

By The Plastic Ono Band

Apple CORE 2001 – December 12, 1969

Yoko composed the two songs on the second side of the album recording the Plastic Ono Band's performance at the Toronto Rock 'n' Roll Revival Concert.

mrs. lennon's new single –
mrs. lennon b/w midsummer new york
is on apple records. apple 38
from her forthcoming album FLY –
out soon on SAPTU 101/2
ring
01·247 6694
listen to
mrs. lennon
"Change of pace for Yoko puts her in immediate chart contention as she delivers a most beautiful ballad culled from her just released "Fly" album. Single adds new dimension to artists talents as she can now appeal to both AM and underground markets." Cashbox

A SIDE

(See John Lennon Page 20)

B SIDE

3 **DON'T WORRY KYOKO (MUMMY'S ONLY LOOKING FOR A HAND IN THE SNOW)** *(4.20)*

4 **JOHN, JOHN (LET'S HOPE FOR PEACE)** *(12.00)*

---

7 Instant Karma
(5) WHO HAS SEEN THE WIND *(2.01)*

By Lennon/Ono with The Plastic Ono Band

Apple APPLES 1003 – February 6, 1970

Yoko's third composition to appear on a Plastic Ono Band single, *Who Has Seen The Wind* features Yoko singing solo with instrumental backing from an acoustic guitar (probably played by John), a flute, harpsichord and tambourine.

---

8 YOKO ONO/PLASTIC ONO BAND

By Yoko Ono and The Plastic Ono Band

Apple SAPCOR 17 – December 11, 1970

Yoko's first true solo album (i.e. not co-credited with John) was a companion collection to *John Lennon/Plastic Ono Band*, and was recorded at the same time, with the same musicians (except for one track). The LP was recorded during early October 1970 (except for *AOS*), with John and Yoko producing, using John/guitar; Ringo Starr/drums and Klaus Voorman/bass.

AOS was recorded at the rehearsals for a concert Yoko gave at the Royal Albert Hall on February 29, 1968, with Ornette Coleman/trumpet; Edward Blackwell/drums and David Izenzon and Charles Haden/bass guitars. Contrary to some reports, *AOS* does not feature John on guitar, as he did not perform with Yoko until March 2, 1969, when they both appeared at the Lady Mitchell Hall, Cambridge.

The album sleeve, designed by John and Yoko, was similar to John's album, using almost identical front cover shots (John and Yoko change places) taken by Dan Richter, with a back cover shot of Yoko as a child. The printed inner sleeve, giving song credits, contains a dedication from Yoko "For John with love from Yoko 9/10/70" and an instruction to the record buyer – "Play in the dark". The record features a plain white Apple on both sides.

A SIDE

6 **WHY** *(5.30)*

7 **WHY NOT** *(9.55)*

8 **GREENFIELD MORNING I PUSHED AN EMPTY BABY CARRIAGE ALL OVER THE CITY** *(5.35)*

B SIDE

9 **AOS**

10 **TOUCH ME** *(4.35)*

11 **PAPER SHOES** *(6.58)*

All six tracks were composed by Yoko.

---

9 Power To The People
(12) OPEN YOUR BOX *(3.31)*

"A" side by John Lennon/Plastic Ono Band

"B" side by Yoko Ono/Plastic Ono Band

Apple R 5892 – March 12, 1971

Yoko's fourth Plastic Ono Band "B" side features a line-up of John/guitar, Klaus Voorman/bass and Jim Gordon/drums; it was recorded in February 1971, with John and Yoko producing. Yoko had to re-record her vocals for the song on March 4, after EMI refused to release the single until Yoko had "cleaned-up" the lyrics to the song.

---

10 (13) MRS. LENNON *(4.08)*
(14) MIDSUMMER NEW YORK *(3.47)*

By Yoko Ono

Apple APPLE 38 – October 29, 1971

Yoko's first solo single, which coupled two numbers from her forthcoming double album, *Fly*. *Mrs. Lennon* has John on piano and organ, and Klaus Voorman on bass guitar and bells. *Midsummer New York* features Yoko backed by John/guitar and piano, Klaus Voorman/bass, Chris Osborne/dobro, and Jim Keltner/drums and percussion. The record was released in a plain Apple sleeve, with Yoko's face superimposed onto the Apple on the "A" side.

---

11 FLY

By Yoko Ono and The Plastic Ono Band with Joe Jones Tone Deaf Music Co.

Apple SAPTU 101/2 – December 3, 1971

Yoko's second album, and her first

YOKO ONO

MIND TRAIN / LISTEN THE SNOW IS FALLING

LISTEN NOW RING 297 8221

APPLE 41

double LP for Apple, was recorded at Ascot Sound Studios (John and Yoko's home studio) and at the Record Plant New York during August 1971. It was produced by Yoko and John. Yoko was backed by The Plastic Ono Band consisting of John, Klaus Voorman (bass), Chris Osborne (dobro), Jim Keltner (drums), Eric Clapton (guitar), Ringo Starr (drums), Jim Gordon (drums) and Bobby Keyes (saxophone). Also used on some tracks was the Joe Jones Tone Deaf Music Co., which consisted of eight instruments that played themselves with the minimum of human assistance. The instruments were built especially for Yoko by Joe Jones who had been experimenting with, and developing, such devices since the early sixties.

The front and back cover photographs were taken by John, who is also credited with design of the outer cover. The inner spread shows a collage of seventeen different photographs depicting the musicians' faces superimposed onto a band of gypsies. The majority of the photographs were taken by Iain MacMillan, with some by May Pang, and the gypsies by Kyoko. The two inner sleeves show drawings by Yoko along with song lyrics and credits. The album also included a poster, and a postcard cum order form for Yoko's book *Grapefruit*. The postcard has a small round hole cut out of it, with the caption "Hole To See The Sky Through Yoko Ono '71". The back cover of the album includes a quote from John: "Love is having to say you're sorry every five minutes John '71".

RECORD ONE A SIDE

14a **MIDSUMMER NEW YORK** *(3.48)*

15 **MIND TRAIN** *(16.48)*

RECORD ONE B SIDE

16 **MIND HOLES** *(2.40)*

2a **DON'T WORRY KYOKO** *(4.51)*

13a **MRS. LENNON** *(4.04)*

12a **HIRAKE** *(3.30)*

17 **TOILET PIECE/UNKNOWN** *(0.26)*

18 **O 'WIND (BODY IS THE SCAR OF YOUR MIND)** *(4.23)*

RECORD TWO A SIDE

19 **AIRMALE** *(10.43)*

20 **DON'T COUNT THE WAVES** *(5.19)*

21 **YOU** *(8.54)*

RECORD TWO B SIDE

22 **FLY** *(22.43)*

23 **TELEPHONE PIECE** *(0.25)*

All compositions were by Yoko. *Midsummer New York* and *Mrs. Lennon* had already appeared on a single. *Don't Worry Kyoko* originally appeared as the coupling for *Cold Turkey*, and *Hirake* appeared as *Open Your Box* on the "B" side of *Power To The People*. *Hirake* and *Open Your Box* are basically the same recordings, except that *Hirake* contains the original unexpurgated vocal recording, while *Open Your Box* contains amended vocals (electronically treated to give a muffled echo effect at the end of each line).

Mind Train features John/guitar, Klaus Voorman/bass, Chris Osborne/dobro and Jim Keltner/drums. *Mind Holes* features Yoko singing over John's guitar. *Toilet Piece/Unknown* is the sound of a toilet flushing, while *O 'Wind* features John/guitar, Jim Keltner/drums and tabla, Jim Gordon/tabla, Klaus Voorman/cymbal and Bobby Keyes/claves.

Airmale is the first track featuring Joe Jones Tone Deaf Music Co., with the assistance of John. On *Don't Count The Waves* Yoko plays claves, while John again assists Joe Jones Tone Deaf Music Co., along with Klaus supplying percussion and Jim Keltner tuned drum. *You* features Yoko singing solo with Joe Jones Tone Deaf Music Co., while *Fly* – the soundtrack to Yoko's film of the same name – has Yoko screeching solo until half-way through, when John joins in on guitar. *Telephone Piece* is Yoko answering the phone.

---

12 **(15a) MIND TRAIN** *(4.45)*
(24) LISTEN THE SNOW IS FALLING *(3.09)*

By Yoko Ono

Apple APPLE 41 – January 21, 1972

Yoko's second solo single combined an edited version of *Mind Train*, from her *Fly* album, with another solo composition, *Listen The Snow Is Falling* (which had appeared previously in America as the coupling for *Happy Xmas (War Is Over)* in December 1971). Due to composing credit difficulties, this Plastic Ono Band Christmas single did not appear in Britain until November 1972. *Mind Train* was produced by John and Yoko and features Yoko supported by John/guitar, Klaus Voorman/bass, Chris Osborne/dobro and Jim Keltner/drums.

Listen The Snow Is Falling was recorded during the sessions for *Happy Xmas* between October 28 and 29, 1971. It

APPROXIMATELY INFINITE UNIVERSE YOKO ONO

New Musical Express
January 13, 1973

". . . Yoko has a sense of humour which seems to keep her going. She is the real thing . . .

Yoko is an artist in the throes of creativity, forced to cope with the axe-grinding politics of reality. She won't quit. She'll work it all out and she'll tell the world 'I have a woman inside my soul' and she does."

Melody Maker
January 6, 1973

"The Album, in fact, weeps sensitivity and tenderness. There's a true poetic consciousness at work here . . . a lyricist who can express her pain with as much cogency as Lennon.

. . . she can create a unique ambiance with her voice . . . like that of a child on the edge of tears. And wistful."

New York Times
January 12, 1973

"Approximately Infinite Universe is very much Yoko Ono at many levels."

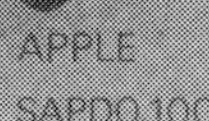

APPLE

SAPDO 1001

was produced by John and Yoko and Phil Spector. Yoko sings a solo vocal supported by John, Klaus Voorman and Hugh McCracken/guitars and Nicky Hopkins/piano and chimes. The record was released in a picture sleeve and features the Apple label with Yoko's face superimposed on the "A" side.

---

13 SOMETIME IN NEW YORK CITY

Record One by John and Yoko/Plastic Ono Band with Elephant's Memory plus Invisible Strings

Record Two by The Plastic Ono Supergroup and Plastic Ono Mothers

Apple PCSP 716 – September 15, 1972

This Plastic Ono Band release featured eight numbers composed jointly by John and Yoko (one with Frank Zappa) and four solo Ono compositions: *Sisters O Sisters, Born In A Prison, We're All Water* and *Don't Worry Kyoko.*

RECORD ONE A SIDE

Woman Is The Nigger Of The World

25 **SISTERS O SISTERS** *(3.45)*

Attica State

26 **BORN IN A PRISON** *(4.02)*

New York City

RECORD ONE B SIDE

Sunday Bloody Sunday

The Luck Of The Irish

John Sinclair

Angela

27 **WE'RE ALL WATER** *(7.11)*

RECORD TWO A SIDE

Cold Turkey

28 **DON'T WORRY KYOKO** *(14.48)*

RECORD TWO B SIDE

(See John Lennon Page 29)

---

14 Happy Xmas (War Is Over)
(24a) LISTEN THE SNOW IS FALLING *(3.09)*

"A" side by John and Yoko/Plastic Ono Band with The Harlem Community Choir

"B" side by Yoko Ono and The Plastic Ono Band

Apple R 5970 – November 24, 1972

Due to composing credit problems with Northern Songs, *Happy Xmas* was delayed for a year after its initial American release in 1971, by which time Yoko had released *Listen The Snow Is Falling* as the "B" side of her second Apple single, *Mind Train.* For this release Apple did not use the original matrix for *Listen*, but cut a completely new master (with a different matrix number).

---

15 APPROXIMATELY INFINITE UNIVERSE

By Yoko Ono and The Plastic Ono Band with Elephant's Memory, Endless Strings and Choir Boys

Apple SAPDU 1001 – February 16, 1973

Yoko's second double album and third solo album for Apple contained twenty-two of her most listenable songs to date. The album was recorded during October and November 1972 at the Record Plant, New York (with two tracks at Butterfly Studio). Yoko and John produced the album using the Elephant's Memory band consisting of Stan Bronstein/saxophone, flute and clarinet; Richard Frank Jnr./drums and percussion; Gary Van Scyoc/bass and trumpet; Adam Ippolito/piano, organ, harmonica and trumpet; Wayne Gabriel/guitar, with Daria Price/castanet.

The gatefold sleeve features photographs by Bob Gruen, with concept by Yoko and John and design by Bettina Rossner. The inner sleeves contain song lyrics while the record labels feature the "Yoko" Apple on the "A" sides.

RECORD ONE A SIDE

29 **YANG YANG** *(3.49)*

30 **DEATH OF SAMANTHA** *(6.16)*

31 **I WANT MY LOVE TO REST TONIGHT** *(5.12)*

32 **WHAT DID I DO!** *(4.12)*

33 **HAVE YOU SEEN A HORIZON LATELY** *(1.54)*

RECORD ONE B SIDE

34 **APPROXIMATELY INFINITE UNIVERSE** *(3.17)*

35 **PETER THE DEALER** *(4.41)*

36 **SONG FOR JOHN** *(2.01)*

37 **CATMAN (THE ROSES ARE COMING)** *(5.29)*

38 **WHAT A BASTARD THE WORLD IS** *(4.31)*

39 **WAITING FOR THE SUNRISE** *(2.29)*

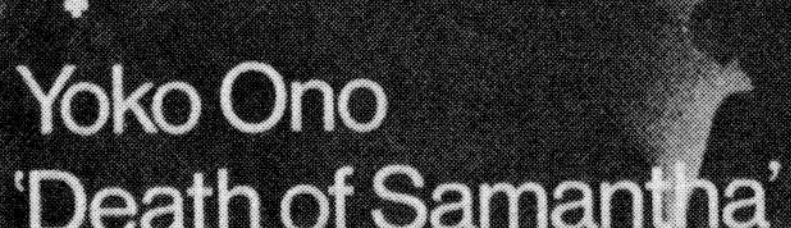

APPLE 47

YOKO ONO
'RUN, RUN, RUN'
B/W 'MEN, MEN, MEN'

RECORD TWO A SIDE

40 **I FELT LIKE SMASHING MY FACE IN A CLEAR GLASS WINDOW** *(4.04)*

41 **WINTER SONG** *(3.35)*

42 **KITE SONG** *(3.18)*

43 **WHAT A MESS** *(2.36)*

44 **SHIRANAKATTA (I DIDN'T KNOW)** *(3.07)*

45 **AIR TALK** *(3.16)*

RECORD TWO B SIDE

46 **I HAVE A WOMAN INSIDE MY SOUL** *(5.29)*

47 **MOVE ON FAST** *(3.39)*

48 **NOW OR NEVER** *(4.56)*

49 **IS WINTER HERE TO STAY?** *(4.16)*

50 **LOOKING OVER FROM MY HOTEL WINDOW** *(3.28)*

All twenty-two songs were composed and sung by Yoko. Although John is credited with co-production, he is not evident vocally or instrumentally to any great extent. *I Want My Love To Rest Tonight* is one of the four songs inspired by John, who supplies backing vocals. The other songs that were obviously inspired by John are *Song For John*, *Winter Song* and *Shiranakatta*. *Winter Song* supposedly features John and Mick Jagger on guitars, although this is not credited on the sleeve. Mick Jagger is mentioned, however, in the lyrics to one song, *I Felt Like Smashing My Face In A Clear Glass Window*.

The basic tracks for *Catman* and *Winter Song* were recorded at the Butterfly Studio. John plays guitar on *Move On Fast* and *Is Winter Here To Stay*, although he is credited on the sleeve as "Joel Nohnn" (an anagram of "John Lennon", minus one "n"). Yoko plays piano on *Looking Over From My Hotel Window*.

---

16 **(30a) DEATH OF SAMANTHA** *(3.45)*
(29a) YANG YANG *(3.51)*

By Yoko Ono/Plastic Ono Band

Apple APPLE 47 – May 4, 1973

This edited version of *Death Of Samantha* from *Approximately Infinite Universe* became Yoko's third British single, being coupled with *Yang Yang* from the same album. The single was released in a plain sleeve and featured the usual Apple labels.

---

17 **(51) RUN, RUN, RUN** *(3.06)*
(52) MEN, MEN, MEN *(4.02)*

By Yoko Ono

Apple APPLE 48 – November 9, 1973

The two tracks from Yoko's third and last Apple album, *Feeling The Space*, were both written and produced by Yoko. Released in a plain Apple sleeve, it was the penultimate Apple singles release (disregarding the solo Beatles' releases which – although appearing with an Apple label – were theoretically still on Parlophone), the last being Badfinger's *Apple Of My Eye*.

---

18 **FEELING THE SPACE**

By Yoko Ono/Plastic Ono Band and Something Different

Apple SAPCOR 26 – November 16, 1973

Yoko's last album for seven years was recorded at the Record Plant, New York, during the autumn of 1973, apparently using many of the musicians that John had used for his *Mind Games* album. They were as follows: Ken Ascher/piano, organ and Mellotron; David Spinozza/guitar; Gordon Edwards/bass; Jim Keltner/drums; Michael Brecker/saxophone; Sneaky Pete Kleinow/pedal steel guitar; Don Brooks/harmonica; Bob Babitt/bass; Jeremy Steig/flute; Arthur Smith/drums; David Friedman/vibes; and Rick Marotta/drums.

John contributed guitar to *She Hits Back* and *Women Power* under the pseudonym of John O'Cean. As on the *Mind Games* album, backing vocals were supplied by *Something Different*.

A SIDE

53 **GROWING PAIN** *(3.47)*

54 **YELLOW GIRL (STAND BY FOR LIFE)** *(3.13)*

55 **COFFIN CAR** *(3.30)*

56 **WOMAN OF SALEM** *(3.07)*

51a **RUN, RUN, RUN** *(5.06)*

57 **IF ONLY** *(3.38)*

B SIDE

58 **A THOUSAND TIMES YES** *(2.59)*

59 **STRAIGHT TALK** *(3.17)*

60 **ANGRY YOUNG WOMAN** *(3.51)*

61 **SHE HITS BACK** *(3.31)*

62 **WOMEN POWER** *(4.49)*

52a **MEN, MEN, MEN** *(4.01)*

YOKO ONO'S SINGLE
WALKING ON THIN ICE – FOR JOHN

John and I were gloriously happy in the first week of December. "Double Fantasy" was in the top ten. It was just a matter of time for it to go up to number one since we still had two weeks to Xmas and it was selling well. We kept saying, "We did it, we did it," and hugged each other. "What are we going to do when it's number one, John?" "I'll take you out to dinner." "That's a date?" "That's a date." That meant dressing up time: John in his suit and me in drag. He would put the diamond pin on his lapel, a birthday present from me. Then we would end up going to a quiet, dark restaurant where nobody could see us except us. But that was our idea of fun. "Mother, help me put this diamond pin on, will you?" I hear him saying.

"Yoko, you paid your dues, and you produced a top ten record. Don't let them kick you around anymore. When you talk to them, just remember that. They have to respect you now. Just look them in the eye and say I'm a top ten artist, in your mind, okay?" he said, over and over again. "Don't worry, John. I look them in their eyes anyway." "That's because you're crazy," he laughed. "But you're a commercial success now, Yoko; you don't know what that means. It means dollars and cents, and they understand that." "Sure, John."

"Walking On Thin Ice" was what we were remixing that night. The past weekend we had listened to the song all day and night. It was as if we were both haunted by the song. I remember I woke up in the morning and found John watching the sunrise and still listening to the song. He said I had to put it out right away as a single. He wanted to be on the B-side of it. I didn't think that was wise. "Nobody's going to listen to the A-side then." "Hey, I've got a good idea. How about sending just the A-side to the DJs and keep the B-side a total secret until it's sent to the shops?" "Nice try, John. You know it's not going to work." Later, John agreed with me. "You're probably right. We have to put you out as a solo artist." In our minds we were a team. In the world's mind it was John Lennon and his Missus who got lucky. I caught him looking at the grey streak in my hair. He caught me looking at his cheekbones. We were old soldiers. "Let's really give it to them. Let's make it a rule that we won't release any photo of us unless we are kissing or looking at each other." That'll really go down well, I bet," I laughed. He laughed, too, looking pleased that he made me laugh. The family who laughs together stays together, I thought.

"It Happened" was a song John loved. "It's a hit." "No way." "You wanna bet? I'll make it a hit," he said. I remember thinking "Why this one?" John had found the song amongst my old tapes two weeks before the night.

Getting this together after what happened was hard. But I knew John would not rest his mind if I hadn't. I hope you like it, John. I did my best.

Yoko
Jan. 24 '81
NYC

Single Includes Lyric Sheet

K 79202

Also Available
Cassette Single With A Bonus Third Track

K 79202 M

Due to the lack of any specific information on British copies of the album, it has not been possible to provide musician credits for individual tracks which were written and produced by Yoko.

---

19 **(Just Like) Starting Over**
(63) KISS KISS KISS *(3.38)*

"A" side by John Lennon

"B" side by Yoko Ono

Geffen Records K 79186 – October 24, 1980

As with their earlier Plastic Ono Band singles, John and Yoko's first single for seven years comprised an "A" side by John and a "B" side by Yoko. Both tracks were from their *Double Fantasy* album. For chart statistics relating to *(Just Like) Starting Over*, see John Lennon section (page 42).

---

20 **DOUBLE FANTASY**

By John Lennon and Yoko Ono

Geffen Records K 99131 – November 17, 1980

For their first album together since 1972, John and Yoko composed seven songs each to share equally both writing and vocal duties.

A SIDE

(Just Like) Starting Over

63a **KISS KISS KISS** *(3.39)*

Clean Up Time

64 **GIVE ME SOMETHING** *(1.52)*

I'm Losing You

65 **I'M MOVING ON** *(3.17)*

Beautiful Boy (Darling Boy)

B SIDE

Watching The Wheels

66 **I'M YOUR ANGEL** *(3.34)*

Woman

67 **BEAUTIFUL BOYS** *(2.53)*

Dear Yoko

68 **EVERY MAN HAS A WOMAN WHO LOVES HIM** *(4.00)*

69 **HARD TIMES ARE OVER** *(3.12)*

---

21 **Woman**
(67a) BEAUTIFUL BOYS *(2.51)*

"A" side by John Lennon

"B" side by Yoko Ono

Geffen Records K 79196 – January 16, 1981

The second single from *Double Fantasy* featured Yoko's *Beautiful Boys* as the coupling for John's *Woman*. For chart statistics, see the John Lennon section (page 46).

---

22 **(70) WALKING ON THIN ICE – FOR JOHN** *(5.56)*
(71) IT HAPPENED *(5.02)*

By Yoko Ono

Geffen Records K 79202 – February 20, 1981

Yoko's first solo single since 1973, which became her first solo hit when it entered the BMRB Top 75 on February 28 at No. 50, rising to No. 35 on March 14, and staying in the chart for five weeks.

Walking On Thin Ice, written by Yoko, was recorded in late November and early December 1980 at the Hit Factory, New York, and was produced by John and Yoko and Jack Douglas. John and Yoko were re-mixing the song during the night of December 8 when, at approximately 11 p.m., John was gunned down. The recording features John/guitar and keyboards; Hugh McCracken and Earl Slick/rhythm guitars; Tony Levin/bass; Andy Newmark/drums and Jack Douglas/percussion.

It Happened, also written by Yoko, was recorded in 1973 at the Record Plant, New York, and was left over from the *Feeling The Space* sessions, featuring David Spinozza and Hugh McCracken/guitars; Gordon Edwards/bass; Kenny Ascher/keyboards; Arthur Jenkins Jnr/percussion and Rick Marotta/drums. The track begins with a recording of John and Yoko talking whilst strolling through New York's Central Park. The original recording was produced by John and Yoko; John "rediscovered" the song among Yoko's old tapes two weeks before he was shot, and thought it could be a hit, so it was edited and re-mixed by John and Yoko with Jack Douglas.

Before John was shot, *Walking On Thin Ice* was scheduled to be released as a twelve-inch four track EP (along with two of Yoko's tracks from *Double Fantasy*) titled *Yoko Only*. Yoko decided to continue with the release, because John had been so certain that it would be a hit, although the EP format was dropped. The single appeared in a "picture" sleeve with a "Finishing Note" from Yoko, plus an insert containing lyrics and credits.

23 **Watching The Wheels**
(66a) YES, I'M YOUR ANGEL *(2.48)*

"A" side by John Lennon

"B" side by Yoko Ono

Geffen Records K 79207 – March 27, 1981

The third release from *Double Fantasy* featured Yoko's *Yes, I'm Your Angel* as the "B" side. This song is called *I'm Your Angel* on the *Double Fantasy* album, and is likewise credited on the label of this single, only the sleeve crediting it as *Yes, I'm Your Angel.* For chart statistics see John Lennon section (page 47).

24 **SEASON OF GLASS**

By Yoko Ono

Geffen Records K 99164 – June 12, 1981

Yoko's fifth solo album was originally advertised by Geffen Records as including the single *Walking On Thin Ice.* But after *Beatles Monthly* magazine had informed them that the album did not feature this song, Geffen gave the single away free with the album, and changed the advert accordingly. Although it did not enter the *NME* Top 30, the album was Yoko's first to enter the BMRB album charts, which it did on June 20 at No. 70, rising to No. 47 the following week (its final week in the chart).

The album was recorded at the Hit Factory, New York, during April 1981, with Yoko and Phil Spector producing, using basically the same musicians who performed on *Double Fantasy*: Hugh McCracken/guitar and Jew's harp (on *Dogtown*); Earl Slick/guitar; Anthony Davilio/keyboards and guitar (on *No No No* and *Toyboat*); George Small/keyboards; Tony Levin/bass; John Sigler/bass (on *Mindweaver* and *Mother Of The Universe*); Andrew Newmark/drums; David Friedman/vibraphone and percussion; Arthur Jenkins Jnr/percussion; George "Young" Opalisky/soprano and alto saxophone; Michael Brecker/tenor saxophone; Ronnie Cuber/baritone saxophone; and Howard Johnson/tuba. Yoko handled all lead and backing vocals.

The album sleeve caused some controversy, many people considering it to be in bad taste as the front cover picture shows a bloodstained pair of glasses. Cover photography and design was by Yoko, with artwork by Christopher Wharf.

A SIDE

72 GOODBYE SADNESS *(3.48)*

73 MINDWEAVER *(4.24)*

74 EVEN WHEN YOU'RE FAR AWAY *(5.20)*

75 NOBODY SEES ME LIKE YOU DO *(3.12)*

76 TURN OF THE WHEEL *(2.41)*

77 DOGTOWN *(3.21)*

78 SILVER HORSE *(3.00)*

B SIDE

79 I DON'T KNOW WHY *(4.16)*

80 EXTENSION 33 *(2.42)*

81 NO, NO, NO *(2.42)*

82 WILL YOU TOUCH ME *(2.34)*

83 SHE GETS DOWN ON HER KNEES *(4.12)*

84 TOYBOAT *(3.30)*

85 MOTHER OF THE UNIVERSE *(4.23)*

At one time during early 1981, it was reported that Julian Lennon (John's first son) would be assisting Yoko to complete the unfinished numbers left over from the *Double Fantasy* sessions, and that Yoko and Julian were possibly recording an album together. These reports later turned out to be pure speculation, and further reports that two songs being recorded by Yoko were previously unreleased Lennon-Ono compositions, were also unfounded. All fourteen songs on the album were Ono compositions, although the lyrics to *Mother Of The Universe* appear to be based on the "Lord's Prayer". Many non-musical sounds appear throughout the album, including Yoko talking on the telephone, Sean Lennon telling a short story, and four "gunshots" at the beginning of *No, No, No,* which sparked off more "bad taste" controversy.

25 **(86) MY MAN** *(3.59)*
(87) LET THE TEARS DRY *(3.28)*

By Yoko Ono

Polydor POSP 541 – November 26, 1982

Yoko's first single for Polydor – with whom she signed in October 1982 – featured two self-penned songs from her first Polydor album, *It's Alright (I See Rainbows)*. Although receiving considerable airplay and favourable reviews, the single, released in a picture sleeve with photography by Bob Gruen, did not enter the charts.

26 **IT'S ALRIGHT (I SEE RAINBOWS)**

By Yoko Ono

Polydor POLD 5073 – December 16, 1982

Yoko's most commercial album to date, *It's Alright* was well-received by the music press. It contains some of her most conventional work, although this was unfortunately not reflected in sales, as the album did not enter the charts.

The album was recorded at the Hit Factory, New York, during the autumn of 1982, with Yoko producing, using the following musicians: Pete Cannarozzi and Paul Griffin/synthesizers; Elliot Randall and John Tropea/guitars; Paul Griffin, Michael Holmes and Paul Shaffer/keyboards; Neil Jason/bass; Yogi Horton and Alan Schwartzberg/drums; Rubens Bassini, David A. Friedman, Sammy Figeroa and Roger Squitero/percussion; Roy Badal/tabla and Howard Johnson/tuba and baritone saxophone. Lead and harmony vocals were by Yoko, with backing vocals by Gordon Grody, Kurt Yahijian and Carlos Alomar.

The album sleeve was designed by Yoko, with artwork by Bill Levy and Bob Heimall and photography by Bob Gruen. The back cover features a 1982 photograph of Yoko and Sean taken in New York Central Park, with a 1980 photograph of John superimposed on top.

A SIDE

86a **MY MAN** *(3.57)*

88 **NEVER SAY GOODBYE** *(4.25)*

89 **SPEC OF DUST** *(3.31)*

90 **LONELINESS** *(3.48)*

91 **TOMORROW MAY NEVER COME** *(2.25)*

B SIDE

92 **IT'S ALRIGHT** *(4.24)*

93 **WAKE UP** *(3.46)*

87a **LET THE TEARS DRY** *(3.22)*

94 **DREAM LOVE** *(4.55)*

95 **I SEE RAINBOWS** *(3.13)*

Although again many people were expecting (and hoping) that Yoko's new album would contain some of the "Lennon-Ono" numbers left over from *Double Fantasy*, all compositions on the album were by Yoko. Even though the album does not feature any of John's recordings, most of the songs were inspired by him or his memory, and on *Never Say Goodbye* (during the middle instrumental section) John can be heard shouting "Yoko", while Yoko and Sean can be heard talking. At the end of this track, it is Sean who says "Looks like a gigantic plum". Sean is heard again at the beginning of *It's Alright*, attempting to wake up Yoko.

YOKO ONO US

1 **UNFINISHED MUSIC No. 1 – TWO VIRGINS**

By John Lennon and Yoko Ono

Apple T 5001 – November 11, 1968

2 **UNFINISHED MUSIC No. 2 – LIFE WITH THE LIONS**

By John Lennon and Yoko Ono

Zapple ST 3357 – May 26, 1969

3 **Give Peace A Chance**
(1) REMEMBER LOVE

By The Plastic Ono Band

Apple 1809 – July 7, 1969

4 **Cold Turkey**
(2) DON'T WORRY KYOKO (MUMMY'S ONLY LOOKING FOR A HAND IN THE SNOW)

By The Plastic Ono Band

Apple 1813 – October 20, 1969

5 **THE WEDDING ALBUM**

By John Lennon and Yoko Ono

Apple SMAX 3367 – October 20, 1969

6 **THE PLASTIC ONO BAND – LIVE PEACE IN TORONTO 1969**

By The Plastic Ono Band

Apple SW 3362 – December 12, 1969

7 **Instant Karma**
(5) WHO HAS SEEN THE WIND

By Lennon/Ono and The Plastic Ono Band

Apple 1818 – February 20, 1970

8 **YOKO ONO/PLASTIC ONO BAND**

By Yoko Ono and The Plastic Ono Band

Apple SW 3373 – December 11, 1970

While *John Lennon/Plastic Ono Band* was in the Billboard Top 30 album for ten weeks, Yoko's companion album managed a three week run in the Top 200, entering on February 6 at No. 199 and rising to No. 182 the following week. (Tracks and sleeve same as British release.)

---

9 **Mother**
(6a) WHY

"A" side by John Lennon and The Plastic Ono Band

"B" side by Yoko Ono and The Plastic Ono Band

Apple 1827 – December 28, 1970

This single, not released in Britain, coupled one track from both John and Yoko's respective *Plastic Ono Band* albums.

---

10 **Power To The People**
(10a) TOUCH ME

"A" side by John Lennon/Plastic Ono Band

"B" side by Yoko Ono/Plastic Ono Band

Apple 1830 – March 22, 1971

The "B" side to *Power To The People* in Britain was Yoko's song, *Open Your Box*. Capitol refused to allow her to use the song due to its suggestive lyrics, so a track from the *Yoko Ono/Plastic Ono Band* LP was substituted.

---

11 **FLY**

By Yoko Ono and The Plastic Ono Band with Joe Jones Tone Deaf Music Co.

Apple SVBB 3380 – September 20, 1971

Yoko's second solo chart entry, *Fly* entered the Billboard Top 200 for two weeks at No. 199 on November 13, 1971. (Sleeve same as British release.)

RECORD ONE A SIDE

14 MIDSUMMER NEW YORK

15 MIND TRAIN

RECORD ONE B SIDE

16 MIND HOLES

2a DON'T WORRY KYOKO

13 MRS. LENNON

12 HIRAKE

17 TOILET PIECE/UNKNOWN

18 O 'WIND (BODY IS THE SCAR OF YOUR MIND)

RECORD TWO

(Same as British release.)

---

12 **(13a) MRS. LENNON**
(14a) MIDSUMMER NEW YORK

By Yoko Ono

Apple 1839 – September 29, 1971

---

13 **Happy Xmas (War Is Over)**
(24) LISTEN THE SNOW IS FALLING

"A" side By John and Yoko/Plastic Ono Band with The Harlem Community Choir

"B" side by Yoko Ono and The Plastic Ono Band

Apple 1842 – December 1, 1971

---

14 **Woman Is The Nigger Of The World**
(25) SISTERS O SISTERS

"A" side by John Lennon/Plastic Ono Band with Elephant's Memory plus Invisible Strings

"B" side by Yoko Ono/Plastic Ono Band with Elephant's Memory plus Invisible Strings

Apple 1848 – April 24, 1972

---

15 **SOMETIME IN NEW YORK CITY**

Record One by John and Yoko/Plastic Ono Band with Elephant's Memory plus Invisible Strings

Record Two by The Plastic Ono Super-group and Plastic Ono Mothers

Apple SVBB 3392 – June 12, 1972

RECORD ONE A SIDE

Woman Is The Nigger Of The World

25a SISTERS O SISTERS

Attica State

26 BORN IN A PRISON

New York City

RECORD ONE B SIDE

(Same as British release.)

RECORD TWO

(Same as British release.)

YOKO ONO
NEW ALBUM
SEASON OF GLASS

INCLUDES
'WALKING ON THIN ICE'

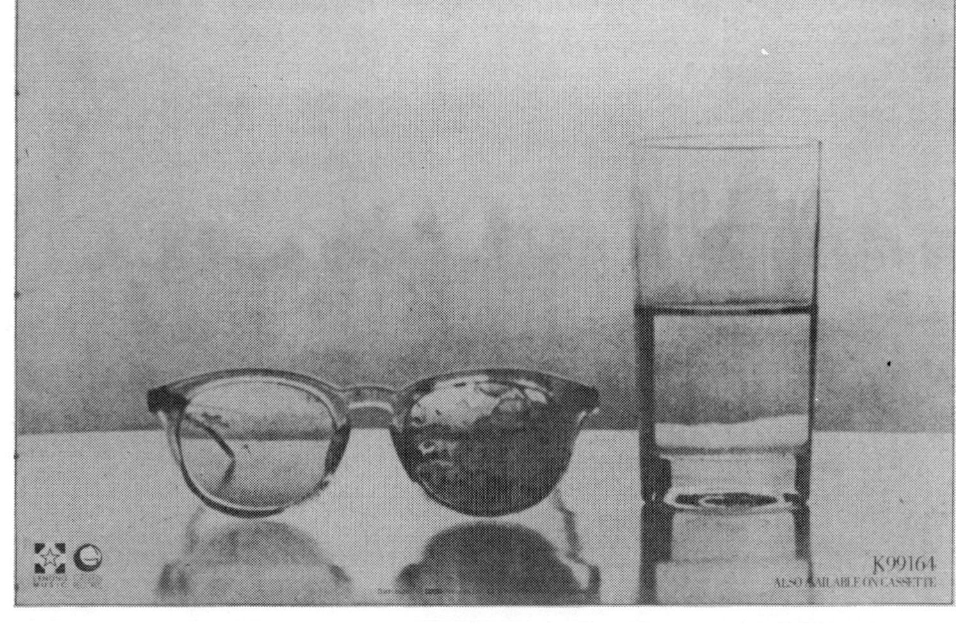

16 **(48) NOW OR NEVER**
(47) MOVE ON FAST

By Yoko Ono and The Plastic Ono Band with Elephant's Memory

Apple 1853 – November 13, 1972

The second Yoko solo single in America featured two tracks from the *Approximately Infinite Universe* album, and was not released in Britain.

---

17 **APPROXIMATELY INFINITE UNIVERSE**

By Yoko Ono and The Plastic Ono Band with Elephant's Memory, Endless Strings and Choir Boys

Apple SVBB 3399 – January 8, 1973

Yoko's third solo album, and third to enter the lower regions of the Billboard Top 200. It entered the charts on February 24 at No. 198, and rose to No. 193 on March 10 (its fourth and final week in the chart). (Cover same as British release.)

RECORD ONE

(Same as British release.)

RECORD TWO A SIDE

(Same as British release.)

RECORD TWO B SIDE

46 I HAVE A WOMAN INSIDE MY SOUL
47a MOVE ON FAST
48a NOW OR NEVER
49 IS WINTER HERE TO STAY
50 LOOKING OVER FROM MY HOTEL WINDOW

---

18 **(30a) DEATH OF SAMANTHA**
(29a) YANG YANG

By Yoko Ono/Plastic Ono Band with Elephant's Memory, Endless Strings and Choir Boys

Apple 1859 – February 26, 1973

A second release from the *Approximately Infinite Universe* album featured the same tracks that were later released in Britain.

---

19 **(62) WOMEN POWER**
(52) MEN, MEN, MEN

By Yoko Ono

Apple 1867 – September 24, 1973

The American single from the *Feeling The Space* LP featured *Women Power* as the "A" side, as opposed to *Run, Run, Run,* the favoured track for the British release. The "B" side, however, is identical.

---

20 **FEELING THE SPACE**

By Yoko Ono and The Plastic Ono Band and Something Different

Apple SW 3412 – November 2, 1973

Yoko's fourth solo album did not enter the Billboard Top 200. (Sleeve same as British release.)

A SIDE

53 GROWING PAIN
54 YELLOW GIRL (STAND BY FOR LIFE)
55 COFFIN CAR
56 WOMAN OF SALEM
51 RUN, RUN, RUN
57 IF ONLY

B SIDE

58 A THOUSAND TIMES YES
59 STRAIGHT TALK
60 ANGRY YOUNG WOMAN
61 SHE HITS BACK
62a WOMEN POWER
52a MEN, MEN, MEN

---

21 **(Just Like) Starting Over**
(63) KISS KISS KISS

"A" side by John Lennon

"B" side by Yoko Ono

Geffen Records GEF-49604 – October 23, 1980

---

22 **DOUBLE FANTASY**

By John Lennon and Yoko Ono

Geffen Records GHS 2001 – November 17, 1980

---

23 **Woman**

(67a) BEAUTIFUL BOYS

"A" side by John Lennon

"B" side by Yoko Ono

Geffen Records 49644 – January 12, 1981

---

24 **(70) WALKING ON THIN ICE – FOR JOHN**
(71) IT HAPPENED

By Yoko Ono

Geffen Records 49683 – February 6, 1981

This single entered the Billboard chart on March 7, 1981. During a ten week chart residency it peaked at No. 58.

---

25 **Watching The Wheels**
(66a) YES, I'M YOUR ANGEL

"A" side by John Lennon

"B" side by Yoko Ono

Geffen Records 49695 – March 13, 1981

---

26 **SEASON OF GLASS**

By Yoko Ono

Geffen Records 2004 – June 3, 1981

This LP entered the Billboard chart at No. eighty-one on June 27. During nine weeks in the chart, its highest position was at No. 49.

---

27 **(86) MY MAN**
(87) LET THE TEARS DRY

By Yoko Ono

Polydor PD-2224 – November 2, 1982

---

28 **IT'S ALRIGHT (I SEE RAINBOWS)**

By Yoko Ono

Polydor PD-1-6364 – November 29, 1982

This LP reached No. 158 on the Billboard Top 200 during Christmas week, 1982.

---

29 **(88a) NEVER SAY GOODBYE**
(90a) LONELINESS

Polydor 810 556-7 – January 25, 1983 (seven-inch)

Polydor 810 575-1 – February 22, 1983 (re-mixed twelve-inch version)

BIBLIOGRAPHY

This book could not have been compiled without researching other books for facts and information. The following is a bibliography of the books used for research, along with other Beatles books, which together constitute a definitive library for any Beatle fanatic.

Abbey Road Brian Southall (Patrick Stephens 1982)
The Album Cover Album Storm Thorgerson (Hipgnosis)/Roger Dean/Dominy Hamilton (Dragon's World Books 1977)
All Together Now Harry Castleman/Walter Podrazik (Pierian Press 1976)
All You Needed Was Love John Blake (Hamlyn 1981)
All You Need Is Ears George Martin/Jerome Hernsby (Macmillan London Ltd. 1979)
Apple To The Core Peter McCabe/Robert D. Schonfeld (Martin Brian & O'Keefe Ltd. 1972/Sphere Books Ltd. 1973)
As Time Goes By Derek Taylor (Davis-Poynter Ltd. 1973/Sphere Books Ltd. 1974)
The Beatles Geoffrey Stokes (W.H. Allen & Co. Ltd. 1980)
The Beatles: A Collection Robert & Cindy DelBuono (RobCin Associates 1982)
The Beatles Again Harry Castleman/Walter Podrazik (Pierian Press 1977)
The Beatles Album File And Complete Discography Jeff Russell (Blandford Press 1982)
Beatles Anniversary Bill Harry (Colourgold Ltd. 1982)
The Beatles: An Illustrated Record Roy Carr/Tony Tyler (New English Library 1975/1978/1980)
The Beatles Apart Bob Woffinden (Proteus Books 1981)
The Beatles At The Beeb Kevin Howlett (British Broadcasting Corporation 1982)
The Beatles: A To Z Goldie Friede/Robin Titone/Sue Weiner (Methuen 1980)
The Beatles: The Authorized Biography Hunter Davis (William Heineman Ltd. 1968)
The Beatles Concerted Efforts Jan Van De Bunt (Beatles Unlimited 1979)
The Beatles Discography Mitchell McGreary (Ticket To Ryde Ltd. 1975)
The Beatles Down Under Glenn A. Baker, with Roger Delernia (Wild & Wooley 1982)
The Beatles' England David Bacon/Norman Maslov (Columbus Books 1982)
The Beatles Forever Nicholas Schaffner (McGraw-Hill Book Co. 1977)
The Beatles Forever Helen Spence (Colour Library International Ltd. 1981)
The Beatles For The Record No author (Stafford Pemberton Publishing 1981)
The Beatles In Help! Al Hine (Mayflower Books Ltd. 1965)
The Beatles Monthly Books Various — edited by Johnny Dean (Beat Publications Ltd. 1963-9/Re-published from 1976)
The Beatles Illustrated Lyrics edited by Alan Aldridge (MacDonald Unit 75 1969)
The Beatles Illustrated Lyrics Volume 2 edited by Alan Aldridge (BPC Publishing Ltd. 1971)
The Beatles In Their Own Words Miles (Omnibus Press 1978)
The Beatles Complete Lyrics (Futura Publications 1974)
The Beatles On Record Mark Wallgren (Simon & Schuster 1982)
The Beatles' Who's Who Bill Harry (Aurum Press 1982)
The Beatles: Yesterday And Today Rochelle Larkin (Scholastic Book Services 1974)
Behind The Beatles Songs Philip Cowan (Polytantric Press 1978)
The Book Of Golden Discs Joseph Murrells (Barrie & Jenkins Ltd. 1974/1978)
The Book Of Rock Lists Dave Marsh/Kevin Stein (Sidgwick & Jackson 1981)
The Bootleg Bible (Hot Wacks Book IX) (Babylon Books 1981)
British Beat Chris May/Tim Philips (Sociopack Pub. 1974)
British Record Charts 1955-1979 Tony Jasper (Futura Publications 1979)
A Cellarful Of Noise Brian Epstein (Souvenir Press 1964/New English Library 1965/1981)
Chart File 1982 Barry Lazell/Dafydd Rees/Alan Jones (Virgin Books 1982)
A Day In The Life Tom Schultheiss (Pierian Press 1980)
Dig It: The Beatles Bootleg Book Volume One Koos Janssen/Erik M. Bakker (Rock Book Centre Publications 1974)
Encyclopedia Of Rock Volumes 1-3 edited by Phil Hardy/Dave Laing (Panthar Books Ltd 1976)
Facts About A Pop Group (Wings) David Gelly (G. Whizzard Pub. Ltd. 1976)
George Harrison Yesterday And Today Ross Michaels (Flash Books 1977)
The Gimmix Book Of Records Frank Goldman/Klaus Hiltscher (Virgin Books 1981)
Grapefruit Yoko Ono (Peter Owen Ltd. 1964/Sphere Books 1971)

Growing Up With The Beatles Ron Schaumberg (Pyramid Books 1976/G.P. Putnam's Sons 1980)
The Guinness Book Of British Hit Singles Jo & Tim Rice/Paul Gambaccini/Mike Read (Guinness Superlatives Ltd. 1977/1979/1981)
The Guinness Book Of Records Norris McWhirter (Guinness Superlatives Ltd. yearly)
'Hands Across The Water' Wings Tour USA Hipgnosis (Paper Tiger 1978)
A Hard Day's Night John Burke (Pan Books Ltd. 1964)
The Illustrated Book Of Rock Records Barry Lazell/Dafydd Rees (Virgin Books 1982)
The Illustrated History Of The Rock Album Cover Angie Errigo (Octopus Books Ltd. 1979)
The Illustrated NME Encyclopedia of Rock Nick Logan/Bob Woffinden (Hamlyn Publishing Ltd. 1976)
I Me Mine George Harrison (Genesis Publications 1980/W.H. Allen 1982)
In The Footsteps Of The Beatles Mike Evans/Ron Jones (Merseyside County Council 1982)
The Joel Whitburn Record Research Series Joel Whitburn (Record Research Inc. yearly)
John Lennon In His Own Words Miles (Omnibus Press 1980)
John Lennon In His Own Write John Lennon (Jonathan Cape 1964)
John Lennon 1940-1980 A Biography Ray Connolly (Fontana Books 1981)
John Lennon: One Day At A Time, A Personal Biography Of The Seventies Anthony Fawcett (New English Library 1976)
The John Lennon Story George Tremlett (Futura Pub. Ltd. 1976)
Lennon And McCartney Malcolm Doney (Midas Books 1981)
Lennon Remembers edited by Jann Wenner (Talmy, Franklin Ltd. 1972)
The Lennon Tapes Andy Peebles (BBC Publications 1981)
Linda's Pictures: A Collection Of Photographs Linda McCartney (Jonathan Cape 1976)
The Longest Cocktail Party Richard DiLello (Charisma Books 1973)
Love Me Do — The Beatles Progress Michael Braun (Penguin Books Ltd. 1964)
The Man Who Gave The Beatles Away Allan Williams/William Marshall (Elm Tree Books Ltd. 1975)
Mersey Beat: The Beginning Of The Beatles edited by Bill Harry (Omnibus Press 1977)
The NME Book Of Rock edited by Nick Logan/Rob Finnis (W.H. Allen Ltd. 1975)
New Rock Record Terry Hounsome/Tim Chambre (Blandford Press 1981)
Nothing To Get Hung About Mike Evans (City Of Liverpool Public Relations Office 1974)
Paul McCartney And Wings Tony Jasper (Octopus Books Ltd. 1977)
Paul McCartney And Wings Jeremy Pascall (Phoebus Publishing Co. 1977)
Paul McCartney In His Own Words Paul Gambaccini (Omnibus Press Ltd. 1976)
The Paul McCartney Story George Tremlett (Futura Pub. Ltd. 1975)
The Penguin John Lennon John Lennon (Penguin Books Ltd. 1966)
The Playboy Interviews With John Lennon And Yoko Ono conducted by David Sheff (New English Library 1981)
P.S. We Love You: The Beatles Story 1962-3 Tony Barrow (Mirror Books Ltd. 1982)
Record Collector various authors/editor — Johnny Dean (Diamond Publishing Group Ltd. 1979 to the present)
Rock Family Trees Pete Frame (Omnibus Press 1979)
Rock File Pete & Annie Fowler/editor — Charlie Gillett (Pictorial Presentations Ltd. 1972)
Rock File 2 as above with various other authors (Panther Books Ltd. 1974)
Rock File 3 as above with various other authors (Panther Books Ltd. 1975)
Rock File 4 as above with various other authors (Panther Books Ltd. 1976)
Rock File 5 as above with various other authors (Panther Books Ltd. 1978)
Rock Legends: Beatles Mike Davies/John Tobler (SB Publishing & Promotions Ltd. 1982)
Rock'n'Roll Times Jurgen Vollmer (Google Plex Books 1981)
The Rolling Stones: An Illustrated Record Roy Carr (New English Library 1976)
Shout: The True Story Of The Beatles Philip Norman (Hamish Hamilton Ltd. 1981)
A Spaniard In The Works John Lennon (Jonathan Cape Ltd. 1965)
The Story of Pop various/editor — Jeremy Pascall (Phoebus Publishing Co./BBC 1973/4/5)
Strawberry Fields Forever: John Lennon Revisited Vic Garbarini/Brian Cullman/Barbara Graustark (Bantam Books Inc. 1980)
Thank U Very Much: Mike McCartney's Family Album Mike McCartney (Granada Publishing Ltd. 1982)
A Twist Of Lennon Cynthia Lennon (W.H. Allen & Co. Ltd. 1978)
With The Beatles: The Historic Photographs Of Dezo Hoffman Dezo Hoffman (Omnibus Press 1982)
Who's Who In Rock William York (Omnibus Press 1982)
Yellow Submarine Lee Minoff/Al Brodax/Jack Mendelsohn/Erich Segal (New English Library 1968)

This index only refers to the Beatles and Yoko Ono's solo recordings, and does not include the "guest" recordings as listed in "With A Little Help To Their Friends". Album titles are in UPPER CASE, and where page numbers are repeated, this indicates that the song appears more than once on a page. The initial letters after each title indicates the section in which the main entry for that title appears.